*Darling Days*

# *Darling Days*

## iO Tillett Wright

**ecco**

*An Imprint of* HarperCollins*Publishers*

HarperCollins
PUBLISHERS
— Since 1817 —

The names and identifying characteristics of some of the individuals featured throughout this book have been changed to protect their privacy.

DARLING DAYS. Copyright © 2016 by iO Tillett Wright. All rights reserved. Printed in the United States of America. No part of this book may be used or reproduced in any manner whatsoever without written permission except in the case of brief quotations embodied in critical articles and reviews. For information address Harper-Collins Publishers, 195 Broadway, New York, NY 10007.

HarperCollins books may be purchased for educational, business, or sales promotional use. For information please e-mail the Special Markets Department at SPsales@harpercollins.com.

A hardcover edition of this book was published in 2016 by Ecco, an imprint of HarperCollins Publishers.

FIRST ECCO PAPERBACK EDITION PUBLISHED 2017.

*Designed by Suet Yee Chong*

Library of Congress Cataloging-in-Publication Data has been applied for.

ISBN 978-0-06-236821-8
HB 11.10.2021

*If it doesn't hurt like hell,*
*it ain't worth a jack shit.*

—MY MA

January 8, 2016

Dear Ma,

Since my first conscious moments, you have been a gladiator to me—the fiercest example of a woman's power I could ever know.

We are some kind of twins, able to see each other in a room of closed eyes, able to hear each other in a world of silence, despite the trauma layered into our story. You are the priestess at the head of my tiny tribe of one.

Since I learned to use a phone and to this day, when our family wants to reach you, they do it through me. I am the whisperer, the only one who can ever locate you in the jungle of New York, because you will always call me back.

When no one could find you to break the news, it fell to me to tell you that your mother had died. The noise that came from you then was an animal pain. The realization that I would also one day lose you was so unbearable that I had to hang up.

For years, we were best friends. Long before the fights and the screaming and the law got involved.

Which is why I feel like I need to say a few things to you before you read this collection of stories intended to capture my life.

People often marvel at my having "turned out so normal." They ask how I'm not angry, how I'm not a fuck-up, why I don't turn around and abuse people.

They say it's extraordinary that I've forgiven you.

I am hardly without effects. I am a vortex of damage. In my brief three decades, I have hurt people, betrayed trust, caused confusion and disappointment. I have sauntered around the shores of an ocean of rage, avoiding what would eventually become a crippling anxiety.

*It's taken thirty years for me to melt the sandstorm of emotions within myself into glass, but now that I have found acceptance, now that I have forged an understanding of happiness and built my own world, I finally grasp the beautiful gift that is the lens I possess. Through it, I can see that instead of a "mom," I have been given a moral compass.*

*Your solitude, your rigorous discipline in your body, the brilliant originality of your vision, as if your eyesight were replaced with a loop from another planet, these things are all gifts to me.*

*Your demons—the visitor that would seep into your eyeballs on so many nights, clouding the kindness, turning your spit to poison—I do not begrudge you.*

*I bow in humbled respect at the feet of your loss, Ma.*

*Since I was a small child, you have recounted the story of Billy, your epic love, and his murder. Nothing has ever touched me or provoked as much empathy in my heart as that; the violence of your loss, so shortly before my arrival in this world. How could I have hated you?*

*I think, even as a tiny tot, I understood; Billy was taken from you, a tragedy without which I would never have existed, and thus, you were to be protected.*

*People call me brave, for getting up on stages and being open about who I am, but I know no other way than to be proud, because of you.*

*I was given the most important gift two parents can give to their child: Your respect. My dignity.*

*So, whether or not you understood that I wanted a clean house, regular meals, and to know which version of you would come home at night; whether you grasped the inappropriate level of professional expectation you put on me as a child who just wanted to play; although your addictions ravaged our relationship for so many years—I understand.*

*I hope, now that we finally know where Billy was put to rest, that we can find a way to his remains, and close the gash that has defined you for three decades.*

*I will do everything I can to help you find peace, so you no longer have to medicate with flavored solvents and pharmaceutical hammers, so you are no longer the loneliest wolf.*

*Because of you, I know forgiveness.*

*Because of you, I know love.*

*Forever,*
*Your Bud*

# PART I

## Heredity

*Her*

## Chapter 1

─ ─ ─

# Babygirl's Gun

*13 Third Avenue, New York City, 1982*

S HE SAID HE GAVE HER THE LITTLE GUN BECAUSE IT WAS
classy and elegant, like her. A feminine twist of metal and
pearl. Lethal, like her. She kept it under her pillow "just in case."

Her bed was, is, and always will be under an open window, this one
looking out onto Third Avenue. In 1981, her pillow filled a head-pistol
sandwich, but she doesn't use a pillow now.

Then, she pulled her bleached blond, bombshell locks into a ponytail
when she slept, always with her man, Billy. Under a pile of blankets in the
winter or sweating naked in the summer, but always with her man.

The window gaped like a loyal simpleton, beaten by the sun or
drooling raindrops, but its mouth never closed. The window stayed
open.

My mother's world was a riot of improvisations, everything in flux
and nothing predictable except the open window and the radio on.
Rhythm in the air. "Life! In the air," she'd say. It stays on. She would
tape over the switch. Nobody fucks with Babygirl's radio.

Later, she would say that there was never a gun in the house. She
would swear to this, like a Mafia wife, blinded by passion or loyalty.
Either way it wasn't completely true. There was a gun under her pillow.
Whether or not he pulled it out before they shot him, nobody knows.

# *Them*

# Birth

*Third Street between Second Avenue and the Bowery,*
*late summer 1985*

I T WAS A FULL MOON, THE LAST NIGHT OF AUGUST 1985. MY mother told my father to turn the video camera on because the baby was coming.

It was sticky hot outside, the kind of air you can feel. She waded uptown through warm pudding, to a swimming pool in Hell's Kitchen. Two weeks before, belly the size of a basketball, she had posed in a bikini at the Russian baths for a young photographer who told her that swimming was the best thing to loosen up her hips for birth. My mother had been swimming every day since.

Sounds travel differently in the summer. Horns are sharper, screams pierce, and catcalls work double time, trailing swinging booty shorts for blocks. In the mid-eighties, streetlights on Ninth Avenue winked on and off over sidewalks cluttered with garbage, the carts of fruit vendors, and the splayed bodies of crackheads, hugging the cement, sharp ribs laid bare in the heat.

Three lanes of headlights cut through the darkness, making Dick Tracy comic books out of countless shady instances of deals in doorways, pupils dilated from a thousand synthetic euphorias, uptown kids in Brooks Brothers and pearl earrings who thought coming to Hell's

Kitchen was coming "downtown" to cop. The beams backlit a fleet of muscle-bound tranny hookers, teetering back and forth on six-inch heels between twenty-dollar tricks. They carried box cutters in their garters in case tonight was the night some dumb motherfucker decided to let his Jesus guilt get the better of him after cumming on their miniskirt. At nearly six feet tall and broad in the shoulders, her eyes raw from the chlorine, Rhonna was perfectly camouflaged within the local wildlife.

They invented the word *glamazon* for women like my mother. Grace Jones had the same severity and stature. Mix one part unicorn, three parts thunderstorm, two parts wounded bull, and you'd have an approximation of the vibe my mother gives off. A wild tiger would be at a disadvantage in a fight. Bleached blond hair sliced at her chin, eyes crystal blue. Her head is carved for the shoulder pad look, all bones and lines, her face anchored by a Greco-Roman nose that dives into crimson lips, full and finely drawn, over ivories so impressive we call them her piano keys. Her muscles twist over her sleek bones like steel cables, and she leads with her chest like a native warrior, her hands made to grip a sword in battle.

The seventies and eighties were a primitive time in New York, a time of robbery, drugs, and rape, so a working model who favored miniskirts and skintight jeans had to be able to show her teeth. She learned to train a look on a man that could make him piss himself. She once carried a busted fluorescent tube through Midtown and shook it in the face of street thugs like a jagged spear.

But that evening, my mother was slow moving, vulnerable, if ever fierce. She looked like a teenager carrying a backpack on her front, because little aside from her belly had grown during the pregnancy. Her hair was swept back, her skin clear and radiant, glowing the way pregnant women do, with a sharp nose and a head of loose blond curls like Alexander. Her bright red denim Daisy Dukes hadn't closed for weeks, so she wore them unzipped and rolled down. Maternity wear didn't enter her universe.

As she walked toward a Times Square teeming with twenty-five-cent peep shows and bargin-bin hustlers waiting for daddies to make their night, a vendor stepped out from under his awning and said, "My god, I've never seen anything so beautiful!"

My parents lived on a notorious block in their day: Third Street, between Second Avenue and the Bowery, an address that is innocuous now. The barnacled gore of used needles and crack pipes, the sludge of despondency, waste, and murder, the freaky traces of poverty clawed into these crappy tenements have long since been bleached out and washed away.

My parents and their scene were there before the gleaming 7-Eleven and the thirty-dollar brunch specials, lounging in their high-waisted jeans, collars turned up, hair teased out, blasting rap and jazz and no wave from boom boxes. Before the East Village was referred to as "the NYU neighborhood," you had to use a pay phone to call your dealer, and you had to shout up to windows to be let in.

The Bowery Hotel, now a glamorous weekend landing pad for movie starlets, used to be a twenty-four-hour gas station that served radioactive vindaloo on Styrofoam plates to my mother in the middle of the night. Two mangy dogs roamed between the pumps, so dirty and caked with exhaust grease that one's fur had turned green, the other one's blue.

The street was no picnic at the turn of the previous century, when immigrants packed each apartment, six to a room. But by 1985, even with the city broke and in chaos, at the tail end of punk, and in the midst of the AIDS and crack epidemics, Third Street stood out for the refinement of its violence, for its kaleidoscopic insanity.

Directly across the street from our building stood the largest men's shelter in New York, which had turned the block into a dumping ground for homeless people from all over the country, the abscessed injection point for the nation's addicted, vagrant, and mad, the Ellis Island of the criminally insane. America had been cutting loose its mental patients for a decade and blending them in with the detritus of society—the failed, the lost, the abandoned—and this toxic brew, refused at every backyard in the country, was being shipped in like barges of garbage and unloaded onto our street, making it the festering point for every fuck-up from as far away as Texas. The result was a low-key permanent riot.

My mother used to look out our window at the crowd, milling around like hypercharged ants, and say: "Look at 'em. America's undiagnosed misfits. They've got to self-medicate to survive, and all they got to work with is hammers, dope, crack, and Night Train."

And many did not survive. At night there were so many homeless people sleeping shoulder to shoulder that you could hardly see the sidewalk. Occasionally, in the morning, an ambulance would come to take away a "late sleeper," leaving a gray silhouette in the concrete where the carcass had drained out.

On the corner opposite the gas station, the Salvation Army had set up a group home for delinquent boys, a half-way house for hopeless cases, which functioned like a prep school for life across the street. Weekly, a police car would pull up onto the sidewalk and two officers would lead a youth out of the building in handcuffs, nailed for robbing and raping a Japanese tourist in a stairwell somewhere.

To add to the stew, one avenue to the east, the infamous Hells Angels had their East Coast headquarters and clubhouse, and occasionally they would tear down the street, thirty to a posse, with no mufflers on their bikes, doing their best to get in a fight.

On the Fourth of July of every year, the Angels would blow up the block. A two-story American flag was strung from the north to the south side of the street, vibrating in earsplitting waves of psychotic heavy metal blasting from stadium speakers jammed into the clubhouse windows. One year an M-80 exploded in a closed trash can and a triangle of galvanized shrapnel tore through the neck of a local Puerto Rican kid, killing him on the spot.

The police did what they could to stay outside of a four-block radius from what they openly dubbed "the asshole of the universe." We called it home.

THREE AND A HALF MONTHS before her dip in Hell's Kitchen, in an apartment overlooking this miasma, my mother was up, at two in the morning, cooking herself something to eat. She had been working out feverishly for the last twelve weeks, trying to lose a stubborn little tire that had swelled around her waist. My father, staring at her in the darkness, saw her left hand draped protectively over her belly, and he knew immediately. It was pictured in a thousand frescos and altarpieces, this graceful, natural gesture of maternity.

"Rhonna, you're pregnant. We're having a baby."

Without context, this could seem like a sweet moment, a wonderful development in a relationship between two young lovers perhaps looking forward to starting a family and realizing some picket-fence fantasy. Let me clear up that misunderstanding; my parents were just hot in the eighties. In fact, if we are going to grope around in the dark closet of existential responsibility, I blame the bathtub. A lot of relationships, and probably a lot of eighties babies, can be traced back to the tenement tub.

Allow me to explain: when you walked into a one-bedroom, railroad apartment in an old tenement, you entered directly into the kitchen. Across from you were the stove and a refrigerator, and two inches from your right elbow was an iron bathtub, encased in white porcelain, a shorty, with little lion's-paw feet, from the turn of the century, crafted for a little person. In our apartment, there was a dark bedroom to the left and a sunny living room to the right.

People tend to underestimate the importance of a tub in the kitchen to establishing the sexual tone of a bohemian existence. It adds a whole new spice when friends take a bath while you're cooking dinner. Sensual mayhem.

Carrying an armful of records and a bottle of whiskey, my mother was all legs and skimpy outfits when she showed up on my father's doorstep. He had run into her before, once lying naked in a triangle of sunlight at the center of a cocktail party on the Upper West Side and another time on the street, clutching everything she owned in two plas-

tic bags. Freshly widowed, she was being ravaged by agonies beyond
her control and stalked by "friends" turned to suitors. Jailbirds who
had started hanging around after the mysterious murder of her husband
by the police.

A week after their second encounter, my parents were both kicked
out of a nightclub for drinking out of their own stashes. Collared by a
bouncer who knocked their heads together, they were tossed, laughing,
into the street. By this point, my father had seen all he needed to cast
her as the unhinged and suicidal Ophelia in an avant-garde film version
of *Hamlet,* which he had been shooting for a few weeks.

AT THE APARTMENT, "Hamlet" slept under a brown blanket in a corner of the living room among his paintings. He was a young friend
of my father's who I would later know as Uncle Crispy—a wiry kid
with a wild head of curls, whose long eyelashes beat down over big,
soft brown eyes, and who talked shit with the raspy voice of a hustler,
like he had a million sentences he had to force through the bottleneck
of his mouth before his dime ran out. Crispy spent his time avoiding
his duties as leading man, flirting with Rhonna, and darting out of the
house.

She, meanwhile, was up every night, howling old torch songs back
into blasting speakers and swigging Johnnie Walker in nothing but a
China red skintight sweater. This perpetually naked tornado of energy
and beauty living in his kitchen caused a great deal of excitement in my
father's life. A great deal indeed. One thing leads to another, and they
were rapidly entangled.

But over the next three stormy months, my father never really saw
Rhonna sleep. As a matter of fact, he can't recall ever seeing her lie
down. Just getting her to sit was a feat, because she was the single most
*up,* physically active person he had ever encountered. Her exercise rou-
tines were particularly radical and savage, as was her diet, and her de-
votion was to staying lean, lithe, and skinny as hell.

Lately, she had been especially vigilant in her exertions, because she felt that she was putting on a little extra weight around the middle, and that wouldn't jive with the nightclub act she was rehearsing every day at a theater nearby. Her efforts to remove this bump had been unsuccessful, and so at two A.M. that night, from the darkness of his narrow bed my father watched her standing at the stove, shielding something deep within herself and in a flash he realized that she *was* protecting something: she was protecting me.

"What the fuck are you talking about? I know my own body. I'm not pregnant. If I was pregnant, don't you think I'd be the first one to know?!"

He insisted, pointing out the evidence, and finally she went out to an all-night pharmacy for a pregnancy test. Within a few hours, they were confronted with an unfathomable truth: they were going to have a baby.

The next morning, shouting and yelping, my father ran straight to the home of his old friend Francesco and his wife, Alba, who had several kids. Alba, seeing that he was terrified, sat him down and in a perfectly relaxed, Italian way, said, "Ilya, this is not something you plan. Babies come with the bread. Each day, the bread is delivered, and one day it comes with a child. There is nothing to do but to accept it."

When he protested that he hadn't a clue how to care for an infant, she said, "Don't worry. The child will teach you everything you need to know. The best teacher in the world is about to be born. They have a device called a scream, and they use it when anything is required. You will know exactly what to do, because the baby will *tell* you. All you have to learn to do is listen. Don't dictate, listen."

My parents never had the intention of being a couple or building any kind of domestic life together, but they made a pact that day: no matter what happened between them, they were going to care for this child, and failing that, they would at least make sure it would be cared for. They agreed: they would respect each other's wildly different styles; they would never fight in front of the kid; and above all, they would never call in the law. No matter how bad it got, no judge would ever dictate what they needed to do with this child.

They explored all the options for a healthy birth, finally settling on a midwife and home delivery. My mother shelved the whiskey and focused her considerable energy on having the healthiest final trimester anyone has ever seen.

Which brings us back to that sweltering evening at the end of August. My father was standing on the corner of Third Street and the Bowery, talking to his friend Jean-Michel about his new fold-up bicycle. The mischievous young painter was wearing a full three-piece tweed suit, sweating profusely, and my father was lecturing him about the dangers of wool in such heat. Dismissing the mothering, Jean-Michel nodded over his shoulder and said, "Maybe you should tend to your own garden."

Turning, Ilya saw Rhonna coming through the traffic on their block. Carrying several bags, she was just slightly less concerned than usual with the cacophony around her, and she looked to be in pain. He rushed to her and, as he helped her upstairs, she told him it was beginning.

"I need to swim."

BY THE TIME SHE returned from Hell's Kitchen that night, the gigantic moon was bursting from the sky, subjecting the city to its powerful tides. There was no question in her mind that the baby was coming. The scattered contractions confirmed as much.

My father picked up the phone and called the midwife they had been training with. Both of them averse to the concept of giving life surrounded by the sick and dying, they had settled on the most natural birth possible, at home. The nunlike woman they had contracted to help them was allegedly the best midwife in town.

Uptight and stroppy, she was someone who liked to play by the rules, so she and my parents had developed a mutual distaste for each other. Regardless, they had confidence in her, and now they were eager for her to come to the rescue. But their worst fears were realized: she told them that she couldn't make it. The full moon apparently had every mother in town popping out their progeny. The midwife inquired about the frequency of the contractions, and when they told her they were few and far between, she said that in the morning, she would send another midwife.

"Someone *else*? *Who*?"

My father was distraught, but my mother was cool. Splayed out naked on the hardwood floor, stretching and sweating, she let out a laugh. She heaved herself into the bathtub and said, "I couldn't give a fuck. I never liked that uptight bitch anyway."

Knees jammed into her teeth, she looked into my father's terrified eyes and said, "I'm happy she's busy."

They made it through the night without a birth, and in the morning my father went down and cleared himself a spot in the mayhem to wait for "someone else." He was wracked with worry, sure that they were going to be given a second-rate apprentice, some fool even less knowledgeable about childbirth than himself. They were headed for disaster.

Through the steaming heat and the crowds of human trash, he saw the shimmering mirage of a jewel. A tiny, elegant woman with a shock of silver hair in a purple silk Saari was making her way through the filthy masses with the graceful strides of a prince. She was holding a piece of paper and checking it against addresses in doorways.

When he saw her his breathing slowed. He sat up straight and watched her navigate the shit show. With perfect authority, she walked straight up to him and said, "You must be Ilya. I am Asoka, your midwife," and shooed him inside. She followed him up the stairs at a clip, firing questions at him in an Indian-British accent hybrid.

"Where is the mother? How often are the contractions? What are the nature of the contractions? Hurry, hurry, hurry."

She burst into the apartment and proclaimed: "Yes, I am a replacement. We have never met before, and you are probably worried about my qualifications. Let me tell you, I have birthed five thousand children with my bare hands, many of them at the foot of the Himalayan mountains. I know what I'm doing. Let me examine you. Get up! Why are you lying down?"

This is the nature of America, a place where immigrants who were doctors and master surgeons in their own countries come to find streets paved with gold, and end up driving taxis. By some idiotic bureaucratic oversight, my stunned parents had stumbled into the care of this wizard, who was not only first rate, but one of the most masterful midwives in the world. Someone who had birthed children under the most extreme conditions—from elevators to mud huts, from Bombay to Liverpool—who the United States didn't recognize as qualified for a birthing license. They could not have felt safer. They were delighted, in awe, in love.

Asoka Roy put her hands on my mother's misshapen belly and made a rather sober face. Feeling around, she discovered that I was backward, sitting spine to spine with my mother.

"Get up, get out of bed, grab a rag, and wash the floor! Like this."

Asoka dropped to her knees and began to demonstrate what she called "the Rock," a sweeping motion with the arms, dragging a rag back and forth across the floor, an activity that moved my mother's hips and was meant to reposition the baby correctly in the birth canal.

This was her philosophy: A woman giving birth is not sick. *You are as healthy as you will ever be. You are doing what you were designed to do, and your body is performing what it was put here to perform, and the last thing you will do is act ill. The* best *thing you can do is use your body and generate as much activity as possible.* This was music to my mother's ears.

Having revolutionized their view of childbirth and assured them that there would be no delivery that night, Asoka went home to sleep. When she returned the next morning, she found my mother in a new state. She was in agony from more frequent contractions, and when

Asoka examined her for the second time, naked on the wooden floor, she found that the baby had not yet turned. On top of that, my mother was dilating very slowly, so it was going to be a long haul.

After thirty hours they were all delirious. Rhonna's belly was stretched beyond anything she could imagine, and her formidable vocal cords were shredded from the screams.

At some point, with that much prolonged pain, your mind loosens and your body takes over. Some ancient mechanism kicks in and puts you into autopilot. You have no control. Things are just happening inside of you.

Thirty-five hours in, my mother rolled up her eyes and checked out, leaving my father, nature, and Asoka Roy each with a hand on the reins.

Asoka realized that if someone as powerful as my mother was unable to ride this out, they would need help. She looked into Ilya's beleaguered face and said, "We are taking her to the hospital."

The little woman and the skinny boy carried Rhonna, screaming the whole way, down three flights of stairs. As they came to the shattered glass of the front door, my father looked out and saw the unimaginable: the gigantic men's shelter was having a fire drill. Seven hundred sweating bodies were teeming over the block and pushing their way up his stoop. Seven hundred shirtless, Newport-smoking vagrants, shouting and hurling things, their voices like thunder, shaking the buildings.

Asoka squawked and my father snapped to, pulling the door open. At that moment, her legs in my father's hands, fingernails digging into her midwife's arms, my mother let out a showstopping scream.

A sea of men, the kind who carried knives in their teeth, went silent. Seven hundred faces turned toward the embattled trio. In awe of the most natural wonder, the sea parted. Hands came out to support them, and slowly, carefully, she was brought down the five concrete steps, bellowing from depths she didn't know she had. Someone brought a taxi from the corner, and they laid her into the backseat, Asoka with

Rhonna, Ilya in the front; they drove through the reverent crowd, and as they turned uptown on the Bowery the parting closed behind them and the roar erupted again.

THE BIRTHING ROOM would be arranged according to my mother's requirements: lights out, music on—jazz, reggae, and blues. Asoka placed my exhausted, overwhelmed father at my mother's feet and ordered him to hold her leg. She told him to soothe her, help her breathe. She elbowed away the doctors and nurses to ensure that my father was a central part of the arrival. Five thousand births and you learn to take no shit.

There was an enormous amount of pain and screaming. I crowned, but I wasn't going any farther. Asoka gave my mother a little cut, and suddenly, I arrived. I had come out backward, covered in slime and blood, but I was a living, breathing little creature.

They put me on my mother's chest. My parents had made a point of not asking my gender, because they had no preference, it changed nothing for them, and they wanted the surprise.

Wrapped in blankets, breasts stretched so big they felt like cement, my mother looked down into the face of a tiny baby girl. To her, I looked like a mango. To my father, I looked like Winston Churchill crossed with a dried apple.

At that moment, both parents hovering over me, my tourmaline-blue eyes popped open. Bang. Hello. Perhaps my infant intuition was trying to catch a glimpse of what would be a rare sight: the two of them together.

My father had been scribbling potential names on napkins for weeks. He was leaning toward a high and a low sound, a line and a disc, an on and an off, a moon and a demigoddess. Jupiter's moon, iO. The most volcanic object in the solar system. Now it was settled.

A FEW HOURS LATER, my ma was ready to go. The doctors tried to convince her to stay the night, but Asoka had demolished their authority before going home to sleep, and Ma wanted to get the fuck out of there.

We went up to my grandparents' house and they took me out for a walk on my first night in this world, bundled up in blankets like a papoose.

Over the next few weeks, my parents took me to jazz clubs, and the theater, and the dance floors at the Limelight and Danceteria. They put me right there on the table and let well-wishers come flocking. Rhonna was going to make sure she didn't raise a shy kid.

*Us*

## Chapter 3

# Fernando

*Lower East Side, summer 1989*

M A ALWAYS SAYS THE DAY I WAS BORN WAS THE HOTTEST day New York has ever seen. Today she took that back.

"Today," she says with a clenched jaw and eyes burning with furious excitement, "is the hottest motherfucking day this town has ever had to melt through."

From where I am I can see the street steaming. Nearly naked bodies all around me are glistening with sweat and glitter, writhing to blaring samba music. I'm at the front corner of a float, moving down Avenue C in the annual Brazilian Day Festival, which is a roaring parade of referee whistles, cowbells, and thunderous beats. As far as I can see, there are women in thongs and headdresses, shirtless men in tiny shorts, and every variation of yellow and green, the colors of Brazil's national flag.

The sun crackles down on hundreds of smiling faces, including my friends Little Sean and Badu, who are hanging off the float with me. Everyone is dancing or singing or playing an instrument, sweating and dehydrated. Several people have climbed onto the back of our float in exhaustion and passed out.

My friends and our chariot are enclosed in a sea of samba school students dressed in all white, hitting giant drums in unison that hang from their waists. It's like an army band, only with a sexy South American rhythm. You can hear the rumble coming from ten blocks away.

I'm so slathered in SPF 70 that my headband keeps slipping down my face. It's hard for me to hold on to the edge of the float because my hands slide off. Sean's mom's boyfriend built this monster of a rolling contraption out of a real boat. He put it on wheels, put a motor in it from a car he took apart, covered the whole thing with sheets and decorations, and now, somehow, it's moving toward Houston Street. I'm sure it's going to fall apart any minute, so I hold on as tight to the edge as I can, swinging my hips to the music and sliding back and forth.

Ma is on the street in front of us, cutting a path down the avenue with tight, hyperactive samba steps, in a sparkling bathing suit hung with glittering tassels that shake with her waist, arms in the air. She dances alongside a fleet of women with bright cloth head wraps and voluminous dresses called *baianas*. They're doing choreographed partner dances with men in tight pants and shirts with big, open collars who swing the women out so that their dresses sweep past them and curl back around.

I love this parade. I love the Brazilians. They have so much life. They love to dance, they love to sweat, they love music, and they love it *loud*. Ma is in ecstasy when she can dance freely like this with these people. I watch her move like an animal fulfilling nature's intentions, sweat pouring from her body.

A space parts between some of the drumming students, and a guy in a purple sequin suit appears on the other side of the crowd. He seems to be honing his focus on my ma, spinning toward her, kicking his legs and waving his forearms. He's a damn good dancer, this guy. Ma spots him and smiles in that demure way when she's willing to consider a dude, and he takes his opportunity.

Poppa stopped living with us right around when my first tooth came in. They couldn't get along. They were never meant to. They couldn't share a life, much less a cramped space, so he found the nearest loft he could and moved out. Now I spend afternoons with him and his new girlfriend, Rita. She's Brazilian, too, and pregnant.

Ma and this dancer guy circle each other, moving like it's their last day on earth, flailing wildly with every ounce of energy they have in them, ignoring the fact that the heat index probably broke an hour ago and even the sun is eager for the moon to take over.

His muscular shoulders are nearly popping the seams on the back of his sequin jacket. I can't even imagine how hot it must be inside there, but he doesn't take it off, he just keeps dancing.

He smiles at my ma, flashing bright white teeth that contrast the darkness of his skin and the jet black of his hair. A gold chain glints on his broad chest, and every time he kicks his legs I notice the ferocity with which they snap back under him.

AS WE MOVE FARTHER DOWNTOWN, it gets hotter and hotter and people are starting to disintegrate in the swelter, but Ma is getting more and more energy. Miraculously, so is purple sequins guy, and they are orbiting each other like burning fire planets, spinning faster, kicking higher, dipping lower.

The band members have started to peel off their shirts and are upending bottles of water over their steamy heads. Just when you'd think it was a lost cause, though, the leader jumps back out in front of the troops and starts banging on a cowbell and dancing to his own beat, furiously blowing on his whistle. With his white T-shirt tied around his head, sweat pouring down his dark face, he starts bounding back and forth in front of the drummers, corralling them back into action. We hit a red light at First Avenue and he uses the pause to coordinate a unified commencement. Ma and suit guy are still dancing, watching the drummers merge back into each other's rhythm. They are the fuse that erupts the parade.

Everyone congregates back in the parking lot of Cuando when they're done, all fired up and yelling and still playing music, high off the energy of the crowd.

Cuando is a massive abandoned public school that stretches across the better part of Second Street, between Second Avenue and the

Bowery. It has no electricity, but lots of artists and junkies squat here.

Nilda and Virginia, two Puerto Rican ladies in their forties, are the matriarchs of the place, keeping the real nasty riffraff out and a campfire going on the roof. They cook up rice and beans and homemade sofrito in a little cement penthouse, a mortar and pestle in one hand and a can of Budweiser in the other.

We go up there and play the drums and soccer and throw balls around with abandon because the roof is enclosed by a huge, high black metal fence that bends in over us, so we can never lose the balls over the edge.

Because there's no electricity it gets gnarly at night in the hallways. When you have to take a piss, you just wander into one of the rooms and find a corner and let it go. Trying to find the bathroom could get you killed, tripping over a sleeping punk or drunk and tumbling down the pitch-black stairs.

The parking lot out front is a big, nasty mud pit with some plywood boards thrown down to make pathways for walking on. It's overflowing with the crowds from the parade, piles of drums, the start of a BBQ in a metal trash can, and the popping bottle sounds that signal the end of a long day.

The street is clogged with the makeshift floats, parked akimbo half on the sidewalk, coming in to dock and be dismantled once the sun goes down and everyone is drunk enough not to give a fuck.

I'm holding a piece of chicken, slathered in BBQ sauce, that Virginia gave me. Half the sauce is smeared across my face, and I am absolutely fine with that. Ma is discussing something with the *baiana* ladies. Everyone has been preparing for the parade for weeks, building the floats and making the costumes, so we all know each other, and it's no surprise when purple sequin guy appears again at Ma's elbow.

He has a strong, fine jawbone, like a jaguar or a puma or something, and deep caramel skin. A scar cuts across his forehead, which, I will later find out, he got from climbing barbed-wire fences to pick mangoes straight from the tree in Brazil.

Flashing his blinding white teeth, he smiles, and says, "Ey . . ."

The *baiana* lady looks at him and in her big, beautiful, rolling Brazilian accent says, "Ohh, Fernando. Honna, this is Fernando. Fernando, Honna," and moves away into the crowd to leave them to work fate. Fernando, smooth as chocolate, in a thick accent, says, "Ey, Honna. We go to another parade in Wash D.C. Why don't you come?"

She looks him straight in the eye, points to me with one lazy finger, and says, "Hey, Fernando, I got a tiny child right heres. We're not going to Washington, D.C."

The way they smile at each other is loaded, and they are both still eletrified from their dance marathon, but they only exchange a few more little pleasantries and he ambles away, resigned to her unattainability.

It's a year before they see each other again. We're walking up Broadway toward Fourteenth Street, and suddenly there he is, with some young buck Brazilian friend of his, taping signs to lampposts for house-painting services. They catch sight of each other and that's it. She brings him home and he never leaves.

OVER TIME I LEARN THIS: Fernando is from Belo Horizonte. He went to *futbol* boot camp growing up, a place where they keep young men in a fenced-in encampment, training and training relentlessly, to become professional soccer players. He ended up playing for the national teams of Brazil, Portugal, and France, until the French stiffed him out of twenty-five grand and he came to New York to be with his brothers. His legs are considered lethal weapons.

He told us that his uncle had shot his wife, in public, at a café in Brazil, and that the police turned their cheek to crimes of passion there. I watched my ma react to that story, and later that night she said to me, "Ah hell, I am never going to Brah-*ʒil*!"

But we knew then that he had the violent gene of jealousy. Ma told me Billy had had it, too. That thing where something comes into people's eyes and they turn into an animal. Over on Twelfth Street, in his new apartment, my father had already started fending off Rita's incinerating jealousy, her X-ray eyes that saw a thousand things that weren't there.

Fernando lives with us now. I like him a lot. He brings home pasta cooked in tomato oil, from the restaurant where he works in the kitchen. He takes me out on his shoulders when he goes selling shit, and he's teaching me the tricks of the trade—how to hustle people into spending more than they know they should on stuff they don't need, just by being charming. He's also teaching me how to be a master soccer player. We get along like gangbusters, and from his shoulders I get a commanding view of the mercantile chaos of the Midtown streets.

We all go to the beach together, and they make out while I build sand castles and make friends with the old people. We eat mangoes together and we dig the salt water. They are really in love, and I like that.

They created a samba act together, Fernando and my ma. At first it was a duet act, and then they expanded it to include other girls, in costumes and headdresses, and then the musicians from the samba school joined them, then eventually the *capoeiristas*. The whole Carioca cachaça klatsch. It was impressive and became a sensation for a little while. They'd do gigs at public schools during the day and club shows at night.

Fernando's jealousy has been getting worse, though. After one of the parties they came home in a cab and apparently he really threw a shit fit with one of the other girls there. It turned into a screaming match on the street, with him yelling nasty things at my ma. When they exploded into the house, I was pretending to sleep, but I listened to them tear into each other, him accusing her of all kinds of things I know she'd never do. My friend Badu was sleeping over, and eventually we got up and watched them yelling in the kitchen, until Fernando reared back and socked Ma square in the face.

I yelped, loud, but I couldn't move. I felt glued to the spot, but Badu ran straight for him and started wailing on his waist. Fernando, in the heat of the moment, kicked him in the shin and my tiny friend crumpled into a crying pile on the kitchen floor. That was a disaster, him kicking a little kid, and Fernando stormed out.

Then things changed, one night when I wasn't there. I was having a sleepover with my poppa and when I came back, something was different. Fernando wasn't warm anymore.

He started shouting Ma down in the street, saying mean things to sink her self-confidence. He gets real insecure and has started accusing her of more and more outlandish shit. She just grabs my hand and keeps walking, but I can always see her holding back tears about it.

Ma has worked out a signal with me that involves a hand behind her back. I'm supposed to slip out and find the cops if she ever gives it.

One night, coming home from the beach, we see a cop car parked right outside our door, two officers in the front seat doing their paperwork by the light of the dashboard. It's a hot night, and the air between Fernando and my ma is thick with heat and tension. Ma starts cooking when we get upstairs, but something lights Fernando's fuse. He starts yelling, his eyes like black fire, and when he hauls off and kicks a cabinet, denting the wooden door, Ma throws me the signal.

I take the stairs two at a time, almost tumbling down, throw open the heavy front door, and wave the cops up.

"Hey! Hey! My ma needs help! Come on!"

A lady cop and her fat partner come in and assess the situation: a burly man panting with aggression, a woman shielding her small child.

The lady cop says to my ma, "What do you want to do with him?"

Heavy in the heart but looking Fernando straight in the face, Ma says, "Just get him outta here. There will be no violence around my little daughter or myself."

So the cops drag him out, and we pack a suitcase with all his shit, including his passport, and drop it down in a neighbor's apartment so he doesn't have any excuse to come breaking the door down.

A few weeks later we're coming home late one night, just Ma and me. We went out to a bar and she had two glasses of wine for the first time in a real long time. As we're coming up to the building, she starts to cry. She's holding my hand and letting out these long, wailing, weeping sobs. It's disorienting to see my rock crumble. I don't know what to do.

We climb the front steps and suddenly she pulls back and puts her fist through the small square pane of glass in the thick metal door. It smashes on impact. This scares me. I've never seen my ma get violent. When I look up into her eyes, she's gone, and there is a new creature there, eyes black with fire.

This sinister force will eventually creep into every crevice of our world. It will corrode our treasured bond, destroy my trust, and cripple my mother. It is the great equalizer, indiscriminate, brutal, and swift in its recruitment, and I will watch as it nimbly swallows my fiercest protectors and leaves all of our lives forever stained.

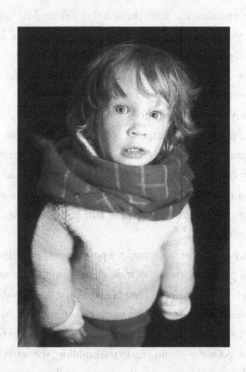

## Chapter 4

# Turning Five

## The Bowery, September 2, 1990

OUR APARTMENT IS LIKE A RIVERBOAT. BIG WINDOWS OPEN out onto the howling street four stories below, and sunlight floats in on the steady breeze. The shifting sky turns our house into a Pantone kaleidoscope, bathing the rooms in dramatic moods and colors, revolving with the weather and the hour. Bright blue, deep orange, burnt red, purple, and rippling swathes of gold. Sunbeams bounce off the licorice-black fire escape, slick from a rain just passed. They hover high above and then plunge into the chaotic street that grumbles and creaks under poverty's aching, struggling ass.

The golden shimmer splashes over the men's shelter and the bedlam slithering around its entrance; a school of bottom feeders in leather vests, torn overcoats, bubble jackets, and bright do-rags; a zigzag of gray jail buses, yellow trees, and sidewalks littered with cigarette butts smoked to the filter.

On warm weekends, the beautiful trannies come down from the Bronx to entertain the shelter boys, get high, and soak the bums for their nickels. There is a heightened pitch across the street right now, because they're here. Sandy, a bombshell with the high cheekbones of a fashion model, is splayed across a picnic table in their fenced-in yard, fawning and fanning herself, sunning and showing off the lavish outfit she sewed, from looks pulled from the pages of *Vogue*. She wears a high ponytail and kind of resembles my ma.

Car horns, distant sirens, Sandy's laughter, and the hissing of a bus all commingle with the sad, honey wail of a saxophone next to my ear. My body is curled around my godfather, James, who is sitting cross-legged on our lacquered wood floor practicing his instrument. I'm wearing a powder-blue dress made of lace and lipstick-red cowboy boots. My long braid is resting on the floor next to me like a sleeping cat.

James is practically my ma's brother. He looks out for her. When she showed up here strung out on Johnnie Walker and grief at the murder of her one great love, James gave her comfort, shelter, safety. He swung his detective cape over her spirit and made sure everybody knew she was under his mayoral protection.

They're a tall, slender breed, with majestic profiles. They look like brother and sister. James slides onto the stages of local hot spots and commands audiences, leading his famous band, playing the sax in his house slippers. Chicks faint like flies for his big pouty lips and his sharp suits. Even practicing around the house he looks like an old Hollywood detective with a jazz fetish. He has a tuft of chest hair that barely peeks out of his wifebeaters and it causes a frenzy.

We are having a party in the community garden on Sixth Street today to celebrate my turning five, and James is on cohosting duty.

Walking there, arms laden with decorations and food, we sidestep split concrete, scurrying rats, and little boys playing stickball across the pavement. The pink ball thwacks into a wall, then a car, then a storefront window, and everybody scatters.

A hydrant is shooting water across Avenue B, and screaming children are pushing each other in and out of the spray. Spanish women with asses overflowing from cheap plastic beach chairs cluck at me and moan, *"Que linda! Que linda!"* This makes me feel embarrassed. I put my head down and frown, making a mental note not to ever wear this dumb dress again.

Ma and James set the party up while I swing my boots back and forth from a big white metal chair. They string chili lights that we found at the ninety-nine-cent store from some high branches over to a rickety shack plastered with concert posters. A cowgirl piñata is hanging from a branch, its ankles swinging a few inches above a broomstick that leans against the trunk, waiting to demolish it.

On a dusty strip of concrete I show off my tap moves to our friends: tall, handsome French Chris who Ma says is "a dead ringer for Alain Delon." He wears a pack of Camels rolled into the sleeve of his black T-shirt. Hammerhead, my dad's giant of a friend who earned his name using construction tools to set people straight on debts. Trixie, with her bright orange hair and kooky Texan outfits, who used to crush pennies into tourist medallions at the top of the Empire State Building. She has a store on Ninth and A called LSD—"Live, Shop, Die." My two beloved aunts, Alice and Olivia.

Alice is my ma's little sister. She moved here a couple of years ago from China, where she went after law school. She's a badass and speaks fluent Mandarin. She's so nice and calming. When Alice comes around you just feel like you can relax because everything is gonna be taken care of. Ma spends hours on the phone with her. They call each other "baby." Alice is always giving me jars of pickles and delicious shit she makes in her little house in Brooklyn.

Alice is elbow to elbow with my pop's sister, Olivia. Seeing them next to each other, you realize they're the same petite, black-haired, shit-together kind of breed. Olivia chain-smokes and is working toward her nine millionth master's degree. She's basically a walking brain with huge eyes and a huger smile. Sometimes she closes her big pillowed eyelids when she's talking to you so she can gather her elegant thoughts in peace. She will own a company one day, with her name engraved in a brass plaque on the building outside.

Olivia is reaching to top off Alice's rosé when a commotion pulls our attention to the garden entrance. My godmother has arrived. She comes bustling through the gate, leading with her bosoms, two cameras around her neck, barking something at the cabdriver over her shoulder. I squeal and run to be picked up and smothered in her ample chest.

My godmother, Nan, is a bodacious, luscious, curvy, cabs-only type person. Her hair bounces in big red curls, and the only makeup she wears is a greasy smear of red lipstick.

Ma says Nan is touched. She says she's got the magical lucky gold pyramid on her shoulder, because everything she touches turns to gold. Currently that theory is holding because in her embrace I'm turning to melted precious metal.

Nan's a night person, so she's pale like bones. We went to visit her in Sicily when I was one, and there she was, the most unlikely person on a beach, spilling out of her black bathing suit, snapping photos of her weirdo friends draped over the volcanic rocks.

Nan and my ma met when Ma was in a movie and Nan was the set photographer. Nan was nuts about Ma and they started chatting. She asked my ma if she would do a lingerie shoot for the first-ever color spread in the *Village Voice*, and Ma ended up, eight months pregnant, laid out on the stone benches at the Russian & Turkish Baths in a swimsuit, being warned not to boil her baby.

Nan was the one who told Ma to start swimming. She asked Nan to be my godmother because Nan was real, and she had the lucky pyramid.

I love Nan, who breezes in, hugs me, gets herself a drink, and goes to say hello to my father and my new baby brother, who's perched on his lap.

Pop is sitting with his wife, Rita, who is spooning some kind of mush into my brother's mouth. Rita is bad news. She eyes Nan and her big tits when she bends over and kisses my pop on the cheek, because

Rita is psycho jealous. She came from nothing, so she's sharp, razor-eyed, protecting what she's got, and I know how mean she can be. Rita would eviscerate a woman for crossing the line. The problem is just figuring out where the line is in her garbled brain.

Rita is a beauty, with thick raven hair, full eyebrows, and a gleaming, deceptive smile. She's moody as hell and she's got that Catholic thing, like she's got spirits running around behind her eyes when her mind is quiet.

Uncle Crispy, the one who played Hamlet, is occupying Pop's ear. Crispy is a close talker. He does this thing where something sparks him and he nails you, telling you how it *really* is, because he is the ultimate authority. On everything.

Crispy is the one who first introduced Ma and Pop, in the middle of Ninth Street when she was running to a dance class. She was in short shorts and Poppa was in a trench coat. Crispy introduced her as "the flame that cannot be extinguished," even though he's the one that can't be put out by the hose of a million people telling him to shut the hell up all the time. The veins in his neck pop out because he'll get so incensed, telling you stories, correcting history.

Nan kisses Crispy's curls, blowing past, and he grabs my pop's elbow, leaning in and saying, "Listen, man, this is the real shit, the way it really went down, okay?"

Across the garden is my poppa's best friend, Yanik, and his wife, Esther, who are the Hungarian John and Yoko of a tribe of expats who escaped from Communist Budapest with the clothes on their backs. They had to literally walk out of the country. They made it to Paris, in their black coats and long beards, then skipped to New York, where a fan gave them a building on Twenty-third Street to build their theater company. They painted the ceilings gold and the entire tribe lives and creates there, next to the Chelsea Hotel, all the children bathing in the one tub in the living room, Colombian coke dealers sneaking in and out to do business with Yanik.

Yanik is tall, angular, and thin, with thick black brows and cavernous eyes that are simultaneously dark and sparkling. He speaks through a lush Hungarian accent, in a voice that should be narrating a twisted movie of *Little Red Riding Hood*. His jaw is bold and defined, and his nose is like a broad landing strip. His perfectly round head looks like nature made it bald so that his mind could be closer to his audience. When he speaks through his full lips and strong teeth, people sit forward and listen.

Yanik and Esther have a daughter, Mira, who I consider my sister. She's the baby vampire of their tribe. Once Ma walked into their family hotel room and Yanik and Esther were sleeping in separate twin beds like coffins, and Yanik was talking and laughing in his sleep.

Yanik is perched on the edge of a child's stool now, the blue plastic feet sinking into the grass. He's holding a fly swatter and a cigarette with a two-inch ash, speaking animatedly to a filmmaker friend in drawling Hungarian. Their language sounds like diamonds rolling around the bottom of a crater lake, lilting and rough at the same time. The two men lean in toward each other, legs draped over their thighs and wrists dangling. Occasional bursts of English reveal that they are discussing a scene the friend shot over the winter.

It was during a historic blizzard that had whited out the entire city. New York normally gives snow a twenty-four-hour window to bedazzle and show off before reducing it to filthy black slush lining the gutters, but this time the powder persevered in the crispy air. Tourists were skiing across Midtown, and everything was muffled under a blanket of crunchy white flakes. Even the hobos were chased indoors by the cold.

Yanik's filmmaker friend sat at our front window and trained his camera downward onto a man stumbling up the street. I watched from behind him as the guy, dressed in nothing but his shirtsleeves, weaved among the desolate cars, clutching his groin like he was in some horrible pain. He hunched over, jerked forward, and lurched into the soft silence, beating a path into our barren block. I looked up the street and the tenements looked like ghost houses.

There was a sweet hobo named Rex who circled the shelter's yard that winter and made the sidewalks in front of it his domain. He was knifed right there during that storm. It took so long for them to realize he wasn't sleeping or drunk that by the time the ambulance pulled up onto the sidewalk, he was frozen solid and partially covered by snow. Two weeks later, we saw the men slipping around in crimson slush. Ma made me look away, and wouldn't speak until the sun was down.

Back in the garden, a petite, muscle-bound man with shimmering, perfectly moisturized caramel skin walks over to the piñata tree, picks up the stick, and turns toward me, grinning. His disfigured face is smashed in and flattened from a decade as a professional prizefighter.

A gold bracelet glints above immaculately manicured fingers as he takes my wrists and hoists me above a halo of clipped black curls. His lisp bespeaks a series of brain injuries when he asks me, slowly, if I'm "ready to tear thith motherfuckah apaht." I tell him I am.

I am sitting on the shoulders of George Nelson, another of Ma's protectors and oldest friends. He'll come over sometimes to take us to dinner in his big Cadillac that he keeps cleaner than a hospital ward. It will take us an hour to go three blocks because he drives around and around, circling the restaurant, looking for the perfect parking spot where the Caddy won't get scratched, because it's his baby. He'll stop along the way to walk ceremoniously around the car like he's circling a racehorse, then open the trunk and get something out, like a pristine jacket.

Ma says that's what happens to people who grow up in filth; they go in the exact opposite direction and become a clean maniac, a germ freak.

Sometimes George will have a flash in the middle of a sentence where his eyes will roll up and freeze under the lids because he's having a punch-drunk moment and his brain is just having a gap. Then he'll pick up where he left off.

A jiggling metallic light bounces off the façades and dirty windows, passes through the high branches, and splashes over George's face. Looking down into his eyes as he carries me over to the noosed piñata, I see that they are crystal brown, like the toffees that old people suck on. Clear caramel.

THE GARDEN PARTY IS over. The cowgirl piñata got smashed into a mess of crepe paper fringes. It was filled with sesame candies, glitter, and honey sticks. Alice is packing up the ruins of the cake with delicious frosting, ravaged by the Hungarians. The chili lights are tangled in a milk crate and the rats are nibbling at a trash bag full of paper plates.

I feel different now that I'm five. As we approach our stoop that night, I am aware of something changing. I want to get this stupid dress off me and burn it. I want to run to the roof naked and light up a sparkler.

When we get back into the apartment I rip off the blue lace, go straight to my box of cowboy-and-Indian stuff, and pull out a tube of war paint. Staring out the window, I put two long smears of color straight across my cheeks, under each eye. I stomp into the hall and climb the steps to the roof methodically, Ma in tow. She's not asking any questions and I'm not giving any answers. I don't have any, I just feel a push in my belly.

I kick the door open with a karate move and rush out into the noisy darkness. The lukewarm air washes over me and I tiptoe around the edge of the roof so as not to wake the neighbors.

Ma is behind me, holding her tiny Minox B spy camera, watching.

I stand at the very edge of the sticky black tar ledge and look out over the snarling city. I'm not thinking, but I'm intent on something beyond what I can see. Something is burning up that I can't place. I clench and unclench my fists. I wiggle my toes. I scratch an itch on my ankle with my foot. I want to scream over the street. Something is aggravating my insides that wants out.

I pull my underwear down, and right there, standing up, I piss.

## Chapter 5

# Alexander Nevsky

A LL HER FRIENDS SPEAK BROKEN ENGLISH.

Ma likes boys with broken teeth and crooked minds, especially if you're from Eastern Europe. If you're hollow eyed, with transparent skin, hemophiliac, with black humor, she loves that. If you can live on a couple of potatoes, if you can build an instrument from garbage, if you speak like Dracula could be a relative, she's yours.

Augustos is the caretaker at the Anthology Film Archives, an immaculate red-brick cinema two blocks from our house that plays only weird art-house movies. It's an old building on the corner of Second and Second where they screen all the stuff that's too strange for general consumption.

Augustos told her he played the saxophone and that they were having a party at the cinema and we should come. It was a huge crew of Lithuanians, flying around, drinking hard liquor, laughing monstrous, old European laughs. They had thirteenth-century gaps in their teeth and big silver rings on their thick jointed worker fingers. They were a joyous bunch, despite clearly being near starvation, with their old weathered peasant faces. A vampire's ball, heaven for my ma.

Lithuania was somehow crossed with Greece, thus the Greek sounding names: Dalius, Audrius, Augustos. But they were extremely Eastern European and they'd served in the Russian occupation armies. They *hate* the Russians, because they served in those armies. We met two brothers, Dalius and Audrius. Audrius was a video artist and a sculptor, and he told my ma, "With Germans, you know when you will die. With Russians, you know *how* you will die."

Audrius explained that Jonas Mekas opened the Anthology cinema in the early seventies. The building is an old police fortress, with catacombs downstairs. They had an architect thin it out, and the catacombs were filled with tables for actual filmmakers, painting on film with spindles, cutting and splicing, etc.

Jonas Mekas came here in the forties, and Audrius told us that Jonas was having lunch with Salvador Dalí while "brother was in concentration camp having leg eaten by dog." Audrius showed us an old photograph of a man in a concentration camp with his leg being eaten by a dog. It was a man they knew, so we figured it was Jonas's brother.

The Lithuanians have parties that go on for several days. Dalius, the younger brother, is a great rock and roll drummer and shreds up the basement with his endless practicing. The sound of his drumming echoes through the catacombs, where he rehearses for days on end, playing on everything—the pipes, the garbage can lids, the trap kit drums down there. Ma loves the backbeat he does, so we go down and she'll dance. He started giving me lessons. I love banging on the drums and making my ma shake around the creepy rooms.

She got the brothers some work doing hard labor jobs, the same ones she does herself, with Stucco Sam, putting up walls, so Audrius would introduce her at parties as "the heroine of New York," and we got carte blanche to see the movies for free. She says we slip in because I'm cute.

EVERY YEAR our landlord will call and say, "We'd like to give you a turkey," because, basically, we're rat-ass poor and they've got some government-surplus turkeys or something. We have to run and grab one or they will be gone, but Ma doesn't trust them. We bring the turkey back to the apartment and stare at it sitting there in a frozen hunk on the kitchen floor and she says, "Surprise fucking surprise. What's the trick up the sleeve behind this shit? Is it radioactive and they needed to dump it on somebody?"

A roast turkey is a feast for a posse like the Lithuanians, so it's a big deal that the landlord has given us one for free.

Audrius has taken a shine to my ma. They've been spending a lot of time together, and last night he came back to the apartment with us. We were walking home with him and we found this old enamel wash-tub big enough to fill a large oven sticking out of the trash. Audrius laughed his Nosferatu laugh, climbed into the mountain of garbage, pulled it out, and we took it back to our house.

This morning, Ma got up real early to figure out how to wrangle the frozen fowl, by now sitting in a puddle of pink fluid, its wrinkly white skin looking frighteningly human as it thawed.

I woke up because the house was boiling from the oven being on, and found them rubbing the whole thing down with olive oil and herbs, stuffing raisins and berries and dry rice up its ass.

They stuck the bird in the basin with the rice and fruit up its fanny, poured six or eight inches of olive oil on it, and put it in the oven to cook. The thing was literally swimming in an olive oil bath.

After many hours the rice simply burned up. It was still hard and greasy, but the turkey was done. Somehow, by laughing and flashing the screwed-up teeth that she loves, Audrius got my Ma to try a tiny piece, even though she doesn't eat meat. They decided it was too good not to share, so the three of us took the basin by its sides and gingerly carried it down the street to the Anthology, the turkey drowning and us slopping oil onto the sidewalk.

This being Thanksgiving, it's one of the most depressing days of the year. Even the bums have found somewhere to go, except the real despondent ones, the ones that have no idea of the date. It's getting cold at night but the heat is not yet rising through the subway grates, or streaming under the locked church doors to warm their cardboard apartments. They're still out there on the empty, gray streets.

Ma reminds us that this is a day of many suicides. She has a poem about the subway on Thanksgiving Day, where absolutely no one is walking around, and the hobos are freezing or sleeping on the trains, and it's such a gloomy, cold, dark thing.

There are new boys working at the theater, and when we walk in they are astonished and thrilled at our offering, because they too were trying to escape this deathly depressing day. This cements our permanent spot on the guest list as far as they are concerned.

That's how we got in to see *Alexander Nevsky* so many times. I can't even count. It's a movie from the thirties about a Russian warrior who saved his people in medieval times, on horseback.

The Gothic Germans, with "Heil Hitler" hands on their helmets, come to destroy and conquer Russia, carrying a tiny organ that plays only a few creepy, dissonant notes. The head German wears a long white beard to his waist and a white floor-length robe, in this frozen tundra. A kind of ghostly camouflage in the snow and the blinding white projector light.

They're carrying him on sticks, the German army warriors, and picking up the little Russian children and tossing them into burning pits. The Russian children look like me—hollow-eyed kids, with the Germans dropping them into giant flames.

There are huge battle scenes with Nevsky and his cavalry, after which the women wander through the burning frozen landscape, between dead horses and their dead lovers and sons and husbands lying there on the white earth. The creepy musical notes make it feel even paler and more desolate. In the burning devastation there are a lot of knights giving thanks, to God, to Alexander, to the weather, and to the thin ice that swallowed up the German army.

Ma got the soundtrack record and we play it at home a million times. I draw along while she describes scenes from the movie that the soundtrack recalls. I draw one of the landscapes and call it "The Burning Pit." She loves it so much she puts it up immediately. She says it's a great drawing and shows it to Audrius when he comes over.

MA AND THE LITHUANIANS will be friends for a long time. Eventually
Dalius and his little classical piano player wife will have ten kids, who
will tear around on their scooters in tiny fur vests. He and the wife will
break up and he'll move into a cramped little room in a boarding house in
Brooklyn, where he'll love feeding the squirrels outside his windows. It's
all about giving away what you don't even have, and that's what my ma
loves so much: gangster socialism, ghetto generosity. He'll go to his construction jobs all day and drink all night and play the drums at his gigs.

Audrius will drop dead at a party while talking to somebody, real
close to his face, just poof, heart stop, fall to the floor, cold dead. Ma
will say, "It's a horrible thing, but what a funny scene for my dear Au-
driosi."

## Chapter 6

# Cutting My Hair Off

*New York and London,*
*August through September 1991*

I T'S BEEN A LONG SUMMER. A LONG YEAR, REALLY. I STARTED kindergarten at my new school, P.S. 3, in the West Village, which has been fun. The teacher is a nice Irish lady, and the kids are pretty cool. There's this one girl, Colette, who I like a lot. She's tough, from the Bronx. She's skinny little thing like me, but her skin is mahogany and she has patches of ivory near her mouth and her eye. She's beautiful. We're friends now.

School got out in June, and Ma and I spent the summer going to the beach. We took a trip out to Montauk with Ma's Australian friend and his kids, and we almost burnt the damn house down with a brush fire. The neighbors got real mad at him, so after that we decided to stick to the city.

Brighton Beach is the next-to-last stop on the F train out in Brooklyn. All the Russian and Ukrainian immigrants settled there because the setup and the view reminds them of Odessa, where my poppa's maternal grandparents are from. They call it Little Odessa.

The area has a wild, Jewish gangster vibe, like anything could happen and probably will, what with Soviet ex-navy toughs with Star of

David tattoos swilling pitchers of vodka in the boardwalk restaurants, wearing mobster track suits and rapper bling.

Saturdays are a hilarious Ukrainian wildlife parade. The older Jewish emigrés walk up and down the seaside promenade in fluorescent nylons and huge Versace shades, like a runway show out of a ninety-nine-cent store.

Sometimes the wind kicks up and it's a blackout sandstorm, people ducking into the restaurants and waiters struggling to hang huge plastic curtains to keep the sand from piling up in the pierogies and the platters of flounder à la crème.

The really old people weather it all and get up for no one. They stick it out on the beach like bleached buffalo skulls in the gathering dunes of filthy sand.

When it dies down the parade is on again.

Sometimes, on holidays, a ring of Hasidic men dance in circles accompanied by some genius pianist fallen to playing yada riffs on a crappy keyboard with massive speakers hot-wired to a car battery or a lamppost. Ten feet away is a man selling Russian pop mix tapes with photocopied jackets, blasting his wares as loud as he can pump it on *his* massive speakers.

The cacophony of the promised land, Brooklyn, US of A, or the next best thing "till we meet in Jerusalem." Little Odessa.

It's also the best place to get knishes and pierogies. There's a place called Mrs. Stahl's, big and open and fluorescent lit, where they sell huge, overstuffed knishes for $1.25 straight from the ovens right behind the glass. Boys covered in flour serve them up to you at the counter, and nobody speaks English, just how Ma likes it. We get potato only, and slather them in gallons of mustard. Ma doesn't stop eating to breathe when she gets to Mrs. Stahl's.

Then we hit the beach with a vengeance. We always go to the left at the boardwalk. That's our spot, our second living room in the vast outdoor house of New York City where my ma actually lives, her real home.

I'm superstitious about switching spots, so by now we know a lot of the regulars. The grandmas and grandpas who came to New York in the depression bring their cheap beach chairs and let their saggy wrinkles hang out in the sun.

There's one real skinny old guy in tight shorts who plays paddleball with me, slowly. I like him because he knows all about Sherlock Holmes, so we can discuss the cases in detail, me struggling sometimes to understand what he's saying through his thick accent. There's Abel, the round redhead in the micro-Speedo with the barrel chest and the big laugh. He likes my ma, but I think he's a sleaze so I always shoo away.

Ma goes out into the water, leaving me with the old man, and swims way out into the deep green, oily waves. She does laps up and down the entire beach, from the abandoned Coney Island parachute tower to the first rocks of Far Rockaway. I'm talking miles, back and forth, for four hours.

My pop told me that on our trip to Positano when I was six months old my ma hit the water at sunup, leaving us together. Ten hours later she reappeared on the horizon in the setting sun. She told us all about a town she discovered down the coast, and the next one after that, Amalfi, and about a sweet freshwater spring in the sea rocks somewhere where she got a drink. Pop would say she is like Odysseus: she has to have help from some spirits in the waves.

She is calm after she comes back into port, back to me on the beach with my old man sitter, smiling and strong. I entertain myself building elaborate sand castles, reading books, playing with the kooks.

There are restaurants on the boardwalk, Volna, Moskva, and others, where the gangsters hang out, where we stop to get bowls of delicious borscht, a beet soup that's native to these guys, and kvass, a weird malt drink that Ma says is the closest thing to beer or Coca-Cola I'll be allowed to touch for years.

Sometimes, after all the swimming, sand in my butt, belly full of beets, we'll walk the two miles down the boardwalk to Coney Island, looping around the very bottom of New York, where all the carnival rides are scattered like neon whiskers on the city's chin.

Where the melancholy sparkling September sun sets, the skyline bursts into spinning lights and flashing ice cream cones. They sell pastel-colored cotton candy in bundles bigger than my whole head (including my hair), long sausages in big, pasty buns, with huge vats of ketchup and mustard that fat kids squirt all over the place and sodas so big I'd have to pee six times. But I'm not allowed meat or sugar.

As the darkness descends, a long chain of tiny lights approaches through the black sky from the east; all the planes with new visitors to New York, advancing slowly in single file, like a string of UFOs, headed to Kennedy airport somewhere up the coast behind us.

We don't do many of the rides because we usually only have money for one, but our favorite is the bumper cars. If we make the trek down to Coney we beeline it straight for the car track, with its blasting rap music and ballistic disco lights. There's a guy in the ticket booth who gets on the mic and yells obscene stuff at ladies walking by to try and get them to come in. It works. They're always laughing and lining up, so it's always a wait to get in.

Ma stands on the side and watches me as I tear around the track. I usually get a blue car. These things really bring out my competitive streak, so I rarely get smacked, but I do a lot of smashing and speeding around.

By the time we're done, I'm completely zonked, and we go across the street to the F train for the hour-long ride home, during which I sleep on Ma's lap. When I wake up we're back on the Bowery, getting Indian food from the gas station on the corner before I hit the pillow once and for all.

Ma has taken to waking up early this year, at seven, before I do, to brush through my hair and get all the tangles out. She loves my hair so much, with its reddish-golden color, and she hums and sings different songs while she does it, brushing all the way through, down to the bottom at my butt. When she's done, she braids it tenderly down my back. These trips to the beach have been making it hard for her to get the brush through my hair.

WE'RE BOTH IN ONE OF YANIK'S CRAZY THEATER PIECES, and it's performing in London. By the time we get on the plane my hair is just one big tangle at the back of my head because we've been at the beach so much.

I've never been to London, but I'm pretty excited about the bobbies and I definitely want to meet the queen.

My head is in my ma's lap in her airplane seat, and she's trying to brush my hair again. She looked down at me a minute ago and said, "Wow. Your little fox-colored head . . . your little fox-colored hair has a red, electric, like a neon red glass highlight. It's like, wow, extraterrestrial. You look like a little fluorescent bag lady, all matted up."

She starts making strange noises when the brush gets stuck. She isn't getting anywhere with getting the knot out, and I think it's breaking her heart. The knots are at the roots.

By the time we get to our hotel in London, a slender building on Gower Street, it's late. Our room is at the very top under the roof. Ma asks Yanik to come up and says, "Yanik . . ."

I see her take his arm, turn her head, and in a grave tone, say, "Cut her hair."

I can almost see her heart fall out of her chest, like when you're on a roller coaster and you go over a big hill and it goes through your feet. It hurts her to say that, or even think it.

But Yanik does it.

Right then he sits me in front of a mirror and cuts my hair off with a big pair of scissors.

The sound of the first snip is invigorating. It makes me sit upright in my chair and stop kicking my feet. *Snip*. He angles the big metal blades to get under the knots, and my hair falls around my shoulders in big clumps. Ma tells him to cut from the top so we can make the long strands into a wig.

It occurs to me that Yanik is bald, and therefore a weird choice of barber. But I'm into it. I lean toward him, and he cuts and cuts. *Snip. Snip. Snip. Snip. Snip.*

The result is drastic, somewhere between a bowl and a helmet. Clearly, the person who wielded the shears is formerly Communist. You can tell by the severity of it. Ma makes Yanik put all my hair in a black plastic trash bag, and he puts it in the corner of the room under the slanted roof.

The next day is my birthday, so they set up a little party for me. Yanik is there with his daughter, Mira, and some of the other actors in the play. I'm grinning and eating cake.

I know Ma's upset, but I'm thrilled with my new cut. It's chin length, and chopped. Not like a boy's, completely, but short enough. I feel free, like I can tear around the way I want to and I won't be hampered by this pretty bouncing braid all the time.

That night I take out my journal and write, "I have now become a boy."

I race up and down narrow cobblestone streets, imitating people's accents in pubs. Ma and I go on seed-gathering adventures in the parks and back alleys, picking flowers and filling bags with a special dirt she wants to take home. We get tea in tiny, ornate green cups at cafés full of Middle Eastern men, and Ma even lets me eat a baklava in Brixton. I feel like a real world traveler when we see Big Ben, and Ma takes a million photos.

A few days into the trip, Poppa and Rita show up with my little brother. He's so small, and he's dressed like a little Beatle, with perfect bangs, a London street cap, and a checkered suit. His mom sure keeps him looking sharp.

He's pretty eagle-eyed, too. He can spot a Ninja Turtle doll from one black-masked eye poking over the dashboard behind the windshield of a car two blocks down Carnaby Street.

I want to play with him, but Rita is in a permanent fury and throwing fits. The walls are bulging out of the hotel with the sounds of her shouting and screaming, making a scene, so I leave them alone. Ma says Rita has baby ego problems that make her need to steal attention any way she can.

Ma and I go to the queen's palace and I inquire about visiting her. The guy in the fuzzy hat outside tells me that she isn't in.

"Well, where is she?"

"She's in her castle in Scotland at the moment, but I can give you an address for her lady-in-waiting if you'd like to send a letter."

I take the address, and I know that the lady-in-waiting and I will become pen pals, but the guy in the fuzzy hat can't possibly know that.

When we get back to the hotel, Ma flips out and starts cursing. The bag filled with my hair is gone. She tears the room apart looking for it and then drags Yanik up to explain. He says he forgotten what it was and threw it out with the trash. She almost decks him.

Crushed, tears start rolling down her face. I go over and hug her leg and tell her it isn't a big deal, that I will grow more in no time. But to her we have lost a harvest of a crop I have been growing for years, an actual piece of me, now out in the cold world, where someone can use it for some macumba spell.

Later that night she pets my head as I'm falling asleep and murmurs, "It's like something being robbed from your most intimate . . ."

I'm already used to the short hair now. I can put my pencil behind my ear, my goggles fit better, and hats are a whole new universe. Ma's fingers keep pulling at the ends of my hair and she moans occasionally, sadly.

"It's okay, Ma. Don't worry. It'll grow back. Everything will be the same again."

## Chapter 7

# The Invasion

*Third Street, fall 1991*

THE WAY MA DESCRIBES IT, IT'S LIKE THEY RODE IN FROM Fourth Street on horseback. One day we are minding our own business in the asshole of the universe, and the next day these squares are galloping in, handing out bribes or slaughter as they go. Either you're with them, or you're gonna lose your apartment. It's like the German warriors in *Alexander Nevsky* with their flaming pits, but this is real life.

In the center of the petri dish that is our neighborhood, our building is a shining castle of community that the rest of the block has no concept of. The neighbors have each other's backs and we keep shit running smoothly. We don't need any bureaucracy or government input, we pay $125 a month, straight to the City of New York, they give us the keys to the boiler, and we handle the rest. There's heat when it's cold, and the roof door stays open when it's hot. Period.

Our building repels "normal" people. They'd have to love cockroaches, scalding radiators, and thin walls to want to live here, and then they would have to establish their own niche in the zoo and defend it. Everyone's door is a slab of featureless metal punctured by multiple police locks, because there is a high likelihood that some crackhead or starving vagrant is going to try to lift what little shit you have while you're out or sleeping.

The doors are high and dark, with old transom windows. Every edge is kind of soft-focused due to centuries of thick paint layers that suffocate the original details. When a piece cracks off you can count the richly colored rings, like a petrified tree.

Our building has a broad chest of red brick, festooned with fire escapes, four windows across. There are two windows to each apartment and four apartments on each floor, two at the front and two at the back.

There is a cluster of trash cans to the left of the entrance, and a metal cage to the right where the maintenance men keep their cleaning shit. In the center are five concrete steps, flanked by a pair of ovals like a robust pair of women's thighs, caked in beige stucco.

My poppa says Greek plays always happen in front of the palace, not inside, and I can see why. If it's not old people talking to themselves, misfits forcing conversation on innocent women, or teenagers yelping and lighting fireworks, the stoop is also home to every intimate freak-out, marital spat, and parental screaming match that should play out in the privacy of people's homes. Only an absolute masochist would take the apartment with a bedroom window directly overlooking this chaotic mess. A masochist like Joey Charles.

Joey is known for waving his .44 Magnum out his window and yelling in the middle of the night, which probably means he has more distressing things going on behind his blackout curtains than the noise from the stoop. Ma says he's a paranoid schizophrenic, and that's why she likes him. She's drawn to men with such a disposition, unfortunately. They are a special species, oddballs with too much juice and a violent streak. Sometimes Joey gets taken away to "rest" for a few months, and we keep track of his mail.

Joey is of the breed of thick-skinned, sandpaperlike personalities that are drawn to the life down here, each of them marked by their personal measure of poverty, illness, bad luck, or addiction. Unemployable misfits, worn down by life at the outermost edges of society.

This area is home to a lot of fidgeters and pacers shouting at the sky, people with fuses permanently lit.

Some of them come to slum it on a dare, looking to score cheap. In no time they are snatching at the lowest rungs of the substance ladder to quiet the clanging in their minds.

Some of them are people who have nothing, so they scour the streets and make palaces out of windowless boxes filled with the resurrected spirit of other men's garbage. And then there are the psychos . . .

One day shortly after I was born, a blond Texan kid with a long beard tried to talk his way into our apartment for the night with some Christian gibberish, but my dad shifted me into the crook of his arm farthest from the creepy kid, and told him no way. Later the guy killed a German ballerina and fed her to the homeless in Tompkins Square Park, stewed with onions.

The first memory I have of Joey is when my ma and I were trying to wrangle a stolen three-foot metal street sign that said BROADWAY into the entranceway, and the hall being blocked by his hairy, rotund mass. Stuffed into a beige trench coat with the collar popped up, sweating profusely, he was pounding a brass police lock into its latch. Joey had drilled countless locks onto his apartment door and he was struggling to shut the last one, cursing to himself.

He and Ma exchanged greetings, and unsurprisingly, Joey took a shine to her. He came up a few days later to sit around the kitchen and regale her with stories. They became fast friends.

But back to our building.

When you enter, you are walking into a living organism. Either Joey's screaming accosts your eardrums from the right, or the first door on your left creaks open until the chain snaps taut. A pale, red-bearded face peers out and inspects you as you pass. This belongs to Fritz, an emaciated recluse who locks himself in his apartment for days on end, tinkering with pianos he's hauled in from the street. Fritz only wears one set of black clothes, and he has long bushy hair the color of Tropicana orange juice, which gives him the stretched-out look of a Goth leprechaun. He smokes pot incessantly, and his skin is translucent from never leaving the house.

Over several years of trick-or-treating and kid manipulation, I've managed to get an eyeful of the inside of his cluttered apartment. He has six upright pianos crammed in there, and he's built a loft for his bed above the kitchen. There are plastic bags filled with his stuff all around, hanging from nails banged into two-by-fours that he's painted gloss black. His kitchen is lit by one exposed bulb over a sink piled up with vinyl records and unspooled cassettes.

Once you've made it past Joey and Fritz, the gray-green stairwell starts halfway down the hall. This is a godsend, because beyond that it reeks of cat piss to the point of nausea. The left rear apartment is inhabited by Susan, a diminutive middle-aged woman with unfortunate helmetlike hair and a pinched, perpetually pissed-off face. We call her the Cat Lady because she's got seventeen cats in there that she's "rescued," turning her tiny studio apartment into a feline outhouse.

On the other side of the wall from us is Henri, a pompous French filmmaker with a blond buzz cut and tight suits. When my parents were subletting his apartment, I was conceived on his kitchen floor and nearly born in the living room. We can hear him clomping around in there with his heavy footsteps, yelling into the phone in an exaggerated accent like he's an avant-garde film mogul.

MY FATHER ACTUALLY STOLE OUR APARTMENT. After I was born and he realized subletting Henri's wouldn't last, he kept his eyes peeled for a chance to crack the impenetrable waiting list for this building. One day he spotted our young junkie neighbor wobbling out her door at midnight with a huge overstuffed suitcase. She couldn't make the rent. Three months later Poppa broke in through the fire escape window and stole the place. In New York City a rent-controlled apartment is gold, and he wanted to leave my ma something. It took him a year to con a receptionist at the city to accept a rent check from him, but as soon as she did, they had to give him a lease.

Below us is Peruvian Miriam, who I call the Purple Woman for no apparent reason, and her husband, Miguel. Once, Miguel came up in his pajamas and told us, in his tired, unhysterical way, that there was shit oozing through his ceiling, and could we please make it stop. Our bathroom is the size of a British phone booth, only painted bright green. It's just off the kitchen, and when we opened the door we saw that the toilet had backed up and flooded the room.

Two floors above Fritz is Kevin. He's a sweet Vietnam vet. An Italian biker kind of dude, who likes army pants and fixing things. If we are ever in trouble, Ma yells *"Keeeeevinnnnnn!"* into the air shaft between the buildings, and he comes running down with a two-by-four studded with nails.

Kevin is best friends with Benny, who is the unofficial mayor of the building. Together they take care of shit as it comes up. If the boiler is giving us problems, we call them. If a pipe is leaking, they take care of it. If somebody is selling drugs out of their apartment, Kevin and Benny knock on their door. Kevin and Benny came in to sort out the shit flood, grumbling and cranky, but they handled it for us.

Benny is nearing sixty. He favors khaki shorts and white tennis sneakers, with tube socks pulled up to his calves. He has a receding hairline of clipped dark curls, and I like to watch his skinny muscles ripple when he moves around. He's not much taller than me, but he cares about his body and he keeps weights on his living room floor. He reminds me of a retired tennis pro. He is actually a retired porn star.

His girlfriend and ex-costar, Stephanie, could be Asian, Native American, Latina, who knows, but she's very beautiful, petite, and sugar sweet.

Ma told me how she used to see Stephanie on posters for the peep show spots on Forty-second Street. She was a legitimate star, who went by the stage name of Cynthia Fox. She did the live strip show circuit for a while and made hundreds of films before retiring. She had a drinking problem back then, but not anymore. Not a drop. She told my Ma, "Once you're a pickle, you're a pickle. You never be a cucumber ever again."

Benny and Stephanie's reign over the top floor makes Benny the watchdog of the roof. The roof is our sanctuary. It's our playhouse, our reading room, our rehearsal space, our sun lounge. We live anywhere and everywhere *but* within our apartment, which is the place where we keep our shit and sleep.

When I got chicken pox last year and was quarantined, barred from school, we spent a week up there, every day, hanging out in the sun, just Ma and I. She covered me in so much SPF 70 that I looked like Casper the Friendly Ghost. We played ball, made up stories, she read me books, and we hung out on our Chinese bamboo mats and stared at the sky.

You can see the Empire State Building, the World Trade Center, parts of Brooklyn, a bridge, and a good portion of Midtown. There's the clock in the Cooper Union building on Eighth Street. Our view is a stellar one, and it feels expensive. Every day when we get restless in the apartment, no matter if it's high summer and the roof is soft and stinking of tar, or if it's deep winter and there are lakes of ice and slush on the buckled asphalt, we make our way up there for an homage to the open sky.

Ma likes to watch the day fall, and at night she doesn't like to turn on the lights. We have a candelabra next to the bathtub in the kitchen that is so encased in wax that you can barely tell what it is anymore. We buy cheap Shabbat candles by the box from the corner deli and keep jamming them into the pile of wax. One time it got knocked over and set the curtain on fire.

Ma crawled out the kitchen window once, tied a rope to the drainpipe, and swung herself across the lightwell to the tiny prison window of the bathroom, and farther to the bedroom window in the back. We had locked ourselves out of the bedroom and she had to get in somehow.

With a single trembling candle we sit in the moonlight in our beloved bathtub and we can see the twinkling tops of office buildings way downtown. Fireworks go off in Chinatown and jazz spills out of our radio.

Even the shelter yard can transform itself into a volcanic orchard from this peaceful vantage point. Yellow leaves on the trees helicopter seeds onto the ground, and you can see a sweet little cemetery right over the black wall. Benny says there is a mayor from a hundred years ago buried in there.

So picture this gallery of misfits, ill-suited to any kind of bureaucratic get-together, sitting in a circle in Stephanie and Benny's living room, surrounding a tiny, twitching Italian guy from management, who is telling us that our building is gonna be gutted no matter what.

The government says we need to have a three-piece bathroom, instead of our phone booth toilet and the bathtub in the kitchen. That would take up most of the apartment, which means we'd need to move to a bigger place, which sounds insane.

The guy reaches into his stack of papers and pulls out a pamphlet, as if he has it with him by happenstance. I know this move, and he's not particularly talented at his hustle, whatever it is.

"Unfortunately for all of us, either way the city is stepping in and putting its foot down. All the tenants will be temporarily relocated during the renovations to equally comfortable apartments until you can be moved back into your new houses."

He tries to word this carefully, but when he says "comfortable," half a dozen people snort and snicker. I'm thinking of the red-haired, pothead leprechaun with six pianos, and what *comfort* might mean to him, a kind of joy inconceivable to the man now speaking in American Dream bullshit platitudes. Or what it means to my mom, for whom *comfort* itself is a dirty word.

"I'm just here to make sure that your voice is heard within the program, so that you end up with the situation that you like. I want everyone to be happy."

With this, the diminutive, twitching Italian puts down his stack of papers, much like David must have dropped his slingshot, adjusts his metal watch, and avoids looking at the wreckage he has just caused in two dozen households.

Yanik once said, as he tore apart a red pepper in a ragged train car on his way to a unpaid gig in Ljubljana, "Happiness!? Happiness is overrated!"

## Chapter 8

### The Purple Cape

*Manhattan, October 1991*

WE ARE ON ONE OF THE MANY SETS WE'VE BEEN ON SINCE I started professionally acting when I was two. It is a little art-house movie. The young director is explaining my role to me. As we get to the discussion about my costume, I balk.

"No."

"I'm sorry?"

"No. I won't wear that."

I point.

"Wear what?"

"That . . . It's purple."

"The cape? You don't want to . . . oh, well, I'm sorry, that's not really negotiable. The name of the movie is *The Purple Cape*."

He looks confounded.

"No. I won't."

Hysteria is beginning to form in my chest. I have never felt this way before, like I have an internal line that shall not, under any circumstances, be crossed.

"I can't do that. It's girly."

## Chapter 9

# POPPA . . .

POPPA AND I ARE WALKING THROUGH CENTRAL PARK. THE air is nippy in the fall dusk. The collar of my yellow turtleneck crests just under my now-short hair. I'm about the height of his hip, and I'm holding his hand as we walk through the leafless trees toward downtown.

I see a group of boys playing ball together in a field off to our left. They are playing touch football in a raucous tumble of laughter and elbow jabs. It looks fun. I want to play.

"Poppa, can I go?"

"Sure, bugsy."

Climbing over the low black metal fence, I slow down. I approach them gingerly, because I'm shy. Poppa says I've got an arm like no kid he's ever known at my age. I can throw with speed, power, and accuracy. I can catch, pitch, kick, and I can sink a basket. But with bigger kids, I'm hesitant until I have the ball.

One of the boys, a shirtless kid with black hair and ruddy cheeks, swings around closer to me.

"Hey," I say. "Can I play?"

He barely looks up, only glancing at me sideways. He looks back at his friends. I wonder if he's going to make me ask again. A blond kid holding the ball seems to be the guy in charge. He sees me standing there and jogs over. Now all the boys are looking at me and I realize they are at least two or three years older. One snickers. They start talking to each other. Then the blond kid says, "Are you a boy or a girl?"

I'm a little confused as to why they'd ask me that. What answer are they looking for? Why does it matter?

" . . . I'm . . . a girl."

One snorts, and the blond crew cut says, "We don't play with girls!" as he turns and runs back to the goalpost they've constructed out of piled backpacks.

I'm standing there, hands in my jeans pockets, confused. Angry. Frustrated. Embarrassed. I know I can throw the ball probably better than they can. And I can catch like I've got Velcro in my palms. If they'd just let me show them. What kind of a stupid rule is that? It never dawned on me there'd be any difference.

I look over and my pop is sitting on the black fence, out of earshot. He nods at me as if to say, "What's up? You playing?" I put my chin down toward my chest, thinking, and walk back to him.

"Not gonna play?"

"Nah."

"You sure? Something happen?"

We start walking in tense silence. It continues for a few minutes before I decide the only obvious course of action there is. After I get it I feel much calmer. I take his hand and swing it back and forth, trying to practice my whistle. There is a hopscotch course chalked onto the ground next to the Sheep Meadow and I hop and jump over it.

We stop to watch the little kids on the merry-go-round, and I realize I should tell him. Craning my neck out of my yellow collar, I turn and look him straight in the eyes.

"Poppa, from now on my name is Ricky. And I'm not your daughter anymore. I'm your son."

Pop looks at me for a little while, like he always does, as a person to be reckoned with and not a kid to be told what to do. He doesn't ask for any clarification, and after another moment's thought he says, "Sure. But I'm not telling any lies, iO . . ."

"Well then, say something else, Poppa."

"I'll say you're my kid . . . okay?"

"Okay."

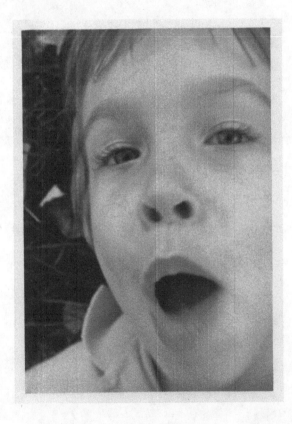

## Chapter 10

# Pee

I AM SEVEN YEARS OLD. EVERYTHING SMELLS LIKE FRESH paint. My belly burns and I'm jiggling my legs. I look down at them in my crisp light blue jeans. They are the high-waisted ones the actors wear in *Top Gun*. I have on my green bomber jacket, too. My Velcro sneakers are gripping the soft linoleum floor.

I have to pee so badly I feel like my belly might burst apart, but I can't go in. I'm in the hallway, just outside the door, waiting.

When I have to pee at school I press my ear against the bathroom door and listen. If I don't hear any voices, I pull the hulking blue sheet of steel open and peek my head inside slowly. If no one is at the sink, I crouch to the floor and check for feet. Then I sprint into a stall and bolt the door quickly.

Standing at the toilet, I kick my sneakers off. I turn around and sit down, with my toes in the backs of my shoes, and pee. That's how I do it every single time. If anyone comes in, it all locks up down there and I can't go. I sit, my little butt sweating and sticking to the toilet seat, praying with everything in me that they don't look through the half-inch crack between the stall and the wall and see me sitting there, full of pee, pants down, a liar.

That would kill me. The thought of that happening is the worst thing I can imagine. It would be like getting struck by lightning. There is no off-duty me who isn't a boy, there is only this, that doesn't match up with my anatomy. But that's my private battle.

There are voices in the bathroom now, so I'm in the hall, jiggling my knees in the peepee dance, waiting. I cross my palms over each other and press them into the wall behind my back, staring at the door. I hear little boys' laughter, like an explosion of machine gun fire. A discomfort grips me that they are laughing at me. I want to throw up. There is a stairwell to my right and I go up six steps and sit down on the black stone. I cross my legs, trying to be sure I don't look girly but stopping the flow.

They are taking forever.

I think about the Hardy Boys. I think about how Frank and Joe are just about to bust into a warehouse and catch the criminal mastermind they've been hunting, and how excited I am to finish this book and go check out another in the series. I think about how good it feels when I go up to the library checkout with four books at a time.

It starts suddenly, the pain, sharp and piercing, below my belly. It propels me upward and I just stand there for a second, stunned. Then I rush down the stairs. At the door to the bathroom I put my hand on the handle, but I can't. I won't do it. I know what is going to happen, but it would be worse if they caught me. I pull my fingers from the cold metal and take a step backward. Maybe I can hold it for a few more minutes.

Laughter from inside.

It's warm at first, on my upper thighs. I can't even look down at myself. It's as though my horror has locked up my neck. I feel like an embarrassed cyborg that someone shut down, frozen, three feet from the bathroom—three feet from salvation—incapable of moving.

Then it's cold. There is a pool of darkness starting halfway up my zipper that spreads all the way down my jeans. I can feel the liquid traveling down my legs. Now it's in my shoes.

That's it. It's done. I don't have to wait here anymore, because even if I could go in, it's all out of me and sloshing around my socks. I turn around and waddle back toward my classroom slowly. I take my jacket off and tie it around my front.

Well, this is really all I need, I think to myself. It's already chaos and torment, now they've got all the ammo they need to tease me until Christmas.

But it would be worse to be caught.

## Chapter 11

# Cartoon Moon

*Central Park, October 1992*

THE SANDPAPER GRIP TAPE ON MY SKATEBOARD IS SCRAPing my knee. All my weight is on my right leg, my left propelling me forward with forceful shoves against the pavement. A fall afternoon whizzes past, crowded with joggers, bikers, tourists snapping photos. Cars aren't allowed to drive through Central Park on the weekends, so the street is free rein. Ma lopes along behind me, unable to keep up, not really trying. Occasionally, she yells my name, but I'm not stopping.

I zip in between joggers' ankles. They hate it when I do that, but Ma and I get a kick out of rattling them.

Keeping my head bent as low to the board as I can, I grip the edges with both hands, body arched forward. I shift all my weight side to side to steer, foot pumping harder and harder. I am tearing down the street so fast that a big hill barely slows me down. As I reach its crest, I glance out over the scenery: pastel rooftops of millionaires' homes on Fifth Avenue; fields covered in leaves the color of pumpkins; trees stripping down for the winter; and a long stream of spandex-clad butts, attached to young, upwardly mobile, mostly white people, out to trim the fat from their midsections in time for their Halloween outfits.

The wind bites at my ears a little, but the exertion is making me sweat. I don't have to push much once I get rolling on the downward slope. Speed gathers quickly and before long it's all I can do to keep my balance as I shred down the hill, both knees on the board, narrowly avoiding plowing into joggers' ankles. My hair is split by the wind and it's hard to keep my eyes open. The question crosses my mind of how I will stop, but I figure I'll just roll it out at the bottom of the hill.

The board starts to quiver underneath me as the momentum takes over. I'm just trying to hold on as the shaking rattles my wrists and gravity tosses me around like the skinny eight-year-old bag of bones that I am. Squinting, blinking furiously, I'm starting to actually get scared. I'm not wearing kneepads or a helmet, so I can't jump off. If it weren't for the rattling sensation vibrating my teeth, and the hard concrete blazing past me in a blur of gray-black, I might think I was flying.

Twenty yards ahead of me, I can see that the road curves to the left and starts to slope upward, thank God, which means I'll slow down naturally.

The board pulls to the right, and I struggle to wrestle it back to a straight course. It doesn't want to cooperate. As the curve approaches, I lean to the left again, but that is a crucial mistake. It throws my weight back the other way, which almost makes the board bite into the wheel. Wobbling calamitously, out of control as I approach the curve, scared and somewhat resigned to fate, I look down at my fingers for a split second and think about how awful it would be for them to get mangled by the speeding wheels. That's when I miss spotting the sewage grate. There is a horrible noise of skull colliding with concrete, and the lights go out.

The first thing I hear in the darkness is a man's voice. He is saying he is a doctor and to let him through. When I come to, there are joggers huddled all around me, and a middle-aged white guy with thin wire glasses and a blue fleece is hovering over my face. Behind him I see a blur of trees and the sky. I'm lying on my back in the street.

Shapes come in and out of focus, and the light feels very bright even though it is almost dusk. Then I hear Ma yelling my name, and the sound of leather soles smacking cement. She must be running toward me. A black lady is telling someone else to back off and not move me in case my neck is broken.

Ma arrives, shrieking, "My bud! My bud! Get outta my way, that's my kid. iO! Can you hear me?!"

It goes dark again.

My whole body tingles when I open my eyes. Ma is real close to me, cradling my head. I move my face to the left to shield my eyes from the bright light. I feel weak. Ma is staring at me, desperate to see if I'm okay. Most of the rubberneckers have disbanded, but a few people are still lingering to make sure I'm not in real dire straits, or dead.

Ma has told them not to call an ambulance. That's not our style. We can't afford it.

My head throbs on the right side where I smashed it into the ground. I reach up and touch it gingerly. I can see a grate between the sidewalk and the street a couple of feet behind us. My wheel must have gotten lodged in it, and it stopped the board short. I was going so fast I flipped over, whacked my skull on the curb, and knocked myself out. Softly, I touch a big knot under my skin near my right temple and feel some blood in my hair.

I flap my lips together, not really able to speak, not really having anything to say but feeling like I need to get something out. I spit.

My shoulders are tense and there is heat in my ears. It sounds like everything is under water, and my belly is hollow. I just want to sleep, but Ma says, "No sleeping, my bud."

I spit again.

I am sluggish and slow to speak, which I can tell is freaking my ma out. She asks me if I think I can stand up. I take stock of my entire body, one inch at a time, and decide that I should probably get up off the cement and get somewhere that I can really lie down. I push myself up off the ground on my forearms, slowly.

It's hard for me to keep my eyes open because things keep spinning, but I'm determined. Ma is behind me, holding on to one of my arms and bracing my back with the other. She is carrying almost all of my weight, but it's still hard to orient myself.

We start to move, very slowly. Someone says something and Ma turns around. It's my skateboard. I need that. Ma grabs it under one arm, and we take a few tenuous steps.

We inch our way out of the park to Fifth Avenue, me staring at the ground, feeling like a cartoon character with birds spinning around his head. It's everything I can do not to barf. On Seventy-second Street, Ma finds a pay phone and puts a quarter in. She has a brief exchange with someone, and we start walking uptown.

IN THE 1950S MY father's father sued *Time* magazine for libel. Whatever he won he plonked down to buy an 1800s carriage house in cash. It sits on a quiet street on the Upper East Side, nestled between an apartment building and a string of brownstones. The curbside trees are manicured, and uniformed doormen greet you as you pass. White people in tasseled loafers and steamed collars load Dean & DeLuca bags and Pomeranians out of Mercedeses and Porsches. This isn't the land of absurd wealth, but it is certainly a haven for members of the spoiled spectrum.

The Tilletts were an elegant couple of unconventional heritage, he a lanky, bespectacled Englishman, with a high hairline and a long nose; she a descendant of Russian Jews from Brooklyn. They met in Mexico in the forties when *Harper's Bazaar,* in its influential heyday, sent Edie down to photograph a pair of English brothers, conscientious objectors who were taking the textile world by storm. She fell in love and stayed.

Eventually, they moved back to New York and got the carriage house.

Although intensely private, my grandparents drew admirers of their delicate designs and bold color choices. Their custom fabrics ended up in stately homes as esteemed as the Kennedy White House. They started a clothing line, with boxy, Asian shapes, androgynous colorways, hand-printed silk ties, and patterned shirts. They opened a boutique in the house, and once upon a time, the Tilletts became notorious for being the first shop in New York to sell men's and women's clothing in the same room. Their genderless shirts were worn by Greta Garbo and President Truman.

Alongside successfully building their design business, they also raised three children. Their youngest son became a radical intellectual artist, who beelined it out of stability and into the hallways of punks, painters, and dope dealers, and eventually the arms of a particular blonde with a penchant for Johnnie Walker and the Ramones. Which is why my now-widowed, septuagenarian grandmother is currently pulling the largest blue Venetian bowl she has from under her sink for her eight-year-old grandchild to use as a puke receptacle after a skateboarding accident.

I don't know Edie very well. Because my poppa now basically lives in Europe, I only come here when he's in town, and that's not very often, so finding myself here is odd. We were within walking distance, though, and my ma was right to assume that the door would be open to us, in any state of need.

The floor where Edie lives is dark and long and exquisitely designed by her. Dim lamps are placed with intention around the classy space, on countertops made of jagged pieces of raw marble, armrests of antique wood, and a low, checkered ivory table.

Edie is small and elegant, with a head of short white curls that look like whipped meringue and a piece of yellow silk tied around her delicate throat. Big glasses dwarf her face, and the sleeves of her thin sweater are rolled up above her tiny wrists. She wears slip-on shoes below her cuffed men's slacks.

Lying on one of the two beige corduroy couches in the center of her apartment, I lean over and lose my stomach into the bowl. This process makes my head feel like it weighs four hundred pounds, and pain shoots through it until I lie back down. That sucks, and I start to whimper. I'm burning hot and can't stop spitting. I just want to sleep.

Ma clutches my hand and rubs me down. She is so obviously uncomfortable in this situation. She calls a doctor that Edie recommends. When she describes my pale skin and freezing temperature, he says I most likely have a concussion, and that the best thing is to bring me into an emergency room either now or first thing in the morning.

She tells me she is going to get me some ginger ale and saltines.

For her to volunteer to give me sugar, things must be pretty serious.

Edie sits at the end of the couch and begins to untie my sneakers. Delicate bird-bone fingers place one shoe and then the other on the black stone floor. Moving quietly, she puts a woolen blanket over me and tucks it in around my edges.

If I didn't have a concussion, maybe I could appreciate the strangeness of this, but my teeth have begun to chatter and I'm just grateful for something warm over me.

Edie stands and rubs her hands up and down her slacks twice, international symbol of distress, before slowly moving into the kitchen. I know she's holding it together for my sake.

She comes back with a crystal glass filled with water and a wet towel, perching her tiny frame on the couch next to me and putting the cold fabric onto my forehead. I get it now; the water is to clear the bile after I puke in the bowl. I fall asleep to her caressing my face.

Ma wakes me diligently every half hour, all night long. Every time, I groan and wave her away because I'm starved for sleep. Once, I wake up retching and lean off the couch and hurl. Ma is sleeping on the floor, but she bounds up and lifts the bowl to my mouth, moaning in sympathy and patting my head. Edie comes out in her long white nightie, silent and ghostly, her skin soft and thin over her veins. She's clutching a tissue and dabbing at her sleepy eyes with it.

By five thirty we're all exhausted, but Ma says it's time to go. She and Edie have a brief exchange about whether it's a good idea, but Ma will have none of it. Today is the shoot for the Cartoon Network commercial I'm in, and I'm going to make it no matter what.

"The show must go on," she says, like a Brooklyn gangster from the twenties, "in sickness and in health!"

Edie knows better than to try to change Ma's perspective, and retreats to her bedroom in the predawn dark.

Ma bundles me up in borrowed cashmere and we go down to the street. The sun is starting to brighten the sky as we walk toward Central Park. I'm entranced by the vulgarity of the bump on my head.

Although I'm slow moving, and my IQ has taken a hit, by the time we get to Fifth Avenue I have convinced myself that I'm fine. Ma wants to believe it, too, even though I'm not talking a ton and I can't keep up with her pace.

Eventually we find the set. A craft services table is set up just off the very road in the park I took my spill on. Ma wraps grape leaves in napkins and keeps stuffing them into her bag until the producer comes over to explain the concept.

It will be a simple day, but it might take a few hours. They're shooting people around New York saying, "SPLOING! BOING! BAM! SPLAT!"

The words take on new meaning now that I've sploing-boing-splatted my brain against the street. I giggle a little too late at my own joke and Ma and the producer look at me sideways. Ma explains what happened, and the producer is concerned. She asks if I need to go to the hospital, it's totally okay, but Ma reassures her that I'm fine.

The producer leaves Ma picking fruit off the table, and I amble away to be alone.

I come to a gravel driveway nearby and am beset with the urge to count how many pebbles it is comprised of.

A half hour later, Ma finds me intently bent over the ground.

"What are you doing, kitty?"

"Couhnthing . . ."

"Counting?"

"Mmhh . . ."

She stares at me, then at the ground. She looks up the driveway, contemplating this. My head feels like someone has pumped smoke into it, and I'm shivering.

"Are you cold?"

I grunt.

"You look pale."

" . . ."

"Stay right here, okay?"

She comes back a few minutes later with the producer, who says, "Hi, iO, honey. Do you want to come do your shot now, so that we can get you outta here? I bet you'd like to go to bed . . ."

"Mmm-hmm."

They have been discussing taking me to the hospital. Ma's silence is heavy. I know she's worried when she stops talking to me.

The producer leads me toward a playground. They stand me next to a tiny Chinese kid in a polo shirt that's striped vertically like a Neapolitan ice cream sandwich. A very enthusiastic guy presents himself as the director, and runs through the sploingo, boingo lines.

I am suddenly overcome with a case of the giggles. The director likes it. The other kid starts giggling, too. It's contagious. The director waves his arms around for the cameras to start rolling. I'm in stitches for no reason, giggling away.

I manage to squeeze out two sets of the lines, and the director calls cut. The words sound like I have taffy in my mouth, but they liked the giggling. A lady with forty different rolls of tape on her belt comes over and takes off a microphone I didn't remember them putting on me, and says, "You're good to go now, sweetie. Thank you."

I hate it when people call me "sweetie."

The hospital is a blur. A man in a lab coat waves a small flashlight in front of my eyes, but it hurts too much, so I close them.

I get frustrated with the chubby nurse in the pistachio scrubs who is keeping me awake. I want ice chips to bring the heat down.

"Eith . . . ."

"What, honey?"

"Eithhh . . . plthh . . ."

Speaking is incredibly laborious. The nurse leaves and comes back with a paper cup with Donald Duck printed all over it, filled with ice shards, and feeds me one. I let it roll across my tongue and slide out the side of my mouth. This makes Ma groan with fear.

The doctor comes back and examines me again with the flashlight. This pisses me off and I whine breathily. I exhaust myself by waving one hand in front of me, hoping it will scare him off. He asks me some questions that I find irritating;

"What is your name?"

"Ughh . . . aaoowww . . . . ."

"I'm sorry?"

" . . . aaeeeeuuuhhh . . ."

"Let's try one more time."

"Aiiiooooo."

I push this last out with great effort. My eyes are rolling back into my lids. He jots something down on his chart.

He looks at my ma and smiles a big cheesy smile, hoping to be encouraging, but she isn't looking at anything but me, intensely, pursing her eyebrows. He starts writing again, and says, without looking up, "Yeah, iO is gonna be fine. She suffered a mild concussion when she took her spill, so you're gonna need to watch out for her progress. The nurse will give you a list of symptoms to pay attention to, but she should be just fine in a few days. If anything gets worse, bring her right back here to us and we'll take care of her. Okay?"

Ma stares at me for a long time, then looks up at him and nods. He extends his right hand, but she sticks out her left, twisting it around to grab his upside down. This throws him.

"Do you live somewhere close by?"

"Yes," she lies.

## Chapter 12

# Zack

THIRD GRADE IS GONNA RULE. I KNOW ALL MY CLASSMATES, and we had Karen last year so I know how to stay under her radar. It's rare that you get the same teacher twice in a row, but through an elementary school version of litigating the adminstrative office, a bunch of us pulled it off.

I am pretty clear on where my place is in the social ecosystem. I'm a weirdo loner kid who everyone is pretty confident is a boy, but they aren't sure. I'm not one of the cool kids by any means, but as long as I don't push my luck I'm chill with everyone. The nerds don't mind me, and so far I've escaped any real brutality by generally being nice.

There is something about being an enigma that earns you a certain holiness. It's easier to leave me alone than to tease me and have to dissect what the hell is actually going on in my underwear.

Ma is gripping my hand, trying to pull me along because we're late, but I am intent on leapfrogging every fire hydrant we pass. At quarter to eight it's a long trek from the Bowery to Hudson Street, basically from one side of sleepy Manhattan to the other, and it gets boring. From our place to Sixth Avenue it's a long stretch of nada. At Sixth, the homeless people start to appear, and occasional drag queens still tottering around from last night. They're entertaining to look at.

Just south of Third Street is a bus stop, and I make sure to always pass between the stop and the lamppost directly in front of it. It's an essential ritual that will dictate the course of the whole day. If I don't pass between them, it won't go well.

We turn up Bleecker from Carmine Street. Then it's a row of Italian bakeries, bread shops, and a record store. My stomach gurgles at the smell of fresh bread, and every day I pull my mom into Geno's for a hot loaf of semolina. I like how it's sweet, and I can scrounge my own thirty-five cents to buy it.

A bar sits on the corner of Bleecker and Seventh Avenue that has a giant plastic yellow cab outside of it and a massive margarita glass hanging over the door. I use this as a landmark. When we pass the cocktail, we are in the home stretch, five minutes to school.

Two blocks up we make a left on Christopher. I like this street because it's quaint and beautiful, overhung with branches and lined with brownstones. It serves as a reminder of all the lives we don't live—quiet, calm, sweet, stable—words I didn't even know were supposed to be associated with how you live your life. There are no bars here, no junkies, no cars blaring bachata, only prim gay men taking their dogs for an early-morning walk, who smile and wave. These guys pick up their dogs' shit with manicured fingers in sandwich bags.

Public School 3 hulks on the corner. The building takes up the better part of a city block. At eleven thirty shrieking and laughter explodes from within, evidence of several hundred children unleashing pent-up fervor, but right now the block is quiet. Everyone is still too sleepy to make a ruckus.

Ma walks me to the top of a stairwell. She checks me in with the security guard and I shoo away through the gym on my own. I pull off a corner of the semolina loaf and cram it in my mouth as I slowly climb the stairs. I don't care about being late. We're late for everything. A sense of urgency has not been instilled in me about lateness; I don't even register it as a problem. My world operates on my time, because that's the only time that exists in my head. It's the third day of the new year and I might as well not set up any false expectations.

One strap of my backpack dangles down over my elbow as I amble up the steps, leaning against the wall as I go. I'm so sleepy. Last night was a late one. The play I'm in had a performance and we went out with the cast afterward. My ma had a wine and got angry. It took us forty-five minutes to walk home from Gramercy at midnight.

When she tried to wake me up this morning, I took a swing at her face. She held me off, but I swung again. At first she was mad but then she started laughing at my tenacity. She sat on the edge of the bed holding my little fist, laughing and laughing and petting my head in that weird way she always does where she doesn't part her fingers and folds her hand, like a ballerina who only bends at the waist. I finally cracked and started to giggle, too. I took another swing at her shoulder out of embarrassment, but she pushed my hand away and kept laughing.

These are the sweet moments. The times when I recognize what I see in other kids with their parents when they're buying chocolate lollipops or driving past us after school. These are the darling days when everything is all good and the beast is calm.

The door to the second floor is heavy. My head is the height of an adult forearm, so I have to lean my entire body backward to swing it open. The hallway is quiet the way that it is only first thing in the morning. I put little nibbles of bread in my mouth as I meander down toward Karen's classroom.

Our class door is covered in colorful index cards with each of our names elaborately scrawled on them. When I push it open, everyone is sitting on the rug, thirty-six shining little faces from every corner of the city. Karen is sitting on a tiny footstool under the blackboard, her big body folded over her knees, talking about what's going to happen today.

Karen is about fifty, with a brush of graying hair, rectangular wire glasses, and a no-bullshit kind of face. She wears oversize T-shirts and jeans with Birkenstock sandals, which combine to make her appear even more imposing.

I like Karen so much. I don't know why. She scares the shit out of me, and getting her to smile is a hard-won victory, but I enjoy the challenge.

That is not happening right now. She greets me with a hard glare over the top of her glasses. For a second I think she's going to say something, but her way of expressing annoyance is to ignore your existence, so she angles her body away and carries on talking.

"So what you're going to do is go into the hallway and line up double file. Find a buddy, and stay on line until I tell you to . . . hey! Andy! *Excuse me*, Andy."

Andy is a special-needs kid. I don't know why he's in our class and not in special ed, but this is his second year in a row with Karen. Dainty and hyperactive, he walks on his toes in a bouncy way that suits his aloofness. He has eyes like holes punched through paper with a pencil. They dart all over the place like he has fifteen thousand thoughts happening at once. He couldn't tell you what eight plus two was if you gave him a half hour to get back to you. He wears T-shirts tucked into his jeans and brags about how his family is Puerto Rican. He has a mullet *and* a rattail. Andy is prone to screaming freak-outs, and sometimes violence, but he's easy to fend off. He is the kind of kid you can hold off by the forehead and he'll keep swinging until he's so infuriated he starts to cry. He can't focus for very long, so Andy's name being yelled across the classroom is the basic soundtrack to the day.

Right now he's doing something on the carpet that he shouldn't, with someone I don't know. As I hang my backpack on a bright yellow hook I look at the new kid.

"Zack! Don't distract Andy, don't do anything while I'm talking but listen to me. Got it?"

I guess his name is Zack. He's wearing a salmon-colored T-shirt and shorts. His hair is sandy blond, also with a mullet, and—Jesus Christ—a rattail, but he takes it one step further because it is wrapped in multicolored thread. He's muscular for an eight-year-old and his eyes are bright, smart, but not particularly warm. He strikes me as angry.

"Got it, kid?"

"Yeah. Sorry."

Before he's gotten the words out of his mouth, his look turns to me, and he stares. Why is he looking at me? I'm trying to ignore it but he is relentless. When I glance back he's glaring. I turn my face back toward Karen. What the hell? But she glares at Zack.

"When we line up, you're walking at the front with me."

Karen considers this a punishment, but last year I kind of liked it when she made me walk with her. I like talking to her better than anyone else anyway. Zack doesn't share the sentiment. He rolls his eyes and flops his chin down onto his chest.

The two lines of children snake from the stairwell halfway down the hall. It's nearly nine now and everyone is starting to wake up. Thirty-six kids makes for a lot of chatter, jokes, and patty-cake games, and a din that perpetually hovers near shrieking splits the hall.

I forgot we were going on a field trip today. It's a big one—we're going to the Brooklyn Aquarium. This kind of thing is usually reserved for the end-of-term summer trip, but we got rained out last year, and part of the joy of having Karen again is that she's making it up.

The whole line is pushed up against the right wall of the hallway. I'm at the back, quietly holding hands with Magda—a tall, bug-eyed dork who favors interpretive dance and snap bracelets. I'm ambivalent about the aquarium, but I'm into the idea of leaving the building.

Then I see Zack and his irritating rattail, to the left of everyone, moving toward me. His eyes are locked on mine. I try to look elsewhere, but I know what's going to happen before it does. He marches up to me and stops a few inches from my face.

Still holding Magda's hand, I look up into his dilated pupils and raise my eyebrows, wordlessly asking him what he wants. There is a slight hint of a smile before he rears back with his left hand and punches me square in the face. The full width of his fist connects with the center of my right cheek, sending an electrical shock into my eyes that instantly makes them tingle and water, prompting me to wonder how everything is so connected inside my head.

He stands there looking at me. Magda is staring, horrified. His eyes are wild, alive, dancing with joy. He scans me for the impact of his attack, but I am doing my best to look unfazed. With a little smile, he says, "I bet you're gonna cry now, huh?"

I square off with him and say, "No. No way."

He laughs a little, spins around, and walks away. He reaches the front of the line at the same time as Karen and I know she has no idea what happened. If I ran to her now, in front of everyone, I'd be a pussy, so I suck it up. Tears start streaming down my cheeks. Poor Magda is worried about me, but she has no idea what to do. She draws herself up to her full height and signals to her friends that something is wrong with me, but no one can be bothered. I just want to disappear.

Salty eye water and snot run silently down my cheeks and I'm trying to catch it all with my sleeve. I just don't understand. What did I do him? Nothing! He doesn't even know me. Why me? There is a piercing feeling in my chest as it dawns on me that someone hates me, for no reason at all, but he hates me.

I watch as Andy smiles at him and they clasp hands behind Karen. The painful sensation sharpens with the notion that everyone is in on something with this new jerk that I am on the outside of.

The aquarium sucks. I don't want to be near anyone or have to do any talking. I trail behind the class all day and I don't even bother to go near the gigantic tanks of sharks. We are a public school, so we can't see the dolphin show, but I don't care, I just want to go home. I keep my head down and do my best to dangle my hair over the lump rapidly forming in my cheek. I can feel it bulging. The skin is hot and tender to the touch. The kid can throw a punch.

As we make our way from tank to tank, I keep an eye on this prick, making sure to stay far away from him. An anger burns through me that makes me want to throw him in the shark tank, or flip him upside down and stuff him in a trash can, or maybe bash his nose in, but I don't think I'd win in a fistfight. His stocky neck tells me as much.

At some point I notice that he is spending an odd amount of time with Barney, the other class oddball. Barney has absolutely no friends, because Barney is a bona fide nerd. He wears glasses that are constantly slipping and dinosaur fanny packs, and he has a watch that tells him when to pee. I stole that watch once last year because I thought it was stupid and to his detriment that he couldn't figure it out for himself. I thought he might be lying, but he pissed his pants. I felt bad and gave it back, apologized to him and his mother, and swore I would never mess with him again. For all his nerdiness, he has a super kind heart, and he forgave me the next day, offering me some of his lunch. Since then we've been on tenuous good terms, but I've put in a lot of work making sure he knows I mean him no harm.

Half an hour later, outside by the penguins, an arm goes around Barney's fat shoulder and I pretend not to see. Zack leans in and says something to him and they both turn to look at me. I roll my eyes and pull my chin into my neck because I think it makes it look thicker and tougher and turn away.

Barney is getting high off the thrill of having someone cool like him and he is turning into a monster in front of me. He no longer looks at me with eyes glazed over by the rich fantasy world of his mind, but with the growing ferocity of a child tempted by a crack at acceptance. I know how he feels. It's a high you don't see coming, when they first talk to you, but it takes no time at all to realize you would do anything to have it never go away, to stay in the inner circle forever. Making somebody else feel like shit is a very small price to pay, and I'd bet money that Zack is selling Barney on that right now.

Everybody squeezes onto the train after lunch. Andy and I are the only ones not yelling or swinging or dancing around the car. All the adults that were already here have moved to other cars to escape the volume. Andy is on his knees facing the window. He's talking to himself, counting the lights whizzing by. I'm in a two-seater at the very end of the car, keeping my head down. My cheek has started to chill out a little bit, but it still hurts like hell. Every time I look up, Zack and Barney give me the heebies, and Karen is too busy to come to my rescue, so I'm keeping to myself. So far, this year is not shaping up to be what I thought it would.

When we pull into West Fourth Street, Karen tries to keep us in line, but it's impossible. Kids stream out through the turnstiles, screeching and tumbling over each other. I have fallen behind everyone and I'm keeping my eyes on the galaxy of gum stains on the ground.

As I start on the steps toward the street, I should see it coming, but I don't. A foot juts out from next to me, and I trip, falling onto my face. I see the side of Zack's sneaker bound up past me. My face is on the corner of the concrete step with my swollen cheek on the filthy ground. Then another shoe comes out of nowhere and actually steps on my head. He doesn't put his full weight into it, but enough for the corner to jab into my face and make it feel like it's on fire. I yelp and make a grab at his ankle. He stumbles up the steps past me. I jump to my feet, praying that no one saw what happened. The last thing I want right now is sympathy. I see Barney's chunky butt waddling up to the top of the steps where Zack is waiting for him. The two boys high-five as I spit on the ground.

The entire walk back to school I don't bother counting cracks. I don't care who falls down the stairs or gets hit by a bus, or has a piano fall on them out of the sky, unless it's Zack and Barney. I know that Barney got duped by a scumbag, so I'm not as angry with him, but I want to scalp Zack's rattail off. My face is swelling and red. I'm angry that my hair isn't long enough to cover the apple forming in my cheek. I don't want any questions, and no one asks any.

Back at school, I make it up the stairs, through the classroom to my book bag, all the way through Karen's speech, and to the end-of-the-day bell without anyone saying anything.

Backpack hugged to my belly, chin propped on it, I'm squatting near the door when the bell clangs. I beeline it to the back stairwell and run down the few flights to my secret spot in the gym where I know no one will bother me. It's a person-sized nook between three walls covered in puffy blue padding, a box with one open side, and when I sit on the ground with my back to the wall I am essentially invisible. Everyone is spilling into the gym to play or read or get picked up by their parents. I know my ma won't be here for another twenty-five minutes.

I pull my knees into my chest and press the not-deformed side of my face into my JanSport, cupping my palm over the tennis ball that has grown under my skin on the other side. Overjoyed to finally be alone, my brain is playing a movie in front of my eyes: the walk to school, the dog shit I almost jumped into when I hopped a hydrant on Bleecker, the half-eaten semolina loaf balled up in my cubby that will be stale by tomorrow, rattails, salmon-colored T-shirts, the first punch, the overwhelming new burden of someone's hatred.

I don't know where to put it all, and I feel a kind of puffed-up deflation. My emotions are wound tight, pushing to the front of my body, ready to explode and yet completely locked away. I want to cry and scream but nothing is coming out. I don't understand. My mind wanders to Cordelia, the little girl who had something burst in her brain and died on the spot in this gym last year. It was a huge deal. There were posters all over the school. Every mother cried and she will forever be this sweet little spirit that everyone remembers fondly. In a morbid corner behind logic, that seems like a desirable outcome to my life.

I stay like this for a good half an hour, pretending I don't hear the cacophony around me. Eventually, a clawing feeling comes over me, a sense that I am trapped in this godforsaken place until my mother comes, and I pull my head upright to search for her, scanning the gym for her distinctive silhouette.

At the other end of the gymnasium, dribbling a basketball, I can see Zack, making new friends like it's his job. What he lacks in height, he makes up for in personality. Too bad I'm the only person he's decided he hates.

Then, like a mirage coming into focus, the wobbling figure of my mother appears. Sweeping through the room like a warrior Viking, in a floor-length black trench coat, carrying two bulging plastic bags and limping severely, she rises over the sea of little people like a spear, moving toward me at a clip. I shift my weight and stand to my feet, swinging my backpack on and pulling my hair in front of the offending side of my face. She strikes me as irritated as she approaches, but I am trying not to look at her.

"Let's go, my bud . . ."

Her words stop short of telling me what dance class awaits.

"What is that?"

Not even twenty seconds have elapsed. She takes my chin in her hand and pulls my face upward, busting the evidence of my inferiority from its cavern of self-pity, into the fluorescent glare of impending vengeance. Her eyebrows contract into themselves and something enters her crystal eyes that reminds me of hot oil.

*"There's an apple in your cheek."*

A new concept enters my mind, one I can't believe I haven't thought of before; my mother, the all-powerful dragon banshee who has sworn to protect me, is my most valuable weapon. I can win *any* battle with her on my side. Chin pointed out at a ninety-degree angle, I tilt my eyes toward hers and I realize what might happen. She speaks through clenched teeth, in a voice so calm it unnerves me.

"Who did this to you?"

My arm shoots out, pointing toward the basketball courts.

"His name is Zack! He just walked straight up and punched me in the face! C'mere, I'll show you."

In a flash I have her hand in mine and I'm pulling her through the gymnasium. Kids move past us in a kind of slow motion, like they're Hula-Hooping and jump-roping in molasses. I am high on anticipation.

Zack is center court when I point him out. He sees me first and flashes a shitty smile that he will regret. Not stopping to put down her omnipresent plastic bag purses, my ma lopes toward him. Standing under her, he barely comes to her ribs, and she looks down into his stunned face and says, "Are you Zack?"

He nods, confused. Dropping her bags on the linoleum floor, Ma grabs him by the shoulders. She presses her hands together and lifts him clear off the ground until his face is level with hers. Terror overwhelms him as he stares at her.

She starts to shake him. With every jerk her speed picks up, and now she's rattling him back and forth like a rag doll, like a maraca. His head snaps back with the every word she says through clenched teeth.

"DON'T. YOU. EVER. EVER. TOUCH. MY. KID. AGAIN. NOT EVER. *EVER!*"

I think he is going to crap his pants. My whole day has turned around. I have never loved my mother more. I am gasping and hopping at the edge of the court. It flashes through my mind that this is probably very, very illegal and maybe she'd better stop, but I'm not going to be the one to say anything.

Everyone in the gym is watching now as she puts him down. Immediately he starts to cry and runs away. Without breaking her poise, she picks up her plastic purses and gestures at me to follow. I scamper after her like a James Brown song is playing on my spine.

We stride down the front steps of the school as giddy as robbers leaving a bank, serious faced and charged up. Not until we hit the corner do I let out a shriek. I leap into the air and high-five her. She smiles for a second, then clenches her big hand into a muscular, scary fist, and says, "NOBODY fucks with my BUD!"

THE NEXT DAY, Zack keeps his distance. He looks like a wounded puppy. Everybody is hesitant to get close to me, too; maybe they fear the thrashing Zack got, but I don't even care. As long as he's not punching anybody, none of it matters.

I feel as though I am part of some secret club with my ma that involves staying away from everyone else, because we are dangerous badasses and they all know we mean business.

After school we go into a bathroom on the second floor because it's more secluded. Sitting on a stool by the sink, I'm watching my ma apply lipstick in the mirror. She's wearing her big trench coat again and her plastic bags are on a stainless steel shelf under the mirror.

There is an overweight woman in spandex pants and a black T-shirt at the mirror opposite Ma's back. We are talking about the audition I'm going on in an hour. It's for something directed by the daughter of somebody famous named Arthur Miller and it's important. Suddenly I am aware that the woman has turned around and is staring at the back of Ma's head. She looks furious, and it takes her a minute to gather her words. She gives me a nasty look, then says to my Ma: "Are you iO's mother?"

Without turning around or stopping the application of her lipstick, my ma says, "Yeah, what about it?"

"You assaulted my son yesterday!"

The look on Ma's face is one of pure disgust, as though this woman has squirted something rancid into her mouth.

"Psh. I didn't assault anybody."

"You have absolutely no right to lay your hands on a child."

"Little prick. Somebody needs to set him straight."

"Your freakish child is out of control, attacking my son, and then you! If you ever go anywhere near my children again I am going to report you to the police!"

You have crossed into an invisible no-fly zone, lady. You are now in aggravated enemy territory, and you just took your foot off a land mine.

Ma looks down at her bags. She sucks her teeth and caps her lipstick. She turns around and, facing this offensive woman, scrapes together everything in her throat and hocks it onto the ground at her feet.

"Fuck you and your aerobics pants, your fat ass, and your monstrous children. Tell your dickhead son to keep his hands off my kid."

With that, she gestures toward me and sweeps out the door. I scramble off my stool after her, leaving Zack's mother fuming and cursing in castrated mom-speak in the second graders' bathroom.

I WISH I COULD SAY that's how it ends. I wish I could report that Zack Sanders had any sense of self-preservation. The near-whiplash incident slowed him down, but only for a bit. Within a month, he was back to top shithead form. Now the morning trip to school feels like a daily plank walk.

The confusion about my gender is just too easy. He preys on my vulnerable weirdness. As a result I'm becoming more introverted. The constant ridicule in front of my classmates is exhausting, and he encourages everyone to be physical in their search for answers. He realized he hit the jugular with a relentless stream of variations on my most dreaded question: WHAT ARE YOU?

At recess, Zack gathers his posse in the bathroom so I'd have to push past them to go, so I have given up peeing. It was a stressful process before, but this makes it completely impossible.

I've become obsessed with not stepping on the cracks in the sidewalk, and my neurotic suspicion games have accelerated to a new level. If I get to the bottom step before the subway comes, Zack will get run over. If I make it to the top step before the door closes behind my neighbor, he'll die.

The unvented anger eventually turns inward, eating at me, creating a violent fantasy life that overtakes my thoughts. Trudging to school in the dead freeze of winter, I dream of stripping Zack to his underwear and making him run the streets barefoot. Feeling helpless, I sit on my stoop and contemplate stringing him upside down and pouring honey into his nose. I think about how he'd squeal when I stick thumbtacks between his fingers and under his nails. Eat an entire plate of fudge and then puke your guts out, you bullying bastard. I think about making him eat a shit milkshake. That one might have been my ma's idea. She always defaults to making her enemies ingest feces.

NINE STEPS TO THE bathroom during morning writing time. Four to the stall. Nine steps back to the classroom. Two steps to my cubby.

Mine is in the middle of three rows of wooden squares stacked on top of each other.

I am reaching for my black-and-white marble notebook when it hits me, a thud and a pain in my left forearm. *Smack*. I don't know what happened. I look down. There is a pencil sticking out of my flesh. I feel my eyebrows go up. I just look at it, the offending object. What is it doing there? I look up and Zack is standing in front of me, arms crossed, smiling wide. I am confused. It takes me a long time to cry out. I only let go and scream when I remember about lead poisoning.

## Chapter 13

# Budapest

*Budapest, Hungary, April 1994*

I'M STANDING IN THE DOORWAY OF THE CAFETERIA AT A THE-
ater in Budapest. Balding men are clustered around wooden
tables, wearing vests and sucking on cigarettes held between thick fingers. They are boisterous and loud, their jokes echoing from the high
ceilings, punctuated by the sound of skin slapping skin when they hit
each other at punch lines. Like sausages on legs, they are rotund in
every way. These men are the lifeblood of this place and all theaters
like it across Europe. They operate the lighting, build the sets, make
castles fly into the rafters, and point spotlights at opera singers. Yelling in Hungarian and gulping steaming black coffee, they embody the
weathered scent of long hours of physical work.

Rehearsal is shut down because Ma is arguing with Yanik over
money. She thinks he should be paying us more. We're getting a salary for the both of us as if we were one actor. He says they can't afford
more. She says fuck you, it's a four-country tour. Now it's a lockout. I
came downstairs to get a sandwich, but I'm stuck at the entranceway,
clutching my forint coin. My heart is in my throat. I am across the
world from my home and I don't speak a lick of Hungarian. I can feel
how thin the thread is that winds me back to my ma and our friends,
easily severed if I make the wrong turn or go out the wrong door.

Then I'd really be lost, in a place where I would have no idea how to find help. Something about this forest of potbellies implies danger.

Hunger splits my stomach like a crack in the earth. This feeling is so familiar it actually helps with the fear by making me feel more at home. I squeeze my fist tight around the coin. Light cuts through the fog from tall cathedral windows, and on the opposite side of the room I can see a counter where a big woman in an apron is trading mugs of beer and things wrapped in napkins for fists of cash. I make a game plan; if I stick to the left wall closely, the way you do when it rains in the city and you don't have an umbrella, I can just retrace my steps back to the door. I check for other doors, but this is the only one like it, so I gather my gumption and make my way to her.

The woman leans over the counter and looks at me. I'm about two feet shorter than the countertop, but I can see a pile of sandwiches in a glass case if I take a step backward. Her broad face melts into a smile, and she says something in Hungarian. *"Nem beszélek magyarul,"* I say. She replies in a shrill, impatient burst. That's the problem with being able to say you don't speak a language in that language. It's a conversation starter. I just stare back at her. She points at the glass case. I nod, and she pulls two sandwiches out. One is long and skinny, the other stout and round. I go for the small one. I can probably afford it.

One of the potbellies is standing at the counter, watching this transaction. He grins, and reaches his hand down to me with an open palm. What, does he want me to climb up his arm to her? "Mahnee." He points to his palm, and at my coin. Hesitantly, I hand it to him, and he gives it to her. He passes me my sandwich and I turn around to leave, but somebody whistles at me like a dog. I turn back, and the potbelly hands me a smaller coin. I didn't anticipate change. Like a toddler, three years is not far enough from Communism for Hungarian culture to adjust itself to the speed walk of capitalist inflation.

From my diminished vantage point I can see a basket with candy wrappers protruding from it. I look at the woman and put on the sweetest smile I have, front tooth missing and all. Eyebrows raised, I point at the coin and then at a Kit Kat bar. The man cackles and the woman says something to him I don't understand. I can see the top of the inside of her mouth when they both laugh and it reminds me of a pit bull. I feel the heat of other people looking at me. The man whistles at me again and motions me closer. I give him the coin, and he hands me the Kit Kat. I'm smiling for real now, and scuttling away along the wall.

Sitting on a closed toilet in the men's room, I break the candy bar open. My shoulders are pinched with tension. If my ma comes in, or if someone tells her I bought candy, there will be a huge scene and a fight. There have been so many fights over sugar, I can't keep track. It is a strictly forbidden substance in our house, along with meat, and generally anything else she feels pollutes the body. I have devised every possible strategy for sneaking it, including a stuffing-down-the-pants-and-socks technique that I have come to call Holocausting. Somehow she always knows. There was one particular instance when my poppa picked me up for a play date and let me indulge in a sticky packaged cupcake from the corner deli—the kind that is so processed you could use it as a baseball, covered in rubbery goo passed off as chocolate frosting, and filled with a bright white cream the texture of whipped Styrofoam. We cleaned up the crime scene really well, drinking water and checking every tooth for evidence before we went back upstairs. Ma was standing over a pot of soup in the kitchen, in direct line of its powerful vegetable smell, but, without even turning around, before we took three steps into the apartment, she said, "Hostess cupcakes." After that I was convinced she was a witch.

I break off one of the four pieces and shove the whole thing in my mouth. The chocolate is warm already, melty, the way I like it best. It coats my teeth with sweet cream. I'm in ecstasy. I break a second bar in half and chew it down in tiny, fast nibbles. If I take too long she'll know what's up. I break the third one into threes, put one piece in each cheek, the third on my tongue, and wait for the chocolate to all melt. The last piece I wrap up again and stuff into my pocket for later.

I take on the sandwich. I figure it's best to eat in that order so the bread will pull the chocolate out of the crevices of my mouth. As I pull apart the pieces of bread, I see it's a salami sandwich, which I love. There is a huge smear of butter on the roll, and a single cornichon. The bread is soft and chewy, almost like a soft pretzel, and the combination of abundant butter and salty meat make my synapses explode. I eat it so fast I'm not breathing. This is a deluxe feast.

On tiptoes, I stand at the sink scrubbing my fingers. I dig under each nail to make sure there's no trace of chocolate. I don't stop until the skin is raw and red. I feel no guilt, only that I've done something forbidden and that getting away with it is imperative so I can do it again. I get the sense that I'm not old enough to know how to outsmart my mother yet, so I have to settle for diligence in my cleanup.

I bound up the marble stairs and tear into the theater with a little more zeal than I should, and walk straight into the eye of a screaming match. The veins in Yanik's neck are protruding and his bald head is engulfed in a flame of purple skin. He is stomping around the area in front of the stage, yelling in a mixture of English and Hungarian, about how his time is being wasted with petty bullshit. If we could just get on with the making of the show, we could be creating something beautiful, but instead we are all forced to haggle over minuscule garbage that is unimportant and boring. For God's sake, move on from this, and move into what is truly important. Creation, questions, answers, no answers, freedom. He is indirectly directing this at my mother, who is standing at the edge of the stage. She appears braced for further battle, enraged and ready to strike, but perhaps a little embarrassed by the scene. Our time in Hungary has changed her. It's as if her wardrobe has taken on the emotion of the postcommunist Eastern Bloc. She wears men's slacks and button-up shirts, all in muted browns, and a pair of Italian leather shoes. Her eyes are a blazing bright blue, glowing with anger now, the only color on her.

She looks at me as I enter and I'm instantly worried she knows what I've done. I'll be punished. But she returns to Yanik and his rant. She fires back at him with something that pushes him beyond the scope of constructive discussion, and someone intervenes. It's Dante from Sullivan Street, a handsome Italian American with a hook nose, deep brown skin, and a crown of bright white hair coifed like a leading man's. His gold cross bounces on his bronze chest as he steps between my mother and Yanik and says, "That's enough. Let's call it a day. Come on, Rhonna, let's go for a swim."

It should be mentioned here that I have almost never seen my ma sit down. In my nine years on this planet, I have never once seen her use a chair as anything other than an instrument to stretch her body over. Except in the act of lying down to sleep, she is a vertical creature. She stands on the subway, on buses, and in bars. We don't often eat at restaurants, and if we do, she is likely to take her food outside and eat it on her feet. She likes to be in natural daylight and fresh air, and standing, at all times. Health, exercise, and physical excellence are her religion.

She takes a classical ballet class every single day. She dabbled in modern and jazz, and not so long ago she was an extra in *Fame* and *Hair*, show-tuning her way around New York, but now it's strictly ballet. Before we came to Europe, I filled in a coloring book on the floor backstage at Radio City while she auditioned for the Rockettes, for the third time. She moves, my ma, and if she can't, she explodes. The first thing she does when we get to a new city is look up the local ballet studios. If she finds nothing to her standards, she turns to swimming. One day I hope she will swim the English Channel and put her stamina to use, and maybe buy me some new shoes.

In Budapest, the public pool is a vital well of sanity for her, and we go almost every day. Dante knows that the only thing that will bring her out of the heat of her argument is the temptation of release, and he's right. She says to me, "Let's go, Kitty," and stomps out the door.

The pool compound is crawling with women and children. There is the occasional man, but this is a predominantly female landscape. A jungle of wrinkled asses spilling out of one-piece bathing suits, and cellulite-stricken arm jiggle. The men wear tiny shorts and have the same sinewy muscles as my mother. The kids look undernourished and energetic, like me. Everyone is Hungarian. This is a city untouched by tourism. The expansive complex of pools is state run and almost strictly for locals. My mother makes a show out of her entrance, strutting out of the building like it's a catwalk, head high, hips swinging, chest forward.

If you were to strut the entire length of the place, first you would see an Olympic-sized pool, with lanes divided by floating buoys, designated for lap swimming. Several middle-aged ladies in shower caps, and one chiseled young man, are working their way back and forth. Just beyond that is a toddler pool for parents and infants, where a few mothers stand in the shin-deep water, dipping their tiny children in and out. Then the teenage hang, a pool of varying depths, teeming with yelling youths, squawking and tossing each other in from the sides. Finally, farthest away from the ruckus, is the lazy hangout pool. It isn't as deep as the teenage basin, and mostly the shy, awkward kids are milling about here, playing with plastic dinosaurs, practicing their water dancing and kung fu moves, talking to themselves, narrating undrawn cartoons. This is my domain—the realm of the weirdo. Here I can be alone, not be picked on, not have to admit that I don't speak the language, and not have to fit in. Here I can spend time with my thoughts, make up characters, really loosen up.

I fill an hour with conversations with myself, punctuated by canonballs and belly flops and discussions with imaginary friends in foreign accents. The sun is beginning to go down, and I figure my ma is probably close to being done with her lap swimming, so I get out of the pool. Shivering a little in my shorts and bare chest, I make my way over to her. I can see her long, muscular form, cutting through the water with powerful strokes. I wonder to myself how swim caps work, and how amazing it is that hers can hold all that hair underneath it. As she makes her turn by my feet she glances up and smiles at me. She is calmer now, like a creature in its habitat. Another lap, another turn, and I reach down and tap her hand. She stops. "Hey, Ma, what do you wanna do?" She takes quick, deep breaths. "Go back and play. Dante is still here somewhere. He'll take you home when you're done. Okay?"

I walk along the concrete edges of the basins, balancing my weight like a tightrope artist, until I'm back at my station. There is a little girl there, even younger than me, splish-splashing around with her father. I watch them as he grabs her under the armpits and lifts her high up out of the water, then dunks her back in. She squeals and kicks her feet with joy. It dawns on me that I don't really know how to swim. My doggy paddle is solid, but everything else I only know how to fake. I think about my poppa and where he is right now.

At the start of the tour he joined us for ten days in northern France, working on the play with Yanik. The cast stayed in a quaint hotel with a rickety staircase that I would climb with breakfast for my ma to eat in bed. I made it into a fairy tale about staying at the Ritz. She would wrap food in napkins and hide it for later. She is the great master of Holocausting, and we can live for a week on what she stashes away from leftovers. Ma got furious when she found out Poppa was sleeping with Yanik's pretty assistant, even though it had been years since they'd had any obligation to each other. She thought it was tacky with the mother of his child around. When we left to perform in Antwerp and Amsterdam, Poppa took me to Paris. On a houseboat on the Seine, he took a piss off the side. When I demanded to do the same, he handed me a watering can and I shrieked with delight. I don't know when I'll see him again, but I make a mental note to ask him to teach me to swim when I do.

I move around the edge of the pool, tightrope balancing, until I'm three feet from the little girl and her father. He is speaking to her encouragingly in Hungarian, making cute noises and blubbering sounds, as she giggles and thrashes her way through the water, upheld by his big hands. The sun sinks a little farther as I sit and watch them. My feet are dangling and my toes start to feel a little pruney. I look around for Dante, but I don't see him. Maybe he's in the teenage pool.

The father is taking the little girl out of the water on his shoulders, speaking to her, probably telling her it's time for dinner. I look around again. No Dante. I stand up and scour as far as I can see, in all the pools. No Dante. With a small twinge of fear, I look back toward the lap swimmers for my ma, but I can't see that far. I feel like it would be better to stay here in case Dante comes by than to run and look for her when she's probably already gone. I could miss both of them, and then I'd be screwed.

Within a half hour, the weirdo pool is empty and streetlamps have started to come on. The city buzzes and clanks outside the chain-link fence, but a silence rolls across the still waters of the pool complex. I am not afraid of a lot of things, but the silence of solitude knots my insides. I'm trying to distract myself by doing one-armed handstands on the bottom of the pool, pointing my legs straight up and out of the water. If I can hold it long enough, maybe I'd be able to do one outside the water, with both hands. I have to hold my nose when I go under, but the last time I do it I stay under too long and panic a little, so I let go. Water floods my nose and throat and I come up coughing and gasping. I'm over it. Where's Dante? I look around. Almost everyone is gone, and it's nearly dark.

Pulling myself out of the pool by my forearms, I look around. Dante wears bright orange swim trunks, so he should be easy to spot. Maybe he's reading a book in one of the chairs, drying off. I scan the chairs with my eyes. No tanned skin, no orange shorts, no gold cross. No Dante. A cold feeling begins down where pee happens, like my insides are pulling together, as I start walking toward the lap pool. My eyesight isn't the greatest; maybe if I get closer I'll see him. The feeling turns to adrenaline as I see that the lap pool is empty. I know, intuitively, that Dante is gone, and so is my ma. I stand there, my heart fluttering so fast it's making me feel queasy, searching the landscape in desperation. No Dante.

Barefoot and dripping water, I turn on my heel and head for the main building, hoping to catch my mom. Shirtless, in my trunks, I approach an old man mopping the floor. "Excuse me?" He ignores me. "Excuse me, sir? Do you speak English?" He shakes his meaty head. The feeling in my belly turns hard, like a stone. I look around him. The locker rooms are to my left, but the building is pretty much abandoned. I step toward them, praying that someone will come out so I don't have to go in. I really, really don't want to go into the women's changing room. My breathing is heavier. The old man says something in Hungarian and I turn around. He is talking to a big woman in a pink shower cap, who has come in from outside. She looks me up and down, and in broken English says, "Help you? You need it help?" I nod at her and ask if she speaks my language. "Little bit." "My mother . . . she's not here . . ." "Come." She motions and pulls me behind her. At the door to the locker room, I slow, hesitant to go in. I don't want to make anyone uncomfortable, because I look like a little boy, but the woman pulls me by the wrist. It's hard to describe the mixture of shame and defeat that rises up like vomit when I realize how little it takes for me to buckle. Just entering this room makes me feel like everyone in there will know that I'm a girl, which puts a sharp pain into my solar plexus. I hate this so much, but how else will I get home?

A few older ladies are scattered around the steamy room, performing their solitary rituals of preparation for the outside world. I try and keep my head down. My lady says something to the room in Hungarian. A few women shake their heads, and one says something back. They discuss for a few sentences, and the new woman approaches. She is tall, round in the middle, and has clipped, silver hair. Her upper arms are thick and loose like bags of milk. She speaks to me in English, asking me what's going on. I explain. I'm American. My name is iO. I'm seven. I'm here with my mother, but her friend was supposed to take me home and he never appeared. I'm acting in a theater piece in town. She asks me if I know the name of the theater. Miraculously, I do. She says something in Hungarian to the other woman, who is at a locker, dressing. She shrugs. The woman with the silver hair tells me to sit on the bench and wait.

I keep my head down, embarrassed, desperate for the woman to finish. I glance up once and get an eyeful of massive, saggy breasts, and that's enough for me. She asks me if I have any clothes. I tell her my mother has them. She clucks. One quick sound, but I sense what she means by it. I feel defensive of my ma. She's trying.

The cold belly thing eases up a bit now that I'm speaking English with someone, and I imagine myself in a storybook. I'm even a little excited to be on a mysterious, dramatic adventure. Lost! In a foreign land! But only because I'm sure this lady will get me home. Or maybe she won't, and I'll be stranded here, in Hungary, and I'll have to live off scraps I find in the trash.

The woman with the silver hair finishes dressing and tells me to come with her. She hands me a T-shirt, which I put on over my wet shorts, and we leave. She leads me around the back of the building, past the pools, to a single-story stone house. Immediately, my skin starts to tingle. She has brought me to a police station. Of all things that I could do to anger my ma, the worst possible sin is to end up in the care of the cops. She hates the pigs, and she is vocal about this fact. I don't know what's worse: being a stranded runaway in Eastern Europe, surviving off scraps of trash, or being brought home by the police.

I sit on a bench in the entranceway, fiddling nervously with the gigantic T-shirt I'm in, while the woman tells the police my deal. She says a clipped, polite "Good-bye" as she sails out the door. Being soft is not the Hungarian way. Now she's gone, too, and I'm plunged back into the darkness that exists between languages.

It's a good hour of waiting before two uniformed guys come out and gesture for me to follow them. They have young, kind faces and the flat skulls of most men here, but they aren't weathered and wrinkled yet.

They lead me to the parking lot and unlock the back door of an ancient squad car. Everything is green, their uniforms, the paint job, the interior. I'm fascinated with the inside of the cop car. Instantly, I feel like a criminal and get into my role. I sit on my hands behind my back, as though they're cuffed. I contemplate how I'd try to pry the door lock up with my teeth. Maybe I could smash the window open with my head if my hands were restrained.

There is a stiff-brimmed green sergeant's hat on the shelf above the backseat, and I gingerly reach for it. The guy in the passenger seat spots me in the mirror and nods that it's okay to put it on. He smiles at me. I smile back. I pull it over my small head and it flops over half my face. I salute at him. He laughs. I sit up straighter in my seat and stare out the window, saluting and murmuring orders, imagining I was a commander of a fleet of tanks.

We drive through the gray city, which looks tired and smells of cigarettes and pickled fish. I convince them to turn the siren on for a part of it, just by gesturing and smiling a lot. I make jokes and pretend to be a silent movie comedian, using my actions to make them laugh. They are amused by the little performer they've been charged with.

By the time we pull up, I'm almost sad to have to leave them. I see a big sign with the name of the theater on it, and Yanik and Ma outside. Yanik's wife, Esther, and Dante come out when they see the cop car. My guys converse with Yanik in Hungarian before they let me out, but my ma is not happy about waiting. She's furious, I can tell by her face. When they open the door, she snatches the hat off my head and throws it on the ground. The cop doesn't have time to react to this before Ma pulls me away.

MA IS PULLING ME by the wrist up a cobblestone street. Generations of deprivation live in the faces we pass. I look up, beyond the crumbling architecture, the leaning structures of damp concrete, toward the gray sky. I can feel a black power swirling amid the clouds. This place makes my spine feel cold.

We stop in front of a three-story house with planter boxes at each window. Sometimes buildings make me feel sad. It's a kind of spacial depression, the angle of a roof to the sky, the color of the clouds, whether or not I've been there before. What causes it is a mystery, but some invisible quality of a building makes me want to run sometimes. Ma pulls her collar closed over her throat as she takes a set of keys from her pocket. She squints at them in this intense way, where she tilts her head down, as though pointing her horn at them will solve the riddle of what to do with the things. She is too vain for glasses, so she has to improvise a lot. I take the keys from her gently, and put the biggest one in the lock.

We squeeze up a tiny staircase to the second floor and I open the apartment door. The smell of animal piss wafts out in a thick wave that makes me feel like my stomach is sinking through to my butt bone. The couple who own the place are squeezed into their armchairs in the living room. The woman leaps up and bounds toward us. She is short and stout, with dyed black hair pushed up into spikes that scare me. She starts yelling something in Hungarian, but we just stand there, stunned. Her husband, a skinny man, stays where he is, whittling something out of a piece of balsa wood. She goes on and on. My eyes focus in on their pet bird, a little blue finch, that lives in a planter box on the windowsill. Later, I will find out that the bird is dead, but they keep his carcass around for sentimental reasons. Soiled newspaper dots the floor of the cluttered apartment and two ruglike dogs lope about. Ma pulls my wrist and I follow her into the bedroom we are supposed to share for the coming months.

There is hardly room to move for all the stuff piled up in here. A threadbare woolen blanket is draped over a twin bed in the corner. The sky rumbles and cracks as it starts to rain outside. The nasty sensation in my stomach worsens when the overhead light pops on and I can see the stains and animal hair on everything.

Ma is upset, but I'm tuning her out. My mind wanders to the kind policemen. The cold belly feeling was gone when I was with them, distracted, playing, moving, smiling, but now it's back: the familiar ache that comes with being trapped.

## Chapter 14

# My Third Grade Yearbook Poem

*New York, spring 1994*

What someone said when they
were spanked on the day before their birthday. . . .
WHHHAAAAAAAAAAAAAAAAAAAA

Someday I may run away.
Someday I may but not today.

Some night I might
Slip away in the moonlight.

Some night I might
But not tonight.

Someday I may.
Some night I might.
Sometime I might.
But not today or tonight.

## Chapter 15

# The Move

*Third Street, spring and summer 1994*

THE TWITCHING ITALIAN GUY FROM THE BUILDING MAN-agement company was right. The move was inevitable, but we are fighting it. Joey the schizophrenic downstairs started getting death threats. He thinks the management's books are being cooked, so he laid them out on the sidewalk for everyone to see and he started getting threatening phone calls. He put garbage bags over his windows, asked us to hold his mail, and left to "go to the mountain" for a little while.

Shit is all fucked up. It went really sideways when they sealed off the basement and locked the roof. It turns out management is steamrolling us with sham votes, putting dead people's names on the ballot.

Ma has been staging revolt in every way she knows how, but most of the neighbors don't want to fight. Henri, whose apartment I was almost born in, capitulated immediately, deciding that whatever the management wanted was best. In response, Ma shredded a bunch of nice men's shirts he had given her and hung them on his doorknob as a symbol of what she'd like to do to him. She spits when he passes us on the street now.

Most everyone has accepted the reality of what's happening and is trying to make the best of it. A woman showed up recently who is in charge of placing us all in our temporary apartments for the renovation. She's a cutesy-pootsie Rasta chick from Harlem who wears plaid skirts and high socks. She has wired-around front teeth and long dreadlocks and Ma says, "She's sexy, but she's a bitch."

Rasta Lady takes us around and shows us a few places, but when she takes us to a one-bedroom directly across the street from a Con Edison energy plant Ma goes haywire and storms out, screaming about "How are you gonna propose to put a single mother and her tiny child opposite an electro power plant?! Why are all these people on medications with diseases? Electro brain diseases? Electro power plant. Fuck you!"

After that Ma stopped cooperating altogether.

It's too hot for even the usual cast of vagrants in the neighborhood. There's been an awful heat wave, and nightfall doesn't bring any relief. It's making the poor people crazy. Fans are jammed into multiplugs, four to a socket, and fuses are blowing all over the place. You can hear regular *pop* noises coming out of open windows, followed by cursing and the clanging around of a sweaty body groping in the darkness for a fuse box.

Kids are sleeping on the rooftops in their underwear. You can see dirty socks dangling off the sides of fire escapes all the way down the block from where we are standing. Fourth Street is a different world. More Spanish is spoken over here than English, and a lot of the management company employees live here, so it always puts me on edge.

Ma is leaning on a buzzer and screaming up into the darkness. It becomes a powerful banshee screech. I have my hands over my ears, embarrassed. It's after midnight. She's wearing a pair of leggings and tattered flip-flops. The veins in her left arm bulge with the weight of her plastic bags while she stabs the bell with two strong fingers on the other hand.

*"Shaaaannon!"*

Shannon Goldfarb's daughter goes to my school. We look up at their windows and the lights are all off. This is mortifying.

We went back to our apartment to sleep, but the door was bolted shut. We know the construction dudes have been in there, but it's still our house. All of our stuff is still inside.

I'm tired. My eyes ache and my jaw stretches out into a big yawn.

"Shannon! Open the door, you piece of shit turncoat motherfucker!"

A light pops on in a window on the third floor. The glass slides up and a confused, disheveled head of hair sticks out.

"What the . . . Jesus Christ, Rhonna."

Ma just leans on the buzzer. Shannon's head pops back out.

"I have a sleeping child! For God's sake, lay off the bell!"

Ma doesn't stop. It's another three minutes or so until Shannon appears at the door. She throws it open. Everyone is braced for a fight. Ma leans close into Shannon's face and says, "They locked us out of our fucking apartment. Our *own* apartment."

She says this like an old Jewish gangster. She sounds like a lockjawed meathead in a detective comic. Somebody who carries a roll of nickels in his jacket pocket.

"That's because everyone is *vacating*, Rhonna."

Ma gets close to Shannon's face, clenching her strong jaw and breathing through her tensely flared nostrils like a bull.

"That is our *home*."

Shannon isn't responsible for what's going on. She's just another tenant like us, but she embraced the change of guard, and, unfortunately for her, can pull strings to get keys to locks late at night.

She looks into Ma's burning tension and the fight deflates out of her. Maybe she thinks about her daughter, sleeping upstairs. Maybe she decides to be the bigger person so that this woman's anger doesn't seep into her own life. Maybe she's afraid for her safety if she doesn't give Ma what she wants.

Shannon's eyes catch mine for a brief second and she looks like she pities me, which makes my spine crawl with shame. Aware of the futility of logic, she says, "Rhonna . . . everyone in your building is vacating. You guys have to move into your new place. The gas went off today, and they're gonna start knocking down your walls in the next few days. You guys have to move or they are gonna move you."

We already know all these things. Ma has stubbornly refused to accept what we have seen every time we've gone home. Kevin is long gone. The Purple Woman, who has always been kind to us, sucked her teeth when she last passed us in the hall, annoyed that my ma is being such a pain in the ass. There are only construction lights in the stairwells now, and the buzzer system doesn't work, which means it's only a matter of time until the shelter boys start looting the place of everything that isn't tied down. Susan and her cats are on Fifth Street; even Joey is installed somewhere else. Every day there are crashing, shredding noises, the sound of walls being busted through and toilets being ripped out. Mexican music blares in the hallways, and the guys ogle my ma. The only other person left in the building is crazy Fritz on the first floor, because the management doesn't know what to do about all of his pianos.

Ma was holding out for a nicer place, to be relocated to an upgrade. The only joint that fit her criteria was a long, skinny one, on the fifth floor of the building closest to the corner of Fourth Street and the Bowery. We were supposed to have moved in two months ago, but Ma hates it. The whole building has a creepy, dark vibe about it, and the people are awful, so we've been sleeping in our beloved old place on Third Street, until now.

Tonight we came home to find a giant padlock screwed onto our door, something that Joey would have installed in a different era, but it was brand new, which means it was put in by the management company. Ma went ballistic. She tried everything to rip and pry it off before giving up and stomping around the corner.

Shannon tucks a stringy curl of salt-and-pepper hair behind her right ear and sighs. She looks at the ground and rubs her eyelids. She's tired. We've been here so many times, and they have had the same discussion, over and over. Ma blames her for being a part of the evil system, Shannon blames Ma for obstructing what everyone else wants and creating a problem. It's a deadlock. Shannon doesn't have the energy to get bitchy anymore, and Ma's rage would stampede her in an instant if she decided to fight, so Shannon, beleaguered, says, "Rhonna, there is nothing I can do this time. I don't have the keys to the padlocks. They told me they were gonna bolt it, and I tried to warn you you had to get out, but there was nothing I could do. For iO's sake, you should just—"

"DON'T YOU TELL ME HOW TO BE A MOTHER!"

Shannon sees immediately that she has made a mistake bringing Ma's parenting into this.

"I'm sorry. I'm not. Okay. There is nothing I can do for you right now, Rhonna."

"Get me the fucking keys, Shannon!"

Ma sticks her foot between the door and the frame.

"I don't have it, Rhonna. I swear to fucking God, I don't have the fucking key to the padlock. I'd give it to you if I did, just so you don't wake my kid up, but I don't have the fucking key. Okay? I don't have it."

There is something believable in the finality of her tone.

Ma sizes Shannon up, her right hand balled into a fist, shoulders hunched forward, staring into her from under her tensed, angry brows. I think she can tell Shannon is telling the truth because she doesn't say anything.

"Okay? Rhonna? I don't have it. I'm going to go to bed now. Please stop ringing my bell. Please."

Shannon gingerly turns and starts to walk back into her building. In that moment she reminds me of a tired old bird: frazzled and confused, half asleep, protective of her little one. I understand her position. I silently wish her a good night's sleep as her back turns and disappears up the stairs.

Ma stands there, foot in the door, seething, watching her go. I am beginning to fear what we will do next. I have no idea where we'll go. We have the keys to the new place, but we don't even have a bed in there. Ma's face is half lit by the brightness of the hallway. Her eyes burn blue as she stares intently at the empty corridor, thinking.

"Ma."

She can't hear me through the jungle of her fury.

"Ma. I'm tired."

She turns her face and looks at me, but it is almost as though she is looking through me, past me, at the fire hydrant behind me. Her face softens when her eyes meet mine, but instantly she is enraged again when she thinks that we have nowhere to sleep because of these assholes.

Abruptly, she pulls her foot from the door and pushes her entire body weight against Shannon's bell again. The noise clangs out into the sticky night.

"Ma! Stop! Let them sleep! She doesn't have the key . . ."

She leans on it some more.

"MA!! Ma! Stop!"

Only when I start to cry does she snap out of it.

"Shit, kitty. Okay. Okay. My little marsupial. It's okay. Let's go."

She pulls me into a hug, tight against her strong chest, before taking my hand and standing up. We start walking, but I have no idea where to. Tears roll down my face slowly for half a block. I'm scared.

At the corner, Ma stops at a pay phone. She rummages through one of her plastic bags and comes up with a quarter. She lifts the receiver and dials a number. She waits as it rings. She hangs up before the answering machine comes on, retrieves her quarter, and tries again. This time someone picks up.

"Hello? It's Rhonna."

WE SLUMBER-PARTY ON A friend's floor, and when we get back to our building in the morning, they have begun to drain the boiler of its oil.

It has spread lazily across the sidewalk in thick black slicks, and the whole building smells like fuel. Construction workers are crawling all over the place, hauling bags of plaster out to a big green Dumpster and pulling the old metal footplates off the stairwell. Ma loved those footplates.

As we come up the stairs to our floor, several men pass, coming down the hallway from the direction of our apartment. Looking past them, we see that the only open door is ours. They were coming out of our house! Three smug, smiling Mexican guys, carrying things.

"Hey!" Ma yells, as she realizes what is going on, but they are already down the stairs and gone.

My heart falling through my stomach, we step into our beloved steamboat palace. It looks ransacked, all of our things strewn around. My favorite table, shaped like the inside of a grapefruit, stands awkwardly in the center of the kitchen, and a pile of Sheetrock covers our bed. Then I see it: there, on the floor of the living room, in the corner under the window leading to the fire escape, is my piggy bank, smashed. I have been saving every lucky penny I picked up on the street, every forgotten quarter I scored in pay phones I check every time I pass one, every nickel from the floor of Joey's car. I was saving to buy supplies for the tree house I've been dreaming of, and I must have had a fortune in there. Now there are only a few pennies left, strewn among the shattered chunks of pink plaster. The pig's eyes are intact, severed from its ears, and something about its sad face, broken on the ground like that, sends a sharp pain through me. It's the feeling of having been violated. I don't have anything, why would someone take that from me?

When Ma spots the piggy bank, she goes scarlet. I know what that look in her eye means. Someone is going to pay. Her nostrils go wide, and her eyebrows come down.

Then she sees the box.

Of all holy things in our lives, the ultimate, most sacred possession we have is Ma's box of photos of Billy and their time together. I join her in anointing this my most important possession, too, because it seems to carry the essence of her soul in it, and I love her soul.

It is an old box, filled to the brim with Polaroids and Minox prints, of Billy alone, on roller skates with kneepads and no shirt on, in nothing but a bathrobe and socks, in their old apartment, of them together, her towering over him in heels and a blond bouffant, him in a zoot suit and her in sequins. Some are of her alone, posing next to a Christmas tree or diving into crystalline Jamaican waters.

This box contains all the visual evidence that the love of her life was a living, breathing man. Billy Balls stomped this earth, and the only proof outside of people's hearts is in that box. Now, the box is upturned and emptied out onto the floor amid the filthy rubble.

I know my ma. I know she loves every single little treasure in this place, every garment in every trash bag on the floor, every minuscule drawing of mine that she's kept since I was tiny; my belly button is in a drawer over there in the corner. She cherishes the soup pot, my little table, and the prince shoes I wore to Aunt Alice's wedding, but *nothing*, no matter what, is more important than that box of photos, besides our own lives.

Her eyes go from shock, to horror, to blazing furious murder as she stares at its flung carcass. She bends, slowly, from the waist, straight down to the floor, and stands it upright. She curses quietly and begins talking to herself.

She delicately brushes each photo off as she puts it back in the box. I crouch down to help her, terrified and curious as to what she's gonna do about this violation. After we have collected them, we realize that some are missing. She stands, eyes wide open, and lopes into the corridor. I follow her, down the stairs, through the hall, and out the front door.

She strikes the stance of a general, staking out a battleground on the stoop, searching back and forth. She spots a man, a few paces away, showing some photos to another dude. Eyes blazing, she lopes down the steps, two at a time, toward him.

He's a Mexican guy, a good foot and a half shorter than my Ma. I watch from the steps as she charges directly for him, while he laughs and makes an obscene gesture, oblivious to the tornado headed his way.

She snatches the photographs from his fingers and gets right up close to his face. He tries to save his dignity by puffing out his chest and saying something to her, but there isn't a whisker of doubt as to who is in charge. He hands over all the photos he has, and she spits, square between his eyes. I think I make out a "motherfucker" before she walks away, but it's hard to be sure.

NOW OUR BATHTUB is rolling down the street.

Pop's enforcer friend Hammerhead and two of his Puerto Rican boys hoisted it onto a dolly and they're struggling it toward the Bowery. A plumber chick we found is carrying the brass pipes from the tub and sink. Ma has her hands loaded with plastic bags, clothes, and cigar boxes full of treasures. I'm a few paces behind, with an overflowing backpack.

The move is real. We are dismantling our castle piece by piece, inch by inch. Once she got the photographs, we went straight to the corner and called my pop. He called Hammerhead, and an hour later there were three guys and this butch chick in our apartment, taking apart everything that Ma said to.

One of them stood watch at the door, in case anyone from management tried to tell us we didn't have the right to take the sink, or that the molding wasn't supposed to come off the walls. Fuck that. We ripped out everything we wanted. I was tasked with stuffing my things into any random bags I could find and collecting my books.

When it came to the tub, Ma explained to Hammerhead that I was practically born in that tub. I had taken every bath of my life in it, and it was my birthright. He didn't argue. The Rasta Bitch did, though. She showed up halfway through and they got into a screaming match about it. Finally, she understood that the only way Ma was gonna agree to go was with the claw-foot tub and the old basin sink, and the powder-pink toilet seat, too, so she turned around and left, cursing, waving her clipboard, and smacking her gum against her gold tooth.

All the windows were open but the outlets didn't work, so we couldn't turn a fan on, and it's hotter than hell outside today. Literally. I can't imagine there is a place where human souls exist that is hotter than our block at this moment. Watching the men struggle the bathtub down the stairs made me want to cry for them.

All of Fourth Street is creepy, but our new building is from another planet. The door is shitty black steel, and there are fluorescent lights in the hallway. As we push through the foyer a couple of kids stop playing to size us up. They look like juvenile delinquents.

It makes a helluva racket when Hammerhead's boys start wresting the cast-iron tub up six flights, so the neighbors start filtering out to the hallway to see what's up, and we get a good eyeful of our new surroundings. They look like awful people. Sour, mean-faced spirits, holding bottles of cheap liquor, skin ravaged by cheap drugs.

Hammerhead starts laying into my mom about her needing to get some boxes, that they're not gonna do this whole fucking move in plastic bags in a thousand trips. She says fuck boxes, why the fuck would she spend money on those. The butch girl, impatient with the bullshit, interjects to ask where we want the tub, and starts soldering the beautiful brass pipes together. Finally, Ma agrees that we'll go across to the food co-op and see if they have any boxes they'll give us for free because she's not gonna spend money on them. Hammerhead says he'll take what he can get and goes out to smoke a cigarette.

We do nine trips back and forth, each time taking an armful of stuff. Hammerhead splits after the fourth run. He says he can't keep his boys there carrying teddy bears around the block, so they take all the records and books and furniture, and leave us to do the little stuff.

Ma and Fritz, alone, the last of the Mohicans, dismantle every piece of molding they can find in the old building, and she scoops up wooden doors from the construction trash. She holds one piece out to me and says, "See, Kitty? It's got the original horsehairs in it from the 1880s."

The tenderness with which she caresses the hand-hewn beams, chopped with an ax, the glass, the plaster, the banister. This strikes me. I understand. This building is a part of us. I was born here, it's all I know. We love our apartment so viscerally that when the time comes to stand in the doorway and actually look at it for the last time, we both feel sick.

Holding hands, we watch the sunlight fall onto the beautiful hardwood floors I learned to walk on, naked now, scraped where the bed was and where my crib once stood, littered with scattered, random remnants of our haphazard, bohemian existence. The dwelling of a gatherer and a little dreamer, we kiss it in our minds and take a mental snapshot, forever held in our hearts. We don't say good-bye, we say "sooner" rather than "later." The idea of not returning is unfathomable.

BY THE TIME IT'S ALL DONE I'm so tired I can't stand up. Our bed is in the center of a huge pile of stuff, under the front window of our new apartment, and I flop down onto it on my face. The only light in the room is an awful overhead bulb, so Ma plugs in a clip lamp and sets it on the floor. She stretches over me and opens the window. Our tall mirror leans against a wall next to me, and I watch her in it. She turns on the radio, letting Count Basie and his boys create some familiarity in the room.

Futzing around the piles of clutter in the purple dusk light, Ma starts to cry softly. She doesn't want to be here, or stay in for the night. I know her. She wants to go out and start walking. She wants to go to the edge of the Hudson River and scream out into New Jersey. She wants to kill every single one of the tenants that turned their back on our family of outcasts and cashed in on an idea of gentrified, whitewashed garbage, but she won't, because I'm here and she wouldn't leave me alone. Her kitty needs to rest.

She looks around at the flat, empty white walls, barren of all of our gathered treasure, and pain swims across her face. She reminds me of a puppy in a crate that has been separated from its mother too soon. I watch her with one eye, worried if she's okay. I lay there, thinking about how I can help, until my one eye closes and I fall into a displaced sleep.

## Chapter 16

# He's Got Nuts

EVERYTHING IN THE AUDITORIUM IS BEIGE. THE FLOOR IS amber wood, the lights glow yellowish-white, and the walls are an easy cream. The hardwood slants upward from an elevated stage in the center of the room, sloping up to three sets of doors at the back. We don't usually play ball in here—this is the kingdom of the thespians, poets, and tap dancers among us—but the gym is being renovated today, so they threw some Hula-Hoops and balls in here and set the throng loose.

I am at the top of the slope, with a dodgeball in my hand.

I've been told for years that I have a good arm, and it's something I work on. My ma and I go to the park and I'll drill pitches at her until my shoulder feels like it's tearing out, which we've been doing a lot of since we moved into the nasty new building. I recognize that natural talents crop up in strange places, and it's our job to nourish them. Ball sports are mine, along with acting, and I feel incredibly blessed. It could have been sewing, or cooking, or some other thing I find to be insufferably "girly," but ball sports really work in my favor.

William is a lanky kid, a tower of bones in loose jeans and a plain

T-shirt. A slick of jet-black hair parts in the center of his head, and he wears copper-wire-rimmed glasses. He lives in a gigantic, curved housing complex on Canal Street, overlooking the Manhattan Bridge. I went there once, just because we both lived on the East Side—friendship is a casual act of happenstance when you're nine. William got real quiet when we entered the apartment. It was dark and smelled like broth. His parents were old and traditional, and only spoke to him in Chinese. I kept my backpack on, turned around, and scooted my little butt back out the door.

Now William is across the invisible line that separates victors from victims of my pitching practice. The ball I'm squeezing is squishy red rubber. The pockmark grip pattern makes it look like it has cystic acne. It has less air than a basketball so that when it hits you, it doesn't hurt. I toe the center line, eyeing everyone on the other side. They don't see me and my hidden ball yet. William is flailing around, taunting people, and I hone in on him. As he moves toward the line to my right, I rear back, one arm outstretched, almost pointing at him, and fire the ball like a cannon, straight at his ribs.

The force knocks him back a few steps, and he drops the ball he's holding. He yelps and clutches his side. My team goes wild. I'm smiling. William is not. He yells something at me in Chinese and stares at me intently, as though he's trying to understand something.

THAT AFTERNOON, we're in the stairwell between the second and third floors. I'm hugging the wall, walking down to art class. William comes around the landing below me and looks up. With all the cockiness of the teenager that he isn't yet, he bounds up the steps and plants himself in front of me. His gangly arm snaps out and he grabs my throat before I have a chance to move.

Vaguely, somewhere in the canals of my mind, I am conscious of the fact that this is probably retaliation for defeating him at dodgeball. He squeezes. Then his hand moves downward and he grabs my crotch.

Chip, our resident cool kid and basketball star, is behind him on the landing now. William turns and yells to him, victoriously: "See! I told you, son! He's a boy. He's got an Adam's apple *and nuts!*"

## Chapter 17

# Fourth Street

*January through October 1995*

I'M SITTING IN THE FRONT WINDOW LOOKING OUT INTO THE winter night. We're six floors up, so the snow-muffled sounds of the street feel very far away. I can see over the buildings across from us and into the darkness where I imagine our old house is now. I'd rather see it like this, from afar, than in real life, because this way I can put the neighbors in it, turn the lights on, and feel the warm sun on the floor.

I've been getting a new feeling lately, in my gut. It's kind of a lonely, disorienting feeling, like the world has shrunk. My body is getting bigger but the world around it isn't, and I'm hitting my head on the ceiling, like some kind of organism that's different from the others. I've started to get these weird pangs. It's a feeling like fear, but there's nothing scaring me. People on the street just look like they're in a different world, as if they're walking behind glass. I've begun to wonder if they can see me. I know that sounds crazy, so I keep it to myself.

Our new building is narrow, like the inside of a steeple. It has water-stained walls and radiators that can burn the hair off your arm. A black cast-iron fire escape ricochets down the façade. I like to drag a pillow out there and read. Sometimes I'll drop water balloons on taxis, but mostly I just look at the sky and talk to myself in accents. I'm a parrot, like my poppa and my little brother. If we hear it we can say it like we heard it. My brother can re-sound anything, including machines, beeps, dings, and buzzers. I've heard him do it on the phone and he's only five.

For the first part of the year, my ma's anxieties were mine, too. Whatever she thought was outrageous and corrupt would get me spitting and mad. One palm flat on the stucco, she would stand at the front of the new apartment and argue into the telephone, telling people it was unacceptable to expect a woman and her child to move into a dark cave lit with crappy poisonous fluorescent rings whose vibrations could give you epilepsy, and I would stand atop a chair in the living room and stamp my feet and yell in agreement.

What the housing association told her, that she didn't repeat to me, was that they were due to start renovating our new building within a month of us moving in, and they would start whether or not we were still there, again. They'd just given us the top-floor place to get us to move. It started as a bluff because they wanted her to just shut up and take whatever they gave us, but they didn't know who they were dealing with. Three months later, we were using flashlights to dodge piles of rubble on the pitch-black staircase.

Ma wants an apartment flooded with daylight, skylights preferably, an entire upper floor at best, but that's not how low-income housing works. It's by system; there's an equation dividing how many occupants you have and how old they are by a mystery denominator to determine how many rooms you get. You don't have the choice of what floor you're on, and skylights are a pipe dream. This is not what Ma wants to hear, so the fight drags on.

Ma has been doing her best to hold it all together, even though she's real sad and angry about being in this shitty building. She works a million odd jobs to try to keep our money up enough to eat, but it means we're constantly tearing around from one thing to the next. School is stressful because I'm always on the offensive, waiting for a hand to grope me again or a comment to set off a chain of teasing, so I've started to make myself invisible.

Ma mostly tries to keep us busy outside the house. We spend lots of nights at other people's places and she's signed me up for more dance classes than ever. She got me into a carpentry class once a week, and we've started to go see movies. We get to see whichever ones are nominated for the Oscars because we're members of the Screen Actors Guild. That's a nice change. We've even started sneaking into the second half of a couple of Broadway shows. It's easy. You just wait until intermission and walk back in with the crowd, linger around the lobby until the lights are almost down, and then slide into whatever empty seat you see.

I'm also in a play. It's funny, we're doing an off-off-off-Broadway production of *Oliver!* in a dingy church basement. The actors are plumbers and mattress salesmen who have dreams of Hollywood, and the director sucks. Ma has the lighting guy check my teeth because he said he went to dental school once upon a time. I'm in the chorus. The rest of the kid actors are all these middle-class bunnies with moms who send them to rehearsals with teddy bears and dinner. Hunger is a big theme of the play. I've made some friends there, and one kid, Jeremy, invited me out to his house in New Jersey. We'll see.

Ma said his family stinks of money, so it'd probably be safe for me to go have a sleepover there. I don't like sleepovers much, mostly because I don't know how to act because I've only ever had a few. Also, there are holes in my mismatched socks, and I don't want them to find out somehow that I'm a girl. It's actually a very stressful process, but one of the kids told me Jeremy has a playroom, so I have to go check it out.

HIS MOM WAS WAITING in a big black SUV after rehearsal one Saturday, the heat cranked and steam pouring from the exhaust pipe. She was wearing a thick sweater and the car smelled good. It wasn't just me going to their house; two other friends of Jeremy's were coming, too, Eli and Sam.

I sat way in the back, watching as we drove through the tunnel to

Jersey under the icy river, past the streams of cars and out into the quiet suburbs. I fought the feelings of panic that surged in my throat when thoughts of how to hide the truth from these kids overnight would surface. I didn't feel scared about being so far from home with strangers; in fact, I looked at Jeremy's mom's cropped highlights and wondered if she'd consider adopting me.

I had never seen such a massive house. We pulled up into a driveway behind another gleaming car and piled out onto the lawn in front. The house was like an obese person whose rolls keep spilling out over their waistband, more and more rooms unfolding from the center. More and more windows with curtains behind them. The paint job was perfect.

This was my dream. A real house. Jeremy didn't even stop to look at it when he jumped from the front seat. He just grabbed his backpack, sauntered up to the door, and led us inside. He's used to this, I realized.

There was wall-to-wall carpeting in the living room, and Jeremy's mom told us to take off our shoes when we walked in. I was embarrassed and had a momentary crisis about whether to leave my holey socks on or run around barefoot, but I decided to try and keep the toe tucked under my foot so no one could see it.

I sat on one of two giant couches while Jeremy and his mom poured us all glasses of juice that they pulled out of a massive refrigerator with an ice maker on the front of it. That was one of the fanciest things I'd ever seen and I tried not to stare. It was a lot to take in. I couldn't believe that Jeremy was so unaffected. He didn't even seem to notice how crazy his life was.

When we finished the juice he took us downstairs into the basement. Plush carpet led us into his personal Disneyland; there was a Ping-Pong table, a wall of toys, bikes, Nerf guns, and, most mind-blowing of all, two bean bags plunked in front of a big TV with a Super Nintendo setup and a huge pile of the latest games.

Jealousy shoved me from the back. Jeremy was parading around, showing off all the shit his parents had bought for him and his brother, and he didn't even seem like he cared. I could tell he did because he wouldn't be showing it off otherwise, but I wanted to see that he cherished it all, like I would. We have never had a TV, much less a gaming setup, and I have never been allowed to play video games. At all. Ever.

We played Ping-Pong for a while, the four of us, me and Eli crushing Jeremy and Sam, then his mom called us up for dinner. She said to get changed into our PJs first. I pulled her aside and let her know I only had the sweatpants I was wearing and she said not to worry at all, Jeremy had tons of stuff he'd be happy to lend me.

Upstairs, in Jeremy's bedroom, he was being super nice, going through his drawers of clothes to find me some basketball shorts that I liked. He said, "Hey, you guys wanna see something cool?"

"Yeah."

"Look at this . . ."

He pulled a wad of cash out of his drawer of tube socks.

"I just got it for my bar mitzvah."

He smiled, showing off the wad with the same blasé shtick he was doing in the basement. We all just sort of cooed and *wow*ed and then went downstairs for what they called dinner in this fantasy castle.

It was nuts. His mom made us mac and cheese and fries and didn't even force us to eat any carrots or broccoli or squash. She didn't use any soy sauce or garlic, and it all actually tasted delicious. After we ate, she said it was movie time and put us in front of the TV with bowls of ice cream. That blew my mind.

We watched *Mrs. Doubtfire*, which made me almost pee my pants it was so funny. Robin Williams plays a man living as a woman, making it even funnier, because these kids had no idea I was a Mr. Doubtfire right next to them on that plush cream couch.

We all slept in real beds because they had a guest room with bunks and his brother wasn't there, so we each got our own space. I didn't have any trouble going to the bathroom because the guest room had its own and I could lock the door.

In the morning, I went back into Jeremy's room to change out of his basketball shorts. Being in there alone was too much temptation for me to handle, and I pulled open the sock drawer. Was he really gonna miss it? What did this kid even need a wad of cash for? He had everything he could ever dream of! I put the wad at the bottom of my backpack, folded up the shorts, and went downstairs.

I left it in my bag when I went to school the next day, just because I had no idea where to stash such a thing that my ma wouldn't find it. I planned to figure it out that night. But when we got home, there was a message on the machine from Jeremy's mom asking Ma to call her back urgently. I sat on the bed straining to hear what was being said, but it sounded like my ma was apologetic and upset. There was the sound of a zipper as she opened my yellow backpack, which was hanging on a coat hook right behind her.

I stopped listening. I got under the blanket and put a pillow over my head. I had a deep desire to vanish, to evaporate into the walls, to float out the window through the glass and just go away somewhere else.

Ma came in and stood at the foot of the bed. To be fair, she didn't attack, she kind of gave me the benefit of the doubt. She could have flipped out on me, but she didn't. She asked where the wad of cash in my backpack came from.

"What do you mean?"

"I mean, where did you get the three hundred dollars that was rolled up under your notebook?"

"Willy gave it to me . . . to hold on to for him . . ."

"Willy? Who's Willy?"

"Willy Hart, from my class."

"Willy Hart . . . Willy Hart gave you . . . Why did Willy Hart give you three hundred dollars to hold onto for him? Why does he have three hundred dollars?"

"I don't know . . . from his mom, I think . . ."

My mind was spinning, trying to keep up with and invent my lie as it spilled out of my mouth. The embarrassment I felt was like being dunked in something gross, everywhere on my body and completely engulfing. The urgent desire to disappear leaned into a zone of hysteria. My face was burning with the guilt of lying, but the shame I felt about having stolen some nice kid's money who welcomed me into his house and having gotten so easily busted made me want to be someone else so bad I was pushing the edges of anger. All of this under a pillow while trying to act natural.

Ma hadn't told Jeremy's mom that I had the money; she wanted to talk to me first, which I appreciated.

"Willy Hart gave it to you to hold on to, huh . . . Well, Jeremy's ma just called, and said he is missing three hundred dollars of his bar mitzvah money that was in his sock drawer. She said he showed it to you and the other kids when you were sleeping over there."

Something snapped into place for me, a decision that I was going to stick with this lie, under no circumstances could I tell her the embarrassing truth, partially because it would hurt her that I felt like I needed to steal money to eat. I realized that I had to treat this untruth like anything but. I ripped the pillow off my face, looked her straight in the eyes and shrieked, "Well, why would he accuse me? Because I'm the poor kid? What about Eli and Sam? Did they ask them?! I didn't take his stupid bar mitzvah money, that money is from Willy Hart. He gave it to me and I have to give it back!"

I'm on month two of sticking to this lie now. It's created a great rift between my ma and me. I can tell she feels betrayed, confused about who I am. But I can't let go. I've dug myself so deep into this hole, it would upend everything to confess. The cash is in a cigar box in the closet, next to the box of Billy photos. She's talked to my pop about it on the phone, and he tried to point out to me how ridiculous a coincidence it is that on the very day I visit a kid who loses three hundred bucks, I show up with three hundred bucks in my bag swearing it's from somebody they didn't even know I knew. But I insist, playing to his sympathies. They're both confused. They don't know me to be a liar and don't want to see me that way.

I'm lucky because Ma's kind of distracted. Our new building is practically abandoned now. I don't understand what happened, since I thought this building was a respite from the other soon-to-be-abandoned building, but now they've ripped the mailboxes off the wall here, too. The electricity is spotty and they've pulled the gas main out, so we've been cooking on a camping stove and using candles to see.

I think Ma feels bad about the house. She says everything they're doing is super fucking illegal, but all her attempts to hold management accountable fall flat. She let me get a pet lizard from Canal Street to try and distract me from the misery of it all, but the second he got out of his cage he buried himself in a pile of rugs and probably won't surface until spring. I don't blame him. I'd camouflage myself into a warm spot and disappear if I could, too.

One day there's a knock and it's one of the last holdouts, Nick, one of the two Aleut Indian brothers who are still downstairs. He says to my ma, "Hey, Rhonna, do you smell gas?"

"Oh shit . . ."

They exchange a few words and she goes straight to the phone and calls Con Edison. They send an inspector down and he says, "You have live gas pipes hanging outside your window."

My ma starts yelling about how we live on the sixth floor of a walk-up, and that it's not acceptable for them to gas us, but he tells her it's the landlord's responsibility and leaves. That's when the phone calls start.

Every night when we get home she goes to the little stand in the hall by the door and gets on the phone, calling councilmen, housing aid organizations, pro bono lawyers, trying to rally up some support for us. I hear her telling them that we were abandoned, tricked by a greedy, fraudulent management organization.

ACROSS THE STREET NOW, I can see the junkies who are squatting the top floor of another abandoned building, lighting candles on their mantel. They've been adding to what has become a mountain of wax atop the fireplace all winter. They're night people. No matter what time I wake up, I crane my neck to check on them and the mantel is lit up, dripping onto itself and down to the floor.

There has been a huge snowstorm the last few days, and homeless guys are sleeping in our stairwell. One of the windows is broken and snow is blowing into the pale yellow light in the hall over them as Ma and I come down the stairs. She stops to film it because it is so beautiful.

She's been working with a gay Puerto Rican lawyer dude who has an office on Fourteenth Street. We go up there at all hours for Ma to write letters and make phone calls and try to change the situation, but nothing seems to be working. Sometimes he gives me cookies or jelly beans while I'm waiting on the front couch. I spend hours and hours there, reading. I found a book in the library on being a survivalist. It teaches you how to spear a fish with a sharpened stick, how to cook it over an open fire, how to shelter yourself in a storm, and how to build a debris hut out of sticks and leaves.

I make Ma take me up to Central Park so I can gather piles of leaves and make myself a shelter to hide in. I love small spaces that have walls, even if they're made of leaves, because I can go in and read and no one will bother me.

Six months go by. Everything descends into a hellscape in the building. All the last neighbors move out and they begin construction on some of the apartments. We're literally the only ones left. They ripped up the floor in the entrance hall and put down planks of plywood to make a path. The daily feeling is one of bottomed-out, gut loneliness. Despair. None of the letters Ma wrote did anything. One of the guys who works for management seemed like he would help us, a collegiate redhead named Gabe, but one night Ma called him because our bathroom ceiling was flooding and he said, "Don't call me after dark, Rhonna, I'm meditating."

He hung up. That sent Ma into a shrieking fit of rage. I think it's all getting to be too much for her to handle. We're like refugees up here, just her and me, alone.

Over the summer Pop came to visit with his new girlfriend, Julia, a well-known choreographer who hired him to make everything to do with design for her new company—stages, lighting, posters. We all made a cowboy movie together. I've taken to wearing a Catholic school uniform daily, because I like the routine and how sharp it looks, so we wrote a movie where I was a kid escaping from his Catholic school who runs into some wooden Indians in a cigar shop. We used a storefront across the street to make the cigar shop and my ma and Julia both painted themselves completely brown with body paint and got dressed up as the Indians to costar.

Ma and Poppa got into an argument over the situation in the house and he gave her some extra money, but there's not much he can do, I guess; how my ma spends it is out of his control. I felt super close to him until the money stealing came up again.

He took me out for lots of walks and tried to get me to just cop to it, but I refused. They started ganging up on me, telling me it wasn't the end of the world, that it's much better to be honest and get the guilt off my chest, and finally I relented.

We were at Chelsea Piers just before my birthday. He was picking me up from the batting cages for a sleepover uptown. They cornered me and started peppering me with questions and finally I just didn't want to lie anymore. I blurted out what they wanted to hear and immediately burst into tears. Poppa was going to get me a bike for my tenth birthday, but as soon as I said it, I knew that wasn't gonna happen anymore. Far worse, actually, was that my ma said now that I had confessed, I couldn't have the sleepover. I had to go home to the hellhole and go to bed without dinner. They got in a yelling match about that, during which I sat on the ground and threw rocks into the Hudson River, but in the end she won like she always does. Poppa has been on tour out of the country since.

Ma made me call Jeremy and apologize. I had to go meet up with him and his mom and his brother and shake his hand and give him the cash back. That was mortifying. It took me two weeks to recover. In the meantime, I found some gauze and taped it over my face and told the kids at school that a dog had mauled out my eye.

By Halloween Ma had forgiven me, and we decided to throw a party in the building. There wasn't another soul living there, and it was the creepiest place on earth. We got these cheap goblets in the shape of skulls and Pop told us to put dry ice in them. We lit a ton of candles in the foyer, laid the goblets around, and put on some music. But nobody showed up.

After that I made a sling and told the kids at school I'd broken my arm. They all signed it with hearts.

TODAY WE WAKE UP to a chain saw noise right next to our heads. It sounds like the Hulk is coming through the wall. Ma jumps out of bed and runs next door, only to find a construction crew literally tearing down the Sheetrock. She gets on the phone and starts screaming.

I put on my pants and we come down to the management office, where the Rasta Bitch says our time on Fourth Street is up. We need to move back to Third Street or hit the road.

Ma protests, saying they shafted us, lying to get us out, and now all they have left are apartments in the back of the building. The Rasta Bitch counters, saying that's not true, there are apartments in the front, they're just one-bedrooms, which she's happy to give us. Ma waves an angry arm toward me and delivers a sermon on the inhumanity of forcing a single mother and a growing child into a space half the size of what they need.

This is an impasse. Rasta Bitch knows she's won, because we can't argue an apartment into existing. "Rhonna, you've had nine months to do this an easier way, but those walls are coming down today, so either you go back over to Third Street or we can't help you."

The fluorescent lights allow for no discretion. Every person in the office is openly gawking at the two women battling in the foyer. It crosses my mind how smart it was of them to put in a sheet of bullet-proof plexiglass to shield the secretary. If they were fucking us over like this, how many other people wanted to go postal on them?

"You still have the option to choose which apartment you'd like, Rhonna. There are two two-bedrooms still available, but Mr. Nuñez is on his way over there as we speak to take the upper one for his family. If you'd like to have a say in the matter, I suggest you head over there right now."

My ma is like a dragon. Her nostrils are wide and her eyes are burning fire again, for the fifty thousandth time this year. But she knows she's being backed into a corner.

"I can delay the demolition by two weeks, Rhonna, to allow you time to relocate back to Third Street, but that is absolutely it. You have to come back here today to sign the paperwork on the new place, or the whole thing is off the table and we'll have to serve you with eviction papers."

My ma curses this woman in every way she can think of as the pretty Rasta Bitch ushers us toward the door.

"Okay, Rhonna, that's real mature. Have a nice day."

She slams the door behind us and I hear her throw the dead bolt. She's lucky, that bitch: Ma could pull her apart like a piece of chicken.

OUR OLD BUILDING IS unrecognizable. Everything has been made over, cleaned up, genericized. Fritz is gone, and Joey too. The walls are sticky with fresh paint, divided into a horizon by two shades of colorless beige, and the banister has been painted over so chunks of wood don't skewer your palms when you run down the stairs. The first floor doesn't stink of Susan the Cat Lady anymore, because she and her furry friends have been relocated permanently. The front door has been replaced, the buzzers work, and the lights in the halls cast what my Ma calls *a sterile flood*.

The apartment smells clean and new when we walk in, and I notice for the first time that the floors are wood. The bathtub isn't painted blue, it doesn't have feet, and it is no longer in the kitchen. Light switches work, and I spend a long time contemplating the clean toilet. Best of all, there are two bedrooms, one for my ma and one for me. Three Boy Scout books have already been scoured for every possible tip on how to build myself a bed, make a lamp, and construct a bookshelf for my collection. I jump up a little bit with every step I take and pull my ma's hand. But she's furious. The four windows at the back look out over the brick back wall of La Mama, the theater behind our building, and the ceilings are low. There is no color in the apartment. No air. No light. She is steaming, and suddenly I am no longer loyal to her notions of right and wrong.

## Chapter 18

# Pet Store Rafik

*Fourth Street, October 1995*

I AM LAID OUT ACROSS THE BACKSEAT OF A 1972 PONTIAC, with my face pressed against the sticky beige pleather. My head and toes nearly touch at both ends. The streetlamps are sparkling orange, and every minute or so a cab ambles by, revealing the ceiling in a roving six-inch shaft of light.

It's chilly and dark out. I have a hoodie up over my ears. We are parked outside the Fourth Street building, but we're not going in. We've got a week left there.

Ma is in the front seat, and Rafik is behind the wheel. Rafik runs the pet shop around the corner from my school. We started going in there to get food for my pet lizard, Bullet, but lately we've been going in for Ma to hang out with Rafik. He is Middle Eastern of some sort, maybe Egyptian. He has short black hair and wears a thin gold chain. He might be thirty or forty. Not a particularly smiley character, but he gives me doggy treats that I give to puppies in the park, so he's okay in my book.

We've been dropping by later and later, waiting until he closes, and in the last few days he's started driving us back across town to get home. This is the latest it's ever gone.

Ma is wearing a black coat, brown hair to her shoulders. She put lipstick on, and I know what that means. Her long legs are bent up underneath her like a spider, and her seat is pushed all the way back. Just the fact that she is in a car tells me she must like this guy.

We sit there, double-parked, while they talk for a while. I tried to interject once and Rafik told me to lie down and do some daydreaming. I didn't like that, but I did it.

Now I'm staring at the streetlights, thinking about David Bowie, thinking about the cowboy movie, my new tap shoes. I hear a smacking noise and look toward the front seat. Rafik is leaning over and kissing my ma. He has one hand on her chin, holding her face against his. I see a glimpse of his tongue snaking into her mouth, and I am repulsed. I whip my head back to the window above me and roll my body so that my back is to them, covering my ears.

I lie there, staring at the stitching on the seat, thinking about the Boy Scouts and how I can possibly finagle my way into a troop. It's been a real pain in the ass because everyone wants to see an ID to okay you for insurance stuff, and if they see that, they'll know I'm a girl and ban me. It occurs to me that my "cousin" Aidan, who lives next door, might have a way in (I refer to him as my cousin because I've known him since I was born), and for a second I forget where I am and turn to tell my ma. I spot Rafik's hand reaching across the abyss above the gear stick, down between her legs, and I snap my head back around. Gross.

If I were in the army, I wouldn't have to deal with this. If I were in the army I'd be doing basic training right now, doing sit-ups and pull-ups and climbing over walls made out of mesh. My head would be shaved and I'd have a bed to make every morning, and maybe right now I'd be shining my one pair of awesome boots.

This year, I dressed up as Eddie Munster for Halloween. We drew a widow's peak on my forehead with eyebrow pencil and scored this amazing black velvet suit from a thrift store. Nobody at school knew who Eddie Munster was, but once I told them, they nominated me for best costume in the class.

Last month we went up and spent the night at Ma's friend Matushka's house because we were cold. Ma has a little gig cleaning her pad on the Upper East Side, and when she goes out of town she says we can crash. We set up a mountain of pillows and blankets on the floor in the living room and had a slumber party.

Matushka had breast cancer and had a tit removed. She's made all this art about it so now there are busts of her naked torso all over her house, showing off how she has only one boob and she's proud of it. I think it's great.

She has an amazing sound system and I started trying out tapes while Ma was in the kitchen making tea. One of them really lit me up. A winding electric guitar kicks in right away, hammering out a basic riff, then the drums come in, and a dude's voice sings "doo doo doo doo doo doo doo doo," in a simple, singsong melody. It sent power through me and I started jumping around, dancing. "Rebel rebel," the guy sang, "you've torn your dress. Rebel rebel, your face is a mess!"

I put the tape on repeat, waving my arms and jumping around on all the furniture. My ma came in and started laughing, dancing and clapping along to the rhythm. She started doing the high kicks I love, and swinging her hair around like the drag queens do it, and that made me squeal.

We must have listened to it fifteen thousand times before I realized that he's saying, "she's not sure if you're a boy or a girl." I found my anthem.

Ma told me the guy's name is David Bowie, and he likes people who are a little bit of boy and a little bit of girl. She said she listened to him a lot when she was a teenager growing up in Kansas. When she was dealing with the "vacuous loneliness" she says comes with that age, she would listen to him and somebody named Mick Jagger and go out and dance in the discotheques and at tea dances.

Ma and Rafik are making weird slurping noises that pull me out of my Bowie dreaming, and I start singing "Rebel Rebel" out loud. The slurping noises stop and Ma says, "We gotta go, Rafik. Thanks for the ride."

She smiles and kisses him on the mouth one more time before unfolding her long body out the door. He looks a little wistful, maybe a little uncomfortable, and he adjusts himself in his seat as I climb out past him into the night without saying good-bye.

We will never see Rafik again.

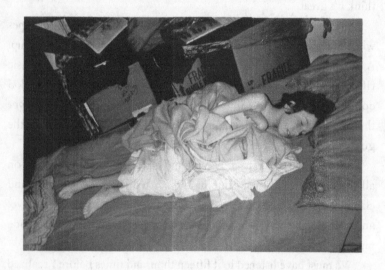

## Chapter 19

# Cold Cuts

*Third Street, Thanksgiving 1995*

WINTER IS A TIME OF DARKNESS. THE SUN IS BUSY IN other places, places where people can pay to frolic in it, places where they use words like *leisure* and *luxury*.

Darkness here comes before you get your day going, and the night is even colder. You clutch your own bones so tight that they start to ache. Hands stay in pockets, buried deep, balled into fists.

It's Thanksgiving Day and everything is wrapped in Christmas lights. It's so cold my skin burns. The air is crystal gray, sliding into slate as the daylight goes. The sky hovers low, like a cramped ceiling, with dark bubbles of frozen slush.

People are bundled up in their layers of wool and cashmere, slashes of eye peeking out between scarves and hats. They dart across the avenues carrying bags filled with thoughtful gifts for loved ones, pulling open the doors to fancy places they plan to leave money in, blanketing the sidewalks in steaming clouds of central heat.

I imagine these people all have houses like Kevin McCallister in *Home Alone*, decked to the nines in ornaments and tinsel and tiny reindeer and Santa and Christmas schlock. Tons of presents spilling out from under a lush tree. I imagine that feels good.

We moved into the new apartment a few weeks ago. It's stark and clean but stuffed with all our junk. I have my own room, which is amazing. I get to put my things where I want to, but I'm not allowed to close the door.

I've been sleeping on an old army cot we got on Canal Street. It's khaki green, the old fold-up kind soldiers would carry around on their backs. It's missing the two posts, though, that keep the cloth taut, so if I don't keep myself positioned just so it claps up around me in the night.

I've got a pile of airplane blankets we took from all the Europe flights, and I've been stuffing sweatshirts into a pillowcase, which works fine as a pillow.

When we first moved in, Ma threw her mattress on the floor, lay down under her Ecuadoran blanket, and went to sleep. She slumbered in the cold, empty room, hibernating like I've never seen her do.

The first morning I woke up to Mahalia Jackson wailing on the radio and Ma weeping. Long, tearing heartbroken noises, like an out-of-tune violin getting pulled on in painful, drawn-out strokes.

She stayed like that, prone, for a couple of days. Eventually the tears stopped, but she still hasn't gotten up. That bugs me out because she never stays down.

I've been asking to go sit on the stoop and I've been taking longer and longer to come back. I started venturing to Fourth Street, and now I've strayed all the way up to the Wiz on Broadway and Waverly. I told her I was playing with Aidan next door, but really I've been at the Wiz every day, watching clips of movies they put on the TVs to show what good quality they are. A Schwarzenegger flick, *Die Hard*—they show good stuff! You just have to be okay with watching the same twenty-minute clips over and over again.

They have a music section that's awesome, too. They have the top twenty-five albums in the country in players along the wall in a back room. Monica, Brandy, Bone Thugs—they've got it all. It's taking me a week to listen through every album up there.

Ma doesn't notice.

The window in my room overlooks the light well, so the nasty pigeons settle on my sill and gurgle their gross song. The morning after we moved in, I woke up to a symphony of coos. The radio was on in Ma's room, but the house was only lit by the few rays of light coming through the windows.

I think that's why she's depressed. She fought so hard for us to get a place with daylight and now we've got a boxy little joint with two views onto brick walls. You have to turn a light on to see in the morning. The ceilings are low, which makes her sad, and there's a fluorescent tube in the kitchen, which is a surefire way to get her going nutty.

I lean over her bony shoulders and ask her if we we're going to the Hungarians' for Thanksgiving this year like we usually do, but she says no and something to the effect of there not being enough space at their house.

This hurts my heart. I feel a wash of shame come over me, wondering what we've done wrong that they don't want us back.

I retreat after that, hanging out in my room and burying myself in Sherlock.

I love Thanksgiving. I love eating so much my belly hurts. I love falling asleep after. I love the sugar high of pecan pie. In fact, I love the mixture of turkey and sugary cranberry sauce so much that the thought stops my reading. I can practically taste the combination as I've had it at so many Thanksgivings with the Hungarians, snuck behind my ma's back.

From where I'm lying, I can see Ma's bed, and she hasn't moved. This is a depressing scene. If I want some turkey and cranberry I'm gonna have to make it happen for myself.

It's so cold that the air almost barks at me when I open the front door. It smells like a mixture of garbage and Christmas.

Halfway to the corner there's a guy on the nod between two

parking meters. At a precarious and impressive ninety-degree angle, he's got a good lean going. Everything in me wants to give him a tiny push, just to see the epic recovery, but it's Thanksgiving, and that wouldn't be kind. So I get real close to his face and shout, "Yo, man!"

His eyes snap open and droop down to half closed immediately. He rights himself and I carry on to the deli.

I grab a can of jellied cranberry sauce and get the dude at the counter to give me a quarter pound of turkey cold cuts for a dollar. Abdullah tells me to take a quart of water for myself and puts everything in a brown paper bag, which I roll up and carry back to my stoop.

There, on the top step, I unpack and lay out my bounty.

Yuppies are coming and going, and our neighbor the Purple Woman passes by, making me wonder if they celebrate Thanksgiving where she's from. Probably not.

I had Abdullah open the can, and I got a plastic fork. It makes the perfect bite when you wrap a slice of turkey around a hunk of cranberry jelly and pop it into your mouth. I've never missed the holiday and I'm not about to start now.

Chapter 20

# Camouflage

*Manhattan, December 1995*

SOMEONE AT SCHOOL WAS TALKING ABOUT WHAT KIND OF cereal they like yesterday and how they go shopping with their mom. I realized that I don't think I've ever been in a conventional supermarket. There's one close to our house but we literally have never set foot inside.

Our eating habits go more like this:

There's a health food store two blocks from the dance studio. We'll have a half hour between classes, or maybe fifteen minutes on the way to an audition, and we'll jet over there. Ma will head to the juice counter and order a large carrot (once I had a shot of wheatgrass and I puked in a trash can on the street). I'll dip to the back and dig through the freezer to unearth one of the Kamikazes I buried in there the day before. Kamikazes are rice shakes that I think are much better frozen (they're really called amazakes, but "Kamikaze" makes more sense).

Twice a month we hit Panna, a closet-width Indian restaurant on Sixth Street, where I always get exactly the same thing: cheese poori (basically an Indian grilled cheese) and raita, which is a yogurt condiment with cucumber in it. On *very* rare occasions I can get lamb curry, but that's only when we're flush. Ma gets a gross spinach dish that takes longer and by the time it comes, I am comatose on the table. I don't know what they put in the food, but I'm almost sure they're drugging me. As soon as we finish eating my eyelids become cement shutters, and I pass out, drooling on the glass tabletop.

Other nights I'll scrape a buck fifty and hit the Spanish deli on Second Avenue for a coffee cup of rice and beans, or, if I've got a little more cash, a pint of chicken lo mein from the takeout Chinese joint. Ma hates that because she says it's rigged with MSG to trick my senses and poison my body, but it's so damn good.

If Ma's not around and I've got three bucks, I'll hit any deli I pass and order the same exact thing: salami on a roll, lettuce, tomato, mayo. Mostly I don't have enough for a sandwich, though; mostly I subsist on toasted bagels with butter, sometimes cream cheese.

It's been kinda gnarly with food lately. The electricity went out in the new apartment because Con Ed shut it off. Ma says the bill doubled since we're in a place with more rooms, so we're running a cable out the window to the Purple Woman's place upstairs. That gives us some light in the front room and the radio, but it means the fridge doesn't work.

Ma says I don't need keys to the house because if the sun is out I should be out in it, so mostly I wait around the dance studio trying to figure out how I can score enough money to sneak away and grab a Happy Meal.

We walked the runway a few weeks ago for a hat designer. There was an Italian model who had a bunch of cash in his jeans in the dressing room. I don't know what I planned to do with a roll of European money, but there was a sweet silver clip so I snagged it. I'm dumb, though, because I was the only one who could have done it, and my ma just about lost her mind when she realized it was me.

The next day, on the way to school, she dragged me into a church and asked the priest if he could give me an exorcism. She told me about how every time she's ever stolen something, anything, no matter what size, something precious to her goes missing. She says she doesn't know how it works, and she doesn't believe in mystical shit, but that's just the balance of things.

So now I don't steal from people anymore. I just sit around staring at people's food, wondering where the hole in the sky is that money and hamburgers are gonna drop out of.

I was on the subway recently and the smell of chocolate floated down the car, rich, milky, and sweet. A little boy was holding it awkwardly between his middle finger and his thumb, smacking his lips from his last bite, watching it melt in the heat of his hands. My tongue sprouted a layer of dew. I wanted to snatch that kid's chocolate so badly.

When you're hungry your mouth waters. Your stomach produces some kind of acids or something and it's like your tongue starts to sweat. There is the vaguest flavor. You can trick your body out of hunger if you replace this flavor.

I have zero shame about going up to the guys at the newsstands in the subway and asking them what I can get for two dimes. Usually a Blow Pop is a safe bet. I go for cherry or sour green apple because it has the most pungent flavor. And Blow Pops last, too. So that's a long time my mouth is telling my stomach I'm not hungry. And then there's gum inside to prolong it further.

Never drink water when you feel like that; it only makes you realize how hungry you are. You want to chew it and eat it, but there's nothing fuckin' there. It's just water filling, or not filling, your little belly.

My strategy to avoid constantly ruminating on my hunger is to steal as much as I can from stores (*not people*), and to distract myself with elaborate getups. I got some costume glue and stuck clippings from my ma's hair all over my face a few weeks ago and told people I was a werewolf lost from the forest and did they want to donate to my fund to return home to my habitat.

We've been spending our evenings in the public libraries, when we're not at school, dance class, or auditions. I got a scholarship to a prestigious ballet school in Harlem, but on the first day the headmaster pulled my ma and me into the girls' bathroom and told her that I couldn't wear my black tights and white T-shirt, I'd have to wear the pink getup required of girls. I ran into a stall and puked. Ma didn't make me go back, but it's destroyed my opinion of ballet. I hate hate hate going to class now. Ma doesn't want to hear it. She said I could do more tap and jazz, and I've started hip-hop, but she says ballet is the backbone of dance, so I have to still take it. At least she took me out of that crazy strict leotard place and lets me go where I can wear my boys' uniform.

I've been taking advanced tap class in the evenings, and two older ladies asked me if I'd give them private lessons. They don't mind that I'm only ten, maybe they think it's cute. For Christmas my grandma Edie got me a pair of Chucks and my ma put taps on them! I've been way up in the front of class right next to the teacher, walking around on my toes, and the ladies have been paying me a little bit to teach them the basics. Needless to say, I've been snagging secret Happy Meals when I can.

But mostly there's no food. Ma is generally in a bad mood and doesn't seem to get hungry much. She hates the apartment and never wants us in there, so she's taking more ballet than ever and she's looking real skinny. I have to remind her about Panna lately, which is weird, and she never cooks, even though we have a stove now. We only go to the apartment late at night and we leave first thing in the morning. If we're home for a longer stretch, I'll light some candles in my room and read while she blasts old songs in the big room and belts along.

Anyway, supermarkets: we have this Kamikaze ritual, which has me stabbing a plastic knife down into the bottle furiously while Ma waits for her juice. I wander the aisles as I do this, dodging butts and occasionally miscalculating. Today I'm in full camouflage—pants, shirt, jacket, hat, and greasy face paint. I *love* camouflage. I love all things army, so this is my dream suit.

We're in a health food store on West Houston Street, and Ma is looking at some Chinese teas, talking to me about body health, but I'm not listening. I'm concentrating on my Kamikaze and getting it smashed up enough to drip in my mouth when a familiar voice calls our names. It's my godmother, Nan!

She glides up the aisle and sweeps me into a huge, warm hug. Chewing on my tongue, I continue slamming my knife into the Kamikaze while she asks my ma all kinds of questions about how we are. She compliments my outfit and asks what the occasion is.

I shrug. "It's Tuesday . . . ?"

She laughs deep and hearty and long, squeezing my shoulder. Something about her just feels cozy, like she sleeps in rabbit furs or bathes in milk. She smells like expensive flowers and first-class plane tickets. I want to tell her I'm fucking hungry, but I'm way too embarrassed to say that to my godmother. I don't want her to think Ma can't provide.

Nan asks if I want to hang out outside with her while my ma shops, so we sit on a bench and chat. Mostly we talk about school and some stuff she's been doing, and she asks if she can take my portrait. I tell her sure, I like having my picture taken, especially while I'm in my dream suit.

She takes a couple of frames in front of the newsstand on the corner before my ma comes out and we say good-bye. Part of me wants to go home with Nan. Part of me wants to go home with everyone who seems like they have a nice, warm, safe place. I wonder what her house looks like and if there's a room there for me. But my place is with my ma, and I know that.

A few weeks later one of Nan's assistants calls and says the *New York Times* wants to use the photo she took of me in their magazine and is that okay. Ma says it'll be good for my career, so of course they can, and do they pay models. No, they don't, the girl tells us, but she'll get us some copies for sure.

The next Sunday we stop at the newsstand and pull the magazine out of the paper. Holy shit, there I am on page 51, under a headline that says "Portrait of the American Child, 1995." Ma starts laughing and says, "Yeah! My bud! And they don't even know you're a girl!"

Ma doesn't think it's strange that I live as a boy. Boys have all the fun, girls have tons of restraints. She gets it. She thinks it takes balls to go up to the African men in the park and tell them I wanna play soccer with them. She respects that. She says who cares, it's not about what I am, it's about the fact that I've got moves. She says if the boys don't even notice anything's up it just means that I've got skills! I love my ma so much in those moments. Then I feel bad for wishing she'd get hit by a bus.

## Chapter 21

# PCS

*Manhattan, February 1996*

I FINALLY GOT A ROLE WITH MORE THAN JUST A FEW SCENES after nine thousand auditions. It's a movie that shoots up in Poughkeepsie for two weeks. Ma says it's so amazing that I got the role and it's gonna change everything. Including school. I'm gonna miss too much, so I need to go to a special place for actors.

There's a private school uptown called Professional Children's School, where all the kids are performers and they make a special curriculum you can take with you to set so you don't screw up your progress in class. It's a crazy expensive place, but they gave me a scholarship, and my grandma Edie is making up the rest.

We were home one night not too long ago, and Ma was really upset. She was yelling into the phone and then at no one, because the house was dark again. The electricity had come back on for a spell, but when we flipped the switch that night nothing happened. Same old story, we couldn't pay the bill, so no lights.

She started making these loud noises that reminded me of a moaning antelope. I'm not allowed to close my door, but I closed it as much as I could and got under the airplane blankets. I lit a candle and tried to read, but I couldn't concentrate.

I yelled at her to stop screaming. At first she was stunned that

I had raised my voice at her, but after a few seconds she went right back to it. I got up and went into her room and said, "Hey. Ma. Ma! Heyyy!"

It was like I was invisible. Nothing. She didn't even look at me, she was just standing in the corner holding a tissue, screaming at the Rasta Bitch like she was in the room. When Ma's real upset like that her voice takes on a different pitch. It's scary. She looks straight through you, and it doesn't register that you're speaking. She can be looking into your eyes and you can be begging her to please stop screaming, but it's like she can't see you. She just goes on and on. When she's in these fits I can usually get away with closing my door, and I do, even though I know she'll yell at me for it later.

I go back into my room and lay down with my pillow on my head. The tension in the air is making me angry and sad, and the darkness is freaking me out. I'm hungry and tired. I want to sleep, I don't want to go to school in the morning, I never want to take another dance class, and I want to just disappear to Europe with my dad.

I start to wonder how that could ever happen. Maybe I can just not get on my return flight when I go visit him. Would that be kidnapping? Would she have him arrested? Would we be international fugitives?

She cries out so abruptly and with such force, I worry she skewered her hand on something. I listen in the darkness, but her rant picks up again and I know she was just emoting. I exhale deeply as fear starts to burn through me.

Ma has been getting worse and worse with these fits and we have fewer and fewer sweet moments between us now. She smashes things sometimes, but she never hits me, although the blackness inks over her eyeballs. It used to be only at night, but now I've stopped knowing which version of her is gonna pick me up from school.

The army cot claps up around my face when I try to roll over and the wooden bar smacks me in the forehead. The shock of this makes me furious and I jump up and scream, *"Fuck!"*

My ma yells at me from the other room to not fucking curse who the fuck do I think I am. This makes me feel like my face is on fire and I ball my fists. I have to let the rage out, so I punch the wall. One, strong, flat punch, and the drywall dents a little. I can see it even in the darkness.

The pain of this brings tears. I slide down the wall and sit on the floor in the pitch black, crying, holding my hurt knuckles. The thing is, I can't call someone and tell them how bad this is, because then I'd be a rat.

Looking over at the candles next to the cot, an escape plan begins to form. Maybe I can show them. What if I burn myself? Maybe then they'll see it and come to my rescue and I won't have to say anything and I won't be a filthy rat.

I scoot across the floor using my not-hurt hand and pick up the matches. I light a shabbat candle and hold it in front of my face. How will I do this? It's a good idea, right? Should I burn my face? No. Then I can't do that movie. That would be super bad. Should I burn my hand? No . . . that wouldn't be bad enough. Maybe I can just burn my hair! Maybe if I burn a bunch of my hair off I can tell some-body that I tried to burn my head off and they'll think that's so bad that they'll say I just can't possibly live here like this anymore. Yeah!

It takes three seconds, and it smells horrible. A big clump of hair vanishes and the air smells like fireworks. Well, that's not gonna work, there's no evidence, I just look like I have a stupid haircut. I grab a nap-kin and go again, this time being careful to catch the singed black bits that fall from the flames.

A COUPLE OF DAYS LATER, I sneak to a pay phone and call Edie collect. I tell her I need to speak to her and can I come over.

Between tap and jazz I bolt out to the subway and go up to the Upper East Side, which is super-duper not allowed, but I'm willing to risk it.

Edie's house is so beautiful and pristine it scares me. I don't want to mess anything up. She welcomes me with a hug and leads me up the stairs slowly.

She's not a warm person, but we have a special bond, Edie and I. Everyone is always telling me not to call her Grandma, because it makes her feel old, that I should call her Edie, but I don't like that. It feels too sterile. I keep calling her Grandma because that's exactly what she is, my grandma, and I don't want to give that up. I want her to know what she means to me.

I'm wearing my fingerless gloves when I tell her I have to show her something. I can't quite bring myself to explain what it is she's looking at when she unfolds the napkin, but I try to telepathically communicate that it's the physical manifestation of how I feel on the inside, trapped in this nasty cycle of darkness and dance class. She doesn't seem to get it.

"It's my hair, Grandma."

"It's your hair? How did your hair get burned and into this napkin, iO?"

The words feel like sharp objects lodged in my throat, but I push them out, at risk of being a dirty rat.

"It got burned on one of the candles in the house. We don't have any lights right now."

"Oh dear! Really? Why not?"

"My ma says she can't pay the bill."

"Ohhh. Oh dear."

She has me call the dance studio and tell my ma where I am, even though I just want to hide. She feeds me some tuna fish and olives and I fall asleep on her corduroy sofa. She tucks a blanket in around my edges like she always does. The cozy feeling makes me want to cry for longing. It makes my heart hurt for some reason, like it's too much of a good thing I want so bad.

At one A.M. the doorbell rings long and hard. I wake up startled and afraid. I'm warm and deep asleep and I don't want my grandma to answer it. The bell goes again, sharp and piercing. A light flicks on in Edie's bedroom and she comes out in her long white nightgown and slippers, shuffling carefully across the black stone floor. I watch her with dread as she moves toward the stairs.

Ma starts yelling my name in the street. I want to die.

I hear Edie try to speak to her sensibly three flights down, but Ma starts yelling up the stairs for me. The thought of her volume hurting Edie's ears makes me stand up and gather my things. I hear her on the stairs screaming for me to come on, let's go, it's time to go home, adventure runaway bullshit playtime in the castle is over.

I'm angry as I drag myself toward the door. She's getting louder and louder, so I bark down that I'm coming and to stop fucking yelling.

When I get down there, Edie is standing in the entranceway in some kind of trance. She looks up at me slowly and licks her lips, unsure of what to do, resigned to the fact that the banshee mother will always win. She asks my ma to wait a minute, goes upstairs, comes back and presses twenty dollars into her hand, beseeching her elegantly to take a taxi.

Ma tries to wave off the money, but Edie won't let her, so we take it, but we still get on the train. Ma is *pissed* that I took off like that and doesn't stop ranting at me the whole way downtown.

When we get off at Bleecker Street I walk real slow so she'll go ahead of me. Trailing behind her up the dark street, glaring at her back with so much hatred, I realize that her shoulders are lopsided and she's wobbling. This pulls my mind out of the sticky swamp of sleepiness and I observe this new development with sharpened eyes. Sure enough, she's limping. She's trying to stand tall and hide it, but there's no denying it, my Viking warrior priestess mother is hurt.

WHEN I GET BACK from the movie shoot, I start at the new school. It's a weird place. Macaulay Culkin, the kid from *Home Alone*, lives next door, in a fancy high-rise with a doorman, with his brother and sister, who both go to the school, plus two other siblings, and their mom.

I imagine their house to be a floor-through place brimming with luxury and all of the toys one could buy oneself if one were a multimillionaire at fifteen.

I try to get close to him at recess. He's like some kind of glowing magnet. If you get into his orbit, maybe his good luck will encompass you, too, and people will want to be your friend or give you roles. We play basketball together in the gym a lot, but I don't think he even knows my name. He's fifteen and I'm ten so I'm just a scrappy runt compared to him.

This school is like the X-Men academy. Everybody has a secret hidden talent that makes them a mutant. We're not like other kids, we're the chosen ones, the ones that get up on the stage in front of the masses and entertain them. The one grain of sand separated out from the beach of humanity and put up on a pedestal to be gawked at. Either because we're so gifted or because we're so freakish. My gender mystery hardly ripples the pool in this circus.

I feel on edge in this fancy school, a sense that I'm out of place. This is compounded when I see that a girl in my new class, Rachel the figure skater, is driven to school every day in a black car with a gloved chauffeur. There's the Korean violinist whose entire rich family moved to New York so she could come here and eventually play at Carnegie Hall. These kids are all on fancy meal plans. Their parents pay hundreds of dollars a semester for them to get the nice meals at lunchtime. I eat the orange Creamsicles out of the dessert cooler because that's what I can afford to buy.

There's a teacher here, Mr. Ryan, a tall skinny white guy, who's in charge of the gym at lunchtime. He's been giving me shit about the fact that I don't eat normal food. He's threatened to not let me play basketball if I don't start eating regularly, but I don't want to tell him it's because I can't afford the food. How would they look at me if they knew that?

It's fucking cold and disgusting out, and it's hard as hell to get here. It's way on the West Side, so I'm late almost every day. They really don't like that here. It's different the way they disapprove in this place. They give you that white-people disapproval frown here, which seems to assess your potential in life based on your performance now. They act like you're showing them your essence, the truth of who you are, based on whether or not you show up late to class.

We have to take three trains to get here and my ma is always late so we're always late. They think it means I don't take school seriously, so they start to take me less seriously, and that sucks—to know people are investing less in you, expecting less from you, because of something that's out of your control.

Lincoln Center is just three blocks away, the place where we're all supposed to end up if we do our jobs right. American Ballet Theatre is there, that's where they put on *The Nutcracker, Hansel and Gretel,* all the ballets and operas and plays that we should be in if we have any talent in us.

The dancer kids stand around outside, loitering with their feet permanently turned out in first position, as if they're showing off that they're part of this tribe.

When we go there I stand up straighter; I remember the thread that's supposed to be pulling my head up from above, straightening out my neck and spine. I turn my legs out so I walk in first position. No slouching. I pretend to be one of the gazelle-ish boys to fit in.

Across the marble courtyard is Juilliard. Hallowed ground. The place where only the most gifted go. The place where I have to end up, to prove that I'm worth anything.

Beyond the American Ballet Theatre and behind the Metropolitan Opera House is the New York Public Library for the Performing Arts. This is where they keep a record of the fruits of all of the many generations of talented performers' labors before me. Cassette tapes with recordings of every Broadway show, VHS tapes of all the old movies from silent to *Star Wars,* sheet music by my beloved Gershwin, recordings of *West Side Story.* All of these to be studied and emulated. By my ma. By me.

I don't want to be here right now, but I have to wait for my ma. She's pulling something for us to practice at home.

It's dark by the time we're ready to go. It's snowing outside and all our layers are damp. It's cold. I'm tired from school and I want to go home. I want to go to somebody else's house. A place where it's warm and there's food getting cooked. It's fucking depressing and I don't want to go to Broadway Dance, but Ma doesn't negotiate class.

We walk past the Met and their restaurant and I want to eat everything they serve, but I know the best I'll get is a free couple of slices of bread. I literally cannot even imagine what their foods taste like. Lush and rich soups. Thick cuts of meat. Hearty potatoes.

Fuck this. I don't want to go to class. I don't want to be trained. I don't want to have perfect posture. Yes I do . . . I just want to go home right now. And I want a piece of cake.

IN A FEW MONTHS, Mr. Ryan will forbid me from playing ball until I eat and we will fight about it in the gym. My teacher, Lucy, will tell me that kind of behavior is unacceptable and scold me in front of the whole class. Embarrassed, I'll stick a hot nail in her weakest spot, telling her maybe her adult braces and hairy legs are why she can't get a boyfriend, and she'll start to cry. The class will then treat me like a pariah, further isolating me in this castle of privilege, and I'll get so sick of the rich kid song-and-dance that I'll freak out and barricade myself in the classroom with a desk, screaming through the door for Lucy and all the rest of them to fuck off.

The administration will politely ask me not to return.

## Chapter 22

# Rocky

*Midtown, spring 1996*

**B**ALLET STUDIOS ARE ALL LINOLEUM AND MIRRORS. A JUMble of stale sweat and skewed body image. People are there for two reasons: either it's their job, or it's how they want to see themselves—lithe and straight backed, twirling through a world where body mass is veiled by impossible grace. Walk down the hall of any dance school, peek in the window, and you will see the same look of determined ferocity, the glare of willpower stretched to its limits, the bulging eyeballs of bodies protesting hell-bent minds.

Dancers dress like a game of Jenga: tights tugged down to the ankle peeking out of sweatpants pulled up to the knee, waistband rolled down to show off their hip muscles, a leotard over jutting collarbones. Bleeding toes are wrapped in tape and shoved in slipper-shaped boxes. At some point someone invented the jazz sneaker, giving dancers a needed break, but wearing them is for sissies. It's like showing up to a gala in sweatpants. If you want to ball, you have to be brazen, a cowboy in tights; rugged, roughed up, stripes earned. Ligaments are torn, bones are cracked, shins are for splints, and good knees are a fleeting gift to the young.

My mother has danced in a single pair of ballet slippers for three years. That is akin to having only one sweater for a lifetime. Your singular protection from the elements, the first thing judgmental eyes size up, the measure of how seriously you take yourself. Their canvas was beige once upon a time, but now they are tattered, black and streaked from the floor, the elastic straps hang loose, and a toe peeks out on the left side. It would be cruel to begrudge her this if ballet slippers were expensive, but they aren't. I know this, and I'm only ten years old. Ballet slippers are cheap, but it has to be important enough to you to go down to Capezio and buy yourself a new pair. My ma doesn't seem to mind.

She's sucking her teeth as we climb the stairs to the fourth floor of the dance school. I have a blue rubber handball in the pocket of my shorts and a piece of gum in my mouth. We have already had a screaming match today. She's been tense since we moved.

She rushes into the dressing room, shedding her trench coat. On a bench by the front door, I bounce my ball and wait. People are already in the studio, stretching their muscles on the gray linoleum, doing exercises. The teacher claps three times, and a piano begins its staccato twang.

My mother hustles out of the dressing room and takes up a place at the barre. Her brown hair is pulled into a high ponytail, and her long back is straight. Her eyebrows are peaked at the arches and her lips are pursed. Her bony arm stretches forward and one finger points at the back wall as she rotates her pointed foot to the rhythm.

I detest this music, this place, the severe looks on all these people's faces, but right now I'm just happy it's not me in there. My only job is to sit and wait. I amble over to the door of the classroom and lean my head against the frame.

The smell of cooked sweat comes in a hot wave, and after a few minutes I'm repulsed. I close the glass door, and when they switch sides, I dart out into the stairwell.

Four flights down, I push a door open onto Forty-seventh Street. Eighth Avenue is to my left, Broadway is to my right, and tourists are swarming. It's too early for the theater crowds, so it's all fanny packs and visors and fingers pointing up from maps. I move toward Broadway, sticking close to the wall. Ma says I'm *perfect elbow height*. This is a hazard in busy Midtown, and more than once I've had a funny bone slammed into my eye socket. She tried to even the scales by telling me to *go for the shins*, but my strategy is to dodge.

Busy being stealthy, I don't see the puppy until he is on top of me. He's black, with two white splotches, maybe ten pounds, and he leaps straight into my arms, almost knocking me backward. Both paws on my chest, he starts licking my face and I sink to my knees, giggling and swatting his drool away. A few paces behind, his owners approach.

"He likes you."

She's a petite black girl, no older than twenty, in a tan T-shirt, her hair twisted into tiny little balls all over her head. Her boyfriend is much taller, skinny in his army pants and T-shirt. He doesn't speak, but she smiles at me. Something about both of them feels yearning and sick.

"You like him?"

"Yeah. He's so cute. What's his name?"

"Rocky."

Rocky. That's what I have always said I would name a dog if I was ever allowed to have one. This trips my mind up. A little piece of my heart falls out.

"You have a dog?"

"No."

"You want one?"

"What do you mean?"

"You can have him."

"Have him?"

"Yeah. You want him?"

I look into his sweet, playful eyes. I'm sunk, done for. For a moment, my mind flashes to my mother, and what she'll say. How she won't like this at all, but that only lasts a few seconds. How could I refuse such a sweet creature? Rocky's tail is wagging and he's jumping up onto me again and again, nibbling at my fingers. My smiling cheeks feel like brittle plaster. Rocky's fur leaves a greasy residue on my fingers.

"Is he sick?"

"Nah. There's nothing wrong with him."

"Why don't you want him?"

"We can't take the right care of him, you know? We busy trying to get by, and I want him to be treated right."

I notice a length of rope around his neck, the other end in her hand. Rocky deserves a leash. She's right, I can take better care of him. I can already envision him in my new bathtub, covered in suds. I'll do everything; I'll walk him, I'll feed him, my ma won't have to do anything, and when I tell her this she won't be so mad.

"So you want him?"

" . . . Okay."

She smiles and hands me the rope. Her boyfriend looks at his pager, unfazed. At the door of the dance studio, the girl bends down and pets Rocky roughly. She says, "Good-bye, my baby," and turns and walks away. I watch their backs, expecting them to turn around and run up to me and say, "*Psych!* Are you crazy? You think I'd just *give* you my puppy?" But they don't. They turn the corner and disappear.

Dizzy with excitement, I pull Rocky into the stairwell. Two flights up, crouching on the floor under a window, I pull his scruffy face close to my own.

"Right now, you're mine. My ma doesn't know I have you, that girl is gone, and for right this second, you are mine."

I touch his ears. His little black snout has a smattering of white spots above his mouth, and the fur is extra soft right there. He bites at my finger, and I wrap my arms around his neck, hugging him close to me. When I sit on the floor in the stairwell, Rocky is as tall as I am.

As we climb the last two flights of stairs, I become jittery. What if Ma's furious? What if she makes me get rid of him? What if there are no dogs allowed in the dance school? How will I explain where I got him? She won't believe me.

The matter is clear to me; I am devoted to Rocky, so if he goes, I go, and I plan to tell her as much. Through the glass door, I watch the muscles in her back ripple as she raises both arms into a half circle above her head. She is on tiptoes, moving diagonally across the studio now.

When she turns to walk back in my direction, her eyes travel to the rope in my hand and the dog attached to it, and her face flies through a quick circus of emotions. Surprise, confusion, irritation, anger. Her gesture is small, but the veins in her arm betray her real feelings. She gestures *NO*. Maybe a little *What the fuck?* and then *Get rid of it.*

I shake my head. Again, the arm says *Get rid of it. NOW.* I shake my head and beckon for her to come. *Please. Come here.* She looks at the class and back to me. *PLEASE. Come here!* She opens the door, and I rush to it.

"Ma, this is Rocky! He's my dog. A girl gave him to me."

"What?"

I repeat myself. She's panting.

"Somebody gave you a dog? Nobody *gives* away dogs. Dogs have fleas, iO. We're not keeping him."

"I'll do everything, Ma! I'll feed him and he can sleep with me, and I'll play with him. Please, Ma, I love him!"

"He's dirty! I don't want a dog in my house. I'm allergic to animals. He's not coming home with us."

"Yes he is! He's my puppy, Ma. You won't have to do anything. I'll give him a bath as soon as we get home."

She closes the door, flicking her wrist dismissively, pursing her lips, and jutting her chin out, eyes back on the class. It is never a good thing when her nostrils flare.

After the class, she stays in the studio, doing the splits on the floor. When she finally emerges, she puts her two clear plastic bags on a bench opposite mine. She leans forward to tie her shoes, bending straight over from the hips. Upside down like this, she unties her ponytail and flips her hair, then she returns upright. She pulls out a bottle of Excedrin and throws a couple into her mouth.

One hand on Rocky's neck, I'm staring a hole into her. She turns and looks at me, then at him. She breathes in deeply, picks up her bags, and moves toward the door. I scramble to follow her.

As we descend, she lays out the rules: Rocky is my responsibility completely. He doesn't come into the apartment—he has to stay in the hall. I have to walk him twice a day, feed him, and she never wants to touch him, because she is *allergic* to animals. I'm so excited I don't even listen. *Yes. Yes. Anything. Yes.*

We go to a pet store nearby where she finds the cheapest leash they have and a bottle of flea shampoo. She pays for them with dollar bills pulled from an envelope in one of her plastic bags.

THE STALE NEW STAIRS fly past two at a time, and before Ma can complain, Rocky is lathered up in the tub. Under normal circumstances, I am forbidden from closing doors, but seeing as there is a wriggling puppy covering the bathroom in bubbles and water, I'm allowed an exception. Secretly, I dry him with my own towel, and slip his new collar around his neck.

My ma is boiling rice when we come out.

"Take him outside."

"Huh?"

"Take Rocky outside."

"But . . ."

"He's not supposed to be inside the house."

"Let me just take him into my room."

"No. Outside."

"You mean like onto the street? Someone will steal him!"

"You can tie him up in the hall."

"Someone will steal him out there, too!"

The argument escalates, but in ten minutes I'm slamming the apartment door and tying Rocky's leash to the guardrail on the hallway window. I push his butt to the floor, pull his front paws out, and lie down next to him. He doesn't want to lie down, wagging his tail and looking at me.

"Come on, boy. We gotta go to sleep now."

Glancing up at the fluorescent bulb that will be burning above him all night, I feel a bubble of worry in my esophagus at the thought of the neighbors stealing him. Wrapping my arms around his neck, I pull him to the floor. He succumbs, and we lie there on the vomit-colored tiles, listening to the pigeons in the light well outside the frosted window.

It is deep dark outside and Ma is naked under her bathrobe when she comes out of the apartment and pulls me inside by the arm. I cry, I kick, I scream, but she just puts a toothbrush in my mouth.

WE HAVE THREE DAYS of walks, trips around the neighborhood, taking Rocky to run, taking Rocky to the Chinese restaurant on Fourth Street, introducing Rocky to the local meatheads, talking to Rocky like he can understand me, hugging Rocky's neck and inhaling the sharp chemical smell of his flea shampoo. I've accustomed myself to fearing he will disappear, and I've started to save up for a tag engraved with our phone number.

Finally, it's Saturday and Rocky is allowed to accompany us. We walk from Third back to Forty-seventh Street. Like a looped tape, my ma is late for class and I'm on my bench. Five minutes in, Rocky and I take to the stairs. We head toward Broadway, and there she is, Rocky's old owner—same boyfriend, same block, different T-shirt. She squeals at the sight of him.

"My baby! Hi, my baby!"

She puts one knee on the sidewalk, pets his head, and smiles. His

tail wags, and he licks her. I am proud of his cleanliness and his leash.
I feel like she must be able to tell that I've been buying him two cans of
Alpo a day with my pay phone money. I smile back.

"You're so clean, baby! He been behaving himself?"

"Yeah. I love him."

"Yeah? That's nice."

She grabs him by the jaw and looks into his face.

"You mind if I take him for a walk around the block real quick?
For old time's sake. I'll bring him right back here."

I look at her petting him and think to myself, who wouldn't
miss him?

"Sure. Of course. I'll wait right there by the door."

"Okay. We'll be back in ten minutes."

Rocky looks up at me and I put my right hand on his head. He
licks it. Saying it out loud would be too sappy, so I'm trying to tell
him I love him with my eyes. I hand her the leash and she smiles in
my direction as the three of them walk toward Eighth Avenue. Again
I watch her back disappear around the corner, followed by Rocky's
excited trot. I sit on a sprinkler valve jutting out of the wall and settle
in to wait.

A woman in a visor asks me which way Broadway is, and for the
first time in a long time I tell her the truth. It's a little victory my ma
and I have over the onslaught of tourists to answer obvious questions
incorrectly. Later, I will wonder if what happened had something to do
with karma.

I don't have a watch, but I know when it's been more than ten minutes. Maybe she took him around a few blocks. The sprinkler is cutting
into my butt, so I walk to the street, balancing my weight on the edge
of the curb, looking up and down. I wish I had my ball, or something
to kill time with.

After half an hour, my stomach starts to feel like I've drunk too
much water, and I go back upstairs. Not wanting to miss them, I race to

the window in the lounge and stick my body halfway out, scouring the street below. I wait.

Sixty minutes in, I am skint on excuses for her. No matter how far she could have walked, she would be back in an hour. My ma gets out of class and it's hard to squeeze the words out to tell her what happened. She doesn't bother getting angry at me for going out alone again, because she can see the crushing feeling happening inside my chest, I'm sure of it, so I stick it back out the window.

Three and a half hours later, my ma is pacing the lounge area, cursing the girl. The woman at the desk gave me a Blow Pop when her shift ended, and she looked like she wanted to cry for me. My stomach aches with disbelief. How could I have been so stupid? Why did I trust this chick? My ma, allergic to animals or not, puts her hand on my head and pets me in her stiff way, never separating her fingers, making a little cooing noise as though my pain is passing through to her, too.

I think about his leash.

I think about the bath.

I think about how cold and hard the tiles in our hallway are.

I think about the sterile flood of fluorescent light.

I think about his neck.

As reluctant as she may be to welcome this dog back into our home, my ma understands that this is my story. She paces the foyer, leans out the window, swears at the girl, drinks water from tiny paper cups shaped like cones, bites her nails, and rearranges the contents of one of her purses, but she doesn't rush me.

At some point I just know it's over. My throat feels like someone slipped a rubber band around it, and I'm too ashamed to look up into anyone's eyes. I just want to leave. I know I'm not allowed to go home becasue the sun's still up, but I'll take a park bench or a bus ride over this.

Trying to walk toward Times Square to the subway, my knees feel weak. It's as though the entire world is in on a secret that I'm not a part of. Here I am, right back where I started. Rocky's Alpo fund is arcade money once more, and I wonder if the girl will ever come back to Forty-seventh Street.

Something in my heart tells me I won't ever see the three of them again. It feels as though real kids live on the other side of some invisible glass, in a place where puppies aren't gifts from teenage junkies and you get to hug them all night.

My ma says we should go lie in the grass in Tompkins Square Park, and I'm too preoccupied to care. I just want out of Midtown.

## Chapter 23

# Orange Juice

*Everywhere, forever and always*

FEELINGS ARE LIKE ORANGE JUICE. WHEN SOMETHING PAIN-
ful happens to you, it's like you're drinking a big, tall, full
glass of orange juice. It's pungent and full of flavor and you get all the
little bits of pulp in your teeth. It's the fullest experience of the flavor of
orange juice.

When you try to tell somebody about what you felt, you're handing them the glass of orange juice, but somewhere in between you and
them, the glass gets half diluted with water. So what they get is sort of
like orange juice, but a heavily watered-down version. They have to
inject the flavor with sympathy and comparisons to things that have
happened in their own lives for it to taste like juice to them. That's why
people are always saying things like "Oh my gosh, yes, when that happened to me . . ." even though it never did, because this thing happened
to you.

My solution is just to hand them two glasses of orange juice. If it's
gonna get cut in half, compensate. Hand them a notion of double the
pain, and by the time it gets diluted by the space between brains, it'll
reach them at just about the pitch of what it actually felt like to you.

That's why I fake all these injuries at school when there's no electricity in the house. That's why sometimes, after a real bad fight, I tell people that my ma hit me, even though she didn't. Even though she never would. But then they get it. They sputter and ooze with sympathy for my hurting bones and I use it as salve for my bleeding heart.

## Chapter 24

# Climbing In

*Third Street, September 1997*

I T'S A TENSION THAT STARTS AT THE BASE OF MY SPINE. EVERY muscle in my butt is clenched. The stakes are high as I turn the corner. The noon light is crisp, sun straight overhead, cold air cutting into my face. I pretend it's a video game—maintenance guys in blue suits are the bad guys who must never see me. A twelve-year-old wandering around at lunchtime by himself is one of the less strange sights in this neighborhood, but still, if one of them casually mentions it to my ma, it will be explosive.

I've worked my way down the block from Second Avenue, and unease ripples through my body as I pass my own stoop. Huddled into the entrance of the building next to ours, I ring apartment 3B. Nothing. I wait. Then I ring again. Still nothing. Lazy motherfucker.

I step out and look up at the windows. One of them is covered by a black trash bag, the other is open. I don't want to do this, but I have no choice.

*"Aidan!"*

It takes a couple of minutes, but the glass rises and my "cousin" Aidan sticks his head out. Gap toothed, handsome, Puerto Rican.

"Yo! Hold up."

Aidan's apartment is pitch black. I can't see what my feet are stepping on, but I've been here so many times I know the way. A long hall stretches from the door, past the bathroom, into a living room cluttered with a plastic-covered couch, a round dining table, and a gigantic television. The smell of grease saturates the air. I bet you could ignite the room if you lit a match. A ripped WWF video game fighter Aidan customized to have blue skin is frozen on the screen, grimacing, holding a chair above his head.

Aidan, shirtless and muscular, short ponytail pulled back, plops back onto the couch. He's grumpy, which means he just woke up. Normally, he's one of the blue suits on the street, working maintenance for management, but he's the only one I don't have to dodge. If shit ever really hit the fan it would be Aidan who I would call to defend me. His place is also typically the only place I can score a meal during the day.

I move through the darkness toward the dining table. I can make out three plates, with leftovers on them. Pork chops, mostly annihilated, but with a little meat on the bones, and piles of white rice. I love Aidan's rice—it's soft and fluffy and buttery. I'm not allowed to eat butter with my ma, so I scarf this first.

Leaving my coat and backpack on, I sit there and quickly clean the plates, shoveling food into my mouth, gnawing little bits of meat off the chops.

Aidan doesn't say a word. He knows to leave me his leftovers. This is our drill. I eat the scraps and leave. This is why he's family; I owe him the weight on my bones. I pick up the plates and put them in the sink when I'm done, give him a quick pound, and head out.

The window in Aidan's shower is tiny, just barely big enough for a body. I toss my backpack and then go out feet first, lowering myself down until my sneakers touch the first ledge. It is an inch of beige brick sticking out from the flat face of the wall three stories up. I would at least break my legs if I fell from here, so I'm careful. My fingers grip the thin black metal of his window frame and I ease myself to the left.

My hand gropes sideways until it touches the window guard of Aidan Jr.'s room. I grip it with one hand and let go of the shower window with the other, bringing my fingers to the sill in front of me. Both hands on it now, I stretch my right foot out diagonally beneath me, groping in thin air for the top of the next window.

Looking down, I can see my backpack on the concrete below. Wind burns my cheeks. I think about what my skull would feel like smashing into the pavement. That's always an option if I get sick of this.

My foot finds the window top, and I transfer my weight, but I've miscalculated. My toe slips off the edge of the brick and flies out underneath me. I yelp as my left arm is yanked taut with the weight of my frame.

Hanging there, three flights above oblivion, my mind exits my body and I see myself from above, as if I were a camera in the sky. Skinny, twelve years old, dark blue baggy jeans, yellow coat. Bones in a bag of flesh, hanging off the side of a tenement building.

I regain my balance and lower myself onto the downstairs neighbor's window guard. If she were to open her curtains she would probably scream. Maybe she would push me off, maybe she would shoot me. Knowing this neighborhood, she would probably hit me in the face with a frying pan.

Inch by inch I move down another flight until I reach a landing. Picking up my backpack, which is empty except for my trusty journal, I walk ten paces to a vertical metal ladder and swing out over an alley that connects the backs of seven or eight buildings behind mine. The carcass of a rat, empty cigarette packs, and used condoms are littered around my sneakers. It's like an urban minefield.

My toes search thin air for the rusted bucket of paint I know is there. It has gathered a puddle in its lid since yesterday.

I make my way across a piss-stained walkway and up the back

steps of my building. One foot vaults me onto a pair of metal railings around the basement entrance and fingers stretch, reaching for the bottom rung of the fire escape ladder. I have shown off my pull-up skills many times in school. I'm the only kid that can do six. For a split second I am grateful as I hoist my body up the eight rungs and onto the first landing.

At the second landing, I can hear a television, so I wait. Making it into an espionage mission, I risk a glance with one eye. My downstairs neighbor, Mr. Nuñez, or one of his seven kids, is watching something in full view of my path. It's too risky, so I reach up for the metal bar between their windows. This way is much more dangerous because I'm essentially dangling over empty space, and if I slip, I'll slam into the railing on my way down, but if he tells my ma he saw me climbing the fire escape in the middle of the day it'll be far worse.

Between the Nuñezes' two windows, I lift my body up onto the handrail, hoisting myself halfway up the next flight of stairs, still out of his view. Something below me moves. I see a head of black hair approaching the window. I scramble up and over the landing and press myself against a wall. My asshole tightens and I pray that whichever Nuñez it is has bad eyesight. I hear the window open, and a cigarette butt flies out. It slams shut. I start to breathe again.

The window to my ma's bedroom looks like it's closed, but I've devised a way to keep it cracked just slightly, so it can be opened from the outside. I press my palms flat against the glass and push straight up. It makes a squeaking noise as it rises. There is a plastic fish tank the size of a shoebox on the windowsill, and in it, a tiny turtle swims frantically toward a rock. The water is muddy with green and brown spots from his shit.

I'm careful not to step on the sill and leave a footprint, so I stretch my right leg out onto the wood floor, bending my body down and in behind me. I listen for any sounds, but the house is quiet. I close the window.

I go straight into my room, just in case, leaving the door open a tiny crack so that if I hear Ma coming I can hide. I'm too nervous to pee, so I hold it.

In my room, I drop my coat and backpack to the floor. I kick off my sneakers and lie down on the army cot. I am out before my face touches the pillow.

## Chapter 25

# A Whole New World

*Baruch Middle School, Manhattan, fall 1997*

M Y NEW SCHOOL IS A PRISON. THEY'RE STRICT AS HELL and they don't care what your excuse is. If you show up two minutes past eight A.M. you have to line up against a wall in the entrance and give them your coat. You can only get it back after you serve detention.

Fuck that. I show up late almost every day and I'm not gonna waste my time in detention. I figured out where they stash the coats, so most days I grab mine, cross myself off the sign-in sheet, and bolt out the side door by noon.

Baruch Middle School takes up an entire city block. It's a low cement cube between Twentieth and Twenty-first Streets, stretching from First to Second Avenue.

My homeroom class is like a foreign country, I see it so rarely. The teacher gave up on trying to tell me off; now she's switched tactics to being proud of me for ever making it at all.

Baruch has a program where you get to eat lunch out of school if you want, but you have to bring your own money. I asked Ma and she gave me a quarter. We can't afford it, so she started sending me with boxes from home. That was mortifying. It was a little takeout container with some lettuce and balsamic and a couple of carrots.

The lunchroom is a screeching hell pit of torment, so I started spending the break with the school secretary, Cheryl. She's a bossy blonde with a raspy voice and a thick New York accent. She likes me, so we sit and talk and I show her drawings and things I've been working on until it's time to go out to play.

You get so hot running in the yard that you take your coat and sweater off and fuck around in just a T-shirt, even in the dead of winter.

All the black and Hispanic cool kids cluster by the basketball court. The mixed-race kids and the weirdos and the white kids run around in fantasy games, tripping out on their imaginations. Cool girls walk around clutching each other in pairs, with flashy nice new sneakers and warm-looking boots. Kids play tag with so much gusto they throw themselves into the walls. A stone drinking fountain is a legitimate danger.

Even boys' voices are shrill at this age, and it's a perpetual cacophony of battle cries and high-pitched alerts from all ends of the yard.

In my first week here they handed me a sheet with a list of classes on it with intimidating names like "algebra" and "biology" and other shit I'd never taken before. I was most excited about gym, because the basketball courts are huge.

On the first day I show up in my sweats, ready to play. The teacher, a stocky guy with black hair on the back of his neck, tells me to go down to the lockers and get changed without looking at me. I tell him I'm already changed but he says I have to go down anyway. I freeze, realizing that the locker rooms are gender segregated.

Dread holds me in place like an obelisk.

"I don't want to go down there. I'm already changed. Can I just wait here?"

"No, you need to go downstairs until we're ready to start class."

"Why?"

He is holding a clipboard when he finally looks up and takes me in, a skeleton in a sweatsuit, trembling underneath his volleyball net.

My center becomes swirled with agitation and I feel like a heat is building in my head that might pop my ears off. Under no circumstances am I going down into the girls' room, where they will laugh and terrorize me, nor am I going down to the boys' because I do not, after all, have a penis.

Hairy neck guy sends me to the principal's office when the panic attack starts and I sit down at Cheryl's desk, snotting and trying to hide my tears.

I guess I look kind of bad. Sleep doesn't happen much in the house, what with the plays and things late at night, plus Ma is in a real bad way. It's like she has a night personality and a day personality. At night she's a menace, mean and screaming, and she does the thing where she stares through me. Then in the morning she's sweeter and softer and pulls me out of bed with a touch of kindness, until I nudge the hive in some small way and she flies off the handle again.

Her hip is bad, so she has to walk slowly, and I don't want to be seen with my mommy, so she only walks me to Fourteenth Street in the mornings. Half the time I cut back down the block and go home to sleep.

I know I look shitty. I must.

Cheryl sends me to the guidance counselor. She tells me that Mrs. Stockhammer is a friend of hers and a wonderful person and that I'll really like her.

Down the two-tone hallway I go into a waiting room covered in illustrations and drawings kids did, made out to "Joanie." She comes out of her office with a forceful stride and shakes my hand with a veiny fist. I'm an undernourished twelve-year-old and she's in cowboy boots but we're standing eye to eye.

She beckons me inside, sitting down with a toss of her blond ringlets, putting her feet up on her desk. What Joan lacks in stature, she makes up for in personality. As she reaches for one of several cups of coffee, I look around the room.

Her brash character, the state of her desk, and the sheer volume of shit crammed onto the walls conjures a distinctly Floridian, posthurricane type of vibe: chaos cut with comedy and caffeine.

She reaches for her purse, riffling through for several seconds, locates a pill bottle, puts two pills in her mouth, washes them down with coffee.

I'm sitting back on my blue metal chair, feeling a lot of things. I'm still stressed out from the incident in the gym, but something about this person is soothing. Familiar. She's raw, real, and I can tell she feels the same thing about me.

"Did something happen in gym class you didn't appreciate?"

She waits with raised eyebrows, sipping her coffee and picking at her finger. She's jittery. She expects me to speak, so I do.

"Well, the gym teacher told me I had to go into the locker rooms . . ."

"Okay . . ."

"The girls' locker rooms . . ."

Joan already knows. There's no way she doesn't. I turn around to see if the door is closed. She walks out from behind her desk, closes it, and sits back down.

"Okay. Talk to me about the girls' locker room . . ."

"Well . . ."

A deep breath. I can't look her in the face.

"I don't belong in there . . . I can't go in there."

"Okay. Why not?"

"Because I'm a boy."

She takes this information like someone offered her a plate of dog meat. She observes it, trying to figure out how to politely decline to ingest it. Coffee is sipped. The silence makes me squirm. She's smart and I want her respect. I don't want to do this dance with her.

"Okay . . . well, what about the boys' room?"

"No. I can't go in there, either."

"And why is that?"

"Because . . . I'm not a boy . . ."

"Okay . . ."

Putting words to feelings is hard, but she's looking at me with appreciation and curiosity, and not like a circus animal. Maybe she gets it. Maybe she finds me refreshing.

JOAN PULLS SOME STRINGS higher up and I start changing into my sweatpants in her office twice a week before I go to play basketball with the boys. This act of kindness solidifies a bond.

Then I miss six days in a row. When I get back, Joan seems genuinely worried about me.

"Where have you been??"

"I got sick."

"What did you get?"

"A tonsil infection."

"That bad? You were out for a week!"

"Yeah. It was pretty bad."

"Did you see a doctor?"

"No."

"No? How did you get rid of it?"

"I gargled with tea tree oil."

"Tea tree oil? What the hell is that?"

I laugh. I like how abrasive she is. I see her outside smoking alone. Her fingertips are yellow from it.

"It's an oil . . . from the health food store. It's good for tonsil infections."

"An oil, huh. Okay. Who told you to do that?"

"My ma."

"Okay . . . did you take anything else for it?"

"No."

"And you didn't go to a doctor."

"No."

"You just stayed home and gargled with this tree oil?"

"Yeah. Mostly. I went to some auditions and two dance classes, too."

"You went to dance class while you had a tonsil infection?"

"Yeah . . ."

"Okay."

She takes a deep breath. Coffee. Nails. She cocks her head and flips her curls over with the back of her hand.

"You want to tell me about your home life?"

It's like a car crash; one minute you're driving along, singing to the radio, and the next minute your head is split open.

Just like that, there is the question I have been silently prodding her to ask.

This is the moment where I go from being trusted to being a rat; where I step out from the animal pact with my ma and enter the system. The establishment will turn me into yuppie scum and I'll rot in a hole, it's that big a betrayal. But it dawns on me I might have options.

I just want to live with my poppa. Just . . . please . . . woman with the curls and the coffee and the many nervous ticks . . . find a way to read my mind so that I don't have to say it and betray her but you will still know how bad it's gotten. As I telepathically communicate with Joan, it dawns on me how little I eat, how little we sleep, and how much we fight. I realize that I hate my world and I want to be with my dad.

My mind bats around the possible outcomes of telling Joan the truth.

"Do you really want to know?"

"Yes . . . I do."

I'm in free fall. I'm a dead man, stepping though one of those movie doorways into the light. I'm stabbing my mother, my best friend, in the throat. I'm tearing up her greatest work of art. Have I become a horrible person? Or is it like the final scene in a tragedy when the hero drives off the cliff 'cause there is no other way out of his twisted, fucked-up life? Looking at Joan, a hornet of fear buzzes up and down my insides.

Something tingles at the back of my brain and tells me that I'm too young to feel all this shit. It's not right. I want to play, I want to stick my hands in some fucking dirt somewhere and watch a cartoon. I've never seen *Sesame Street* and I don't know why.

Then I am overcome by the loneliest feeling. I realize I have to cut myself loose from my own life, from everything familiar to me. Like an astronaut with no suit, drifting, spinning into a dark, soundless void.

In the few seconds before I speak, I age forty years. What I'm about to do is the worst and best move I will ever make. The deepest pain I will ever cause, and the only thing that will save my life. I am going to create a wound that might never heal, but if I don't, I realize I could die.

I'm swimming in apology to my sweet, angry, broken mother. I want to shield her from this, but I'm growing, I'm developing an instinct for my own preservation, and the two desires are pulling me in half.

We made a pact when I was tiny, to protect each other, when she was the wolf and I was the cub. She would raise me, feed me, keep me strong, and teach me to survive. She acknowledged me, sharpened my teeth, gave me eyes to see the real world, and she fed me out of her own mouth.

I think of her thin, vulnerable bones and I start to weep with such abruptness that I nearly throw up. I don't expect this surge of emotion. Her hands, those sinewy fingers that have been stripped raw trying to earn enough to feed me. I'm bent over in my chair heaving up and down with sobs much bigger than my little body.

Joan runs around the desk to me, telling me it's okay.

But it's not. I am in the worst position I could ever be in, forced to choose between my protector and my greatest threat, my antagonist, the emotionally violent, unpredictable animal that shares her skin. The softest fur and the sharpest teeth.

Joan wraps her arms around me, whispering that it's okay to let
it out.

She hooks a finger under my chin and tilts my face up to look at
her. She looks straight into my eyes with so much tenderness that I
find some strength and manage to eke the words out, even though they
make me feel sick with hating myself.

"It's bad."

Chapter 26

—++—  —++—

# Renee

New York, winter and spring 1998

T HINGS MOVE GLACIALLY.

Joan makes the call and nothing happens. Months go by and I figure my case isn't severe enough for the Bureau of Child Welfare to pay attention, but Joan makes her own moves. She gets in touch with my pop and tells him I don't have money to eat, so he sends some money to my aunt Olivia, Olivia gives it to Joan, and each day at lunch Joan gives five dollars to me.

Joan and I talk almost every day that I'm there, which makes me want to go, but classes are a nightmare. I'm so far behind in reading and homework I have no idea what's going on, so I just sit at the window and enviously watch people walk by out in the free world.

There's a police academy a few blocks away and the cadets are always walking around. I admire their crispness.

Kids know there's something up with my gender. They whisper and talk and sometimes they taunt me, but I stay real retreated so I'm usually off their radar. I'm also almost never at school, denying them enough access to figure out where my weaknesses are.

I went to the army recruiting center in Times Square and asked them how soon I could enlist, but they said the absolute youngest was sixteen, which was crushing. I long for routine. I long for someone to tell me to make my bed, starch my shirts, shine my boots. I want to wear a uniform and a buzz cut and wake up at seven A.M. every day and only own one outfit.

One night there's a letter under the apartment door. It's from the Bureau of Child Welfare, saying they'd like to do a home visit to check on the state of the house. Ma loses her shit. I try to look away as she solders profane words together with the blowtorch that is her mouth. She accuses me of ratting right away, talking to these scum, trying to tell them yarns, but I deny it categorically. She crumples the paper and tosses it under a front table.

I look at the apartment, taking in what they would see if they came to inspect: there's an area that's supposed to be a foyer, which is crammed with stacks of wooden windows, doors, and moldings pulled from Dumpsters outside of tenements under renovation. Plastic deli bags, tied off at the top, lie in piles all over the floor, which you have to step over to get to the bathroom.

The tub has a thick black ring around it, remnant of the olive oil Ma covers herself in before her nightly bath. The white tiles are framed in gray-black, never having been cleaned. We only own one towel, which was a hand-me-down to begin with, and we don't have a bath mat. The busted soap dish covered in black mold, the fuzzy tile caulking, and the unfaceable crust inside the toilet bowl.

Three pots sit permanently on the stove holding various Chinese herb concoctions and an unending supply of black tea. The pots are badly burned steel and a thick ridge of filth lines the burners underneath them.

The "living room" is a series of mounds—clothes, records, books, Excedrin bottles, lots of plants, twinkling fabrics, photos, piles of our head shots, candles, old flyers, napkins with poems on them.

The fridge is stuffed with empty bottles of hot sauce, old soup containers, bags of Chinese herbs, and condiment packets. A puddle of brown sludge has gathered on the bottom shelf and seems to have sloshed up onto the walls. There is not an edible thing in the whole fridge.

Ma's futon is nested on the floor in the front bedroom. It's a brief landing spot for the refueling of her rocket ship, a strictly necessary function, not in any way a sanctuary.

The inspectors probably wouldn't like it that we use napkins instead of toilet paper. They probably would think it's weird that we don't have any silverware and there are cockroaches in the drawers. They'd probably ask for a glass of water and be appalled when we told them we don't have any real glasses. They'd *tsk tsk* at my army cot and how it doesn't stay flat, and they'd surely pooh-pooh the fact that we don't have any real pillows.

A visit from them would be a disaster. No wonder Ma canned the notice. They can't break the door down, so she probably figures that if she ignores them, they'll just go away.

IT HAPPENS ON A TUESDAY. I'm on my way down the stairs at school to get my coat and cut out. It's springtime, and I'm pissed that I even brought a coat, because I don't need it. I'm wearing a royal blue button-down plaid shirt, white nylon Adidas pants, and white and blue Air Jordans. My head is shaved into a high-and-tight fade, and I'm wearing my Puerto Rican flag beads.

We just finished fourth period and kids are milling around pre-lunch, digging in backpacks on the stairs, charging around the halls.

I spot the woman from the other end of the school. She's beautiful, with a small afro atop her wiry body. She's wearing skintight beige pants, knee-high boots, and a cropped jean jacket. She hasn't seen me yet, but I know it's her. My first feeling is relief that she's black, then I want to run. Yet something propels me toward her. Everything drops into slow motion and drowns out the cacophony. She looks at me. As I get closer I can see the long, ornately decorated fingernails she holds her files with. I am petrified and enamored.

"Are you iO?"

"Yeah. Who are you?"

"I'm Renee. I'm your case worker from the Bureau of Child Welfare."

I don't ask her where she is taking me because I don't want to sound too accusatory and scare her off, but my heels are also digging into the linoleum.

"I have to call my ma and tell her where I am. She'll freak if I don't."

"I'm sorry, iO, you're not allowed any contact with your mother right now."

Whoa. What?

I woke up there this morning. My clothes are there. That's my home. What the fuck is she talking about?

"Then I'm not going anywhere with you. I have to warn my ma."

My body is alert and erect, poised to spring away from this person. I don't know her and her shackles are already too tight. I bolt into Joan's office.

A girl is talking to her, but Joan can see the hysteria in my face and asks her to come back later. My voice is cracking and my throat feels thick with pain.

"Joan, they're here to take me away."

"I know, honey. It's okay. This is Renee, she's your case worker. This is what we talked about."

Confusion twinkles on her face for a second. I won't look at Renee.

"I need to call my ma, Joan."

"You're not allowed to have any contact with her right now, sweetheart, that's normal."

Something feels like it's ripping inside. My mind is spinning out on how angry Ma will be, how violent she'll become, how Joan is in danger. Tears overcome me.

"Please, Joan!"

She looks at Renee.

"I'm not gonna go otherwise! I can't!"

This is almost a shriek. Joan is startled by my intensity. She puts a chair in front of the phone for me. I tell her the number.

"Broadway Dance Center! How can I help you??"

"Hi. Can I please speak to Rhonna Wright? She should be at the work for trade desk."

"Hold on, please."

There's a beep when she puts me on hold. The silence is painful as I wait. Joan moves to talk to Renee in the vestibule.

Noise floods the line and the receiver clatters while being picked up.

"Hello? Kitty?

"Ma . . ."

"What's up, kitty? Are you okay?"

"Ma . . . the . . ."

I can't do it. It's too hard.

"There's a woman here Ma . . . . the Bureau . . . ."

"What!? What are you saying? I'm at work. I have to go."

"Mom. The Bureau of Child Welfare is here. They're taking me away."

"*What?!* The fuck they are! Don't go anywhere, with *any*body, iO! I'm coming down there right now! That's fucking kidnapping, those motherfuckers . . ."

"No, Ma, listen to me. I did this . . ."

" . . . that fucking guidance counselor. I always knew she was up to shady snake shit, snooping around for some fake-ass fucking problems. I'll kill that bitch."

"Ma. I did this. Not her. I called them. I wanted this. Don't blame her. I want to go to be with my poppa."

There's a silence. She processes this. My face is scrunched up in pain and fear.

"You're just a kid! Why are they listening to you about all this shit? And now the government is involved! Fuck!"

The staccato on this last word makes me jump.

"Ma, I have to go. Don't come down here and attack Joan. I did this. They're not kidnapping me. I just wanted you to know what was happening. I love you."

I hang up the receiver, tears pouring from my face.

I have saved myself and struck her hard.

Now comes the violence.

## Chapter 27

# The Day

*New York City Family Court, May 1998*

MY HOME IS BURNING BUT NOTHING THERE IS MINE ANY-more. The clothes I wear are the only thing I'm allowed and I'm fine with that. My ma is burning, I threw a match in her hair, but I can't dwell on it.

From here out, this is all that matters. I'm almost there. I don't need another shirt. There will be another shirt.

This is a place where you disappear. I feel myself melting, like the wicked witch, but instead of water I've been doused with a case number. I walked through those big stone doors with a social worker's hand on my shoulder, and I disintegrated into dust, blended in with all the invisible children floating through the system.

We are numbers. We are case files. We are the sum of our hearing dates and dental records, grades and attendance sheets. I take orders here. I keep my mouth shut here. I don't trust anyone here. They see a thousand mes a day. I have no sharp edges or defined shape; I'm just another circumstance to be assessed. I poured myself down this unknown drain and now I've disappeared.

But I can work this. I can make it out on the side I want to be on.

When I get there, I can start to act like me again and someone will see me again. My pop will see me. I'll have a face to him, hair, sneakers, feet, and hands. Knobby knees. I'll finally be able to tell him my knees aren't broken. They were never broken. I just wanted him to stay.

*Chapter 28*

# In the Twisted Halls

*New York, May through August 1998*

RENEE LEADS ME, HER NUMB CHARGE, THROUGH METAL DE-tectors and a lobby of disrupted families. I am aware that something monumental is happening. It's a sense of drama come to life, a scary invigorating notion that nothing will ever be the same again.

I am quiet in the elevator. It smells like envelopes and cheap shoes. People in ill-fitting suits sigh as they push buttons with chewed fingernails. Coffee-stained teeth chatter about caseload jargon.

I am breathing.

These are my breaths.

Where am I?

No one knows I'm here.

I am alone.

I wait in a plastic chair in a labyrinthine hallway while Renee goes into an anonymous door. When she comes out there is a woman with her. She has big red curls, glasses, and a smart face. She introduces herself as Sarah and invites me in.

Sarah seats herself behind a big black desk covered in files and trinkets and tells me she is my lawyer. In fact, she says, I have two. On cue, a younger black guy gives a courtesy knock as he strolls into the room, bespectacled too. Ben. Hi, Ben.

He stands, leaning on the end of her desk with both hands, as Sarah starts to talk. I'm not on the ceiling, but I'm not in my body, either.

Behind her halo of curls, the entire wall is covered in framed photographs of Sarah and a little girl, about my age, at Disneyland, camping, at graduation, on her birthday.

"That's my daughter, Ashley."

"Oh. Cool."

They start to pepper me with questions. When was the last time I saw a dentist? Five years ago. How many days a week do I go to dance class? Every day. Do I enjoy acting? Yes. Sometimes. Was it my choice to live as a boy? Yes. Duh. What is our house like? Dark. Infested. I'm not allowed to be there. What do I mean? Like, I'm not allowed to have keys or go there without her. And what time do we usually get home? Late. After midnight. Has she ever hit me? Well . . . not really. But there was an altercation where she kicked me once I was on the ground.

This is a lie. She never hits me. It feels like she does when she screams at me, but she has never hit me. I have these stories in my mind that I've told myself so many times, it's hard to isolate their threads from the truth now. Also, it's the orange juice again. They need to know how it feels.

"Okay. Well, here's the situation, iO. We can do one of three things, and it's really up to you how you want to go forward."

Already this is crazy. This is more power over my own life than I've ever felt before. Finally someone acknowledges that it's my life, too.

"We can either send you back to your mom's house, which might be the easiest; or you can go into a foster care holding situation while we find placement for you; or if there's a family member who can take temporary custody, we can do that."

My head feels thick and full. I look back at the wall of photos. This little girl looks so happy in every picture. I can't remember feeling that lighthearted and smiley. She and Sarah adore each other, at least on paper. Ma documents every second of my life, but all we do is scream at each other now. I want what Ashley has. I want peace and calm and fun and safety.

I ask them if I can have a little time to think about it.

They send me into a conference room across the hall with some french fries and a decadent ginger ale. My Jordans dangle off the chair as I tenderly dip each fry in ketchup, pondering what the fuck I'm gonna do.

I'm in a limbo place in the universe, between cracks. Just me and the shirt on my skinny back.

Then I hear her through the walls. Her voice hits a piercing pitch when she's enraged, like a banshee. Everyone in the building knows she's here and that she's pissed. The familiar sound of her fury tenses all my muscles.

Images of tap shoes and late-night classes fill my mind. I don't want it.

I feel like I did every time she showed up at Edie or Olivia's house to drag me out in the middle of the night—distraught, torn between duty and freedom, loyalty and my peace.

Why? Why, Ma, do you want me to go there so badly? Why do you want me in that dark shithole? Why do we have to stay there? Why is that what you call a life? I know why. Because it's with you, and that's where a cub is supposed to be, with the mother. We are supposed to protect each other.

She and I have a psychic connection. I can feel the pain through the forest of her rage. I know she is afraid. So am I.

Gingerly, I put my feet on the carpet. The delicious fries and soda are irrelevant now that she's here. I don't want them to be, but that's how it works.

Lawyers are milling around the hall, people who rupture families for a living, and they are still moved by the velocity of her anger.

I move toward the door to the waiting room and stick my head out. She is towering over poor Renee, screaming, sandblasting her face with rage.

"This is BULLSHIT! You have KIDNAPPED my CHILD. This is BULLSHIT!! Go and get my fucking daughter . . . NOW!!"

"Ms. Wright . . ."

Renee is overwhelmed, like a news reporter trying to sound coherent on live TV during a hurricane.

"iO was removed from your care by the State of New York. You are going to be formally charged with neglect, and you no longer have custody—"

"NEGLECT?! Fuck you, neglect! I don't neglect iO! What the fuck is she telling you people?!"

I want to look away. This tone makes my throat dry, but I'm scared that if I don't watch she'll win. Some part of me was tempted to just go back to normal when Sarah offered, but I'm so split now.

"She never went to the dentist?! Psh! Of COURSE she goes to the dentist. All the fucking time! News flash! She's LYING to you!"

This hurts. I don't like her calling me a liar. Or a she.

Just then Ma swings her eyes in my direction. Her face changes immediately to a big smile.

"Kitty! Hi, my bud! It's all gonna be cool, my bud. It's just a mix-up."

She blows a kiss at me.

I feel sick.

I pull my head back around the wall.

I don't want it. I can't go back there. They can't let me go back there.

I sprint down the hall into Sarah's office.

"My ma is here! She's pissed! She's lying. She's saying I made it all up!"

"Okay, iO, okay. Don't worry. She can't get to you."

"I want to live with my dad. In Germany. I want to live with my pop. So bad. Please send me to him."

"Okay. Are you sure?"

"Yes. I can't go back there. I won't make it."

My fear is scaring her. I bet, as a mom, this whole scene really bums her out.

I tell her to call my aunt Olivia, because she lives alone. My ma's little sister Alice has a husband and she's pregnant so I don't want to stress her. Olivia doesn't pick up the phone.

Freedom is so close I can smell it, but until I'm out of this building, I won't believe it. Having my ma right down the hall is terrifying. I start picking my fingers. It's like being through a wall from the strongest magnet on earth, watching your chair slide toward it against your will.

Eventually they get ahold of my grandma Edie, and she says she'll come get me but it's gonna be two hours. Olivia is out of the city until tonight, so she'll come get me from Edie then. This is like a jolt of electric hope. Could I really get out of here, not with my ma?

Sarah and Ben have me cross-check some facts on some forms, and poor, shell-shocked Renee takes me down a back hall to another elevator and out to the street.

The air smells different when we get outside, crisp and clean. I can smell soup from a stand on the street. Everything feels like I'm looking at it through a crystal. Each step away gives me life.

I don't even care that Renee checks me in with some police officers, who make me give them everything I have on me. They're nice to me, and they form a human, badge-toting barrier between me and my ma's fury. It's the only time I've been excited about befriending cops besides my ride in the police car in Hungary.

Renee leaves and I wait in a juvenile holding cell for the two hours until Edie arrives, tiny in her cashmere and corduroy slacks, purse on her wrist, tissue rolled into her sleeve. We take a taxi to Eightieth Street, and she sets me up in the bedroom where my poppa was raised. I am having trouble believing what has happened.

Here I am, in Edie's house, and no one is coming to get me. My ma is forbidden from taking me out of here. I've been waiting to be able to have an unadulterated sleepover here my whole life.

I can picture my poppa at eight years old, in this beautiful place, the pockets of his shorts filled with all his collected objects of beauty, making drawings and sculptures, diagrams and models. I can picture him as a man, maybe moving back here and building a home with me, his kid.

Guilt singes my fantasy, flames of worry licking in from the edges. I wonder where my ma is right now, what she's thinking, how she's coping with this. I hope she's not hurting herself, drinking too much, breaking things. I can only imagine how she feels speared by my betrayal.

The thought of her pain makes me cry. I never wanted to hurt her. I just wanted to leave.

Tears usher me into an uncomfortable, exhausted sleep.

Olivia, my fragile mensch of an aunt, comes to rescue me. She and I have always had a bond. I make her laugh so much she can't breathe, and she has the admirable habit of actually listening to people when they talk. Her nervousness used to make me nervous, but now I want to help her out of it.

Olivia recoils from physical contact. She was the most timid of the three Tillett kids, the middle between two loud male personalities. No one even noticed she was nearly blind until she was nine years old. So overshadowed was she by her brothers' rambunctiousness, the family assumed she was just clumsy when she would walk into things, not see who was in the room, or read poorly. This drove her to an inner sanctuary that she carried into adulthood. Her brain operates at a high frequency, and her words are pointed and wise, but they swirl within the tower of her nervous energy as she fidgets with cigarettes and drinks, objects of relief from the relentless electrical storm around her emotional and intellectual isolation.

I, in my semisavage ways, can be a challenge for her, I know this, but she takes me on with a loyalty that makes me want to cry. Here, in my moment of need, Olivia rescues me, even if she is writing her Ph.D. thesis and struggling to pay the rent on her tiny apartment. If she has a floor, it is mine to sleep on.

On the third night, I call. I want to go to my dad, of this I am one thousand percent certain. I just wish there was a way to do it without destroying my ma. Renee, Sarah, and Ben have expressly forbidden contact with her, but I can't not reach out to her. I need to tell her I'm okay.

She doesn't pick up, so I leave her a message, telling her I'm doing fine, I'm staying with Olivia. I'm not in foster care, and she's treating me well. Please don't worry.

The next day there's a voice mail when I get home from school, telling me about three auditions I have coming up. She tells me she's going to leave my audition scripts at Broadway Dance and I have to pick them up.

I feel like there's still a leash on me, but I have some lead now. The collar is looser.

The government gives Olivia a check for taking custody of me. We go to Old Navy and I spend all of it on boxers, jeans, T-shirts, and sweaters. I've never had a shopping spree like this, and it's thrilling to wear new clothes. I buy a pair of Timberlands and a red Yankees hat. I am painting a vision of myself as I want to be.

Olivia takes me to the movies and to see WNBA games. She buys me a jersey from my favorite player and gets me big jugs of soda. We hang out with her girlfriend and eat Chinese takeout in front of the TV. It's my dream, and it seems like she genuinely just wants me to have a little respite. She wants me to be happy.

I tell her I've been trying to reach my ma and she nods quietly, stubbing out her filterless cigarette. She has compassion for the situation.

The court has mandated that I go to see a psychologist, so Olivia takes me down to Midtown in her red convertible. She's too nervous to drive a car in the city, but she has it anyway. She's constantly stalling out in traffic and hitting the brakes too hard. I love it, riding around with the top down, like gangsters, with the cherry-red exterior and white leather insides.

The shrink is a balding, overweight guy behind a desk in the back corner of a fluorescent-lit office. I hate him from the first second I sit down. He says something to the effect of "so why are you pretending to be a boy?" and my brain shuts off. I roll my eyes, lean way back in my chair, arms crossed, and stay that way for the rest of the hour. Clearly, this guy is dumb. He says I have something called "gender dysmorphia" and he wants to address it. He can address the back of my head.

In the elevator, Olivia says she's gonna see if they'd be all right with her taking me to see her shrink. I say it's okay that people don't understand my gender thing. She heaves a big sigh. She doesn't want me to get hurt by these morons.

FINALLY, MY MA AND I SPEAK. She is stoic in her fury, telling me about a new lover she met on the street, Gus, her Puerto Rican "dark angel," a musician from the Bronx who is going to help her conquer all this. She is blaming everyone for this situation except me.

I go to school every day, but it's nearing the end of the year and I've missed so much I'm going to flunk out anyway, so at the end of the second week my pop says I don't have to go anymore.

The more free time I have to sit around the house and be demanding, the more Olivia and I fight. I know I'm driving her nuts, I know I'm not an easy kid, but some part of me thinks that's my right after all this bullshit.

One day we're in the car on the way to her shrink's office and we get in a screaming match about the seat belt. I don't want to put it on and she won't drive if I'm not wearing it. I'm trying to outwit her, but she loses it and I jump out into the street. She peels away, leaving me standing there, my body throbbing with the burn of abandonment that is pervading my whole existence.

Poppa shows up and Olivia tells him she can't do it anymore, he has to make another arrangement. He and his girlfriend, Julia, are the creative directors of a modern dance company, which is now the big-time ballet company of the state theater in some small city in Germany, and they've got a premier coming up that he has to go back for in a week. I beg him to stay. I tell him I'm desperate to go with him. This whole situation is horrible, and can't he stay with me. He says he wishes, but he has to go. He's going to set something up so I'm not stranded, but for now, he's here, and he's fighting to get custody of me himself.

My poppa is pure magic. Everything he touches turns into an adventure. He is a walking imagination. Every tree branch is a character, every cloud a face, every building a cartoon, and every leaf dances with him. We take cabs across town and go to the movies. We cook food and read great books. I laugh so much my stomach hurts, and I am high on the fantasy of getting to live with him.

Poppa goes and meets with Sarah and Ben. They tell him how everything went down, what the plan is with the neglect charges against my ma, and they ask him to come back for a formal interview the next day. He is optimistic that night at dinner, which makes me feel like there is wind in our sails, but when he comes back from the interview his face is dark. He says they turned everything around and accused him of neglect. They asked him if he thought my ma was an unfit parent, and because he refused to bad-mouth her they said he was complicit and questioned whether he was a fit parent. They will file charges against him the next day.

This is really bad. I never imagined that Sarah and Ben could turn against both of my parents. This information stuns me. The idea of being stuck in the foster system makes me nauseous.

We are at Edie's big marble slab table, having dinner with her and Olivia. They can't see the sink in me, but Poppa says not to worry. He's already got a lawyer and he's gonna get this shit all straightened. Olivia gets stressed out and angry. Edie tries to keep the peace. She says she'll pay for the lawyer if that would help. Poppa thanks her profusely. Then he has to leave.

A few days later, we pack up my stuff and Olivia takes me back over to Edie's, where she introduces me to her friend April. She tells me April will be living on the top floor of Edie's house with me, while all the rest of the shit sorts itself out. I don't get it. Who is this woman? Olivia pulls me aside and tells me April is a friend of her girlfriend's who needs a place to live, and has graciously agreed to take care of me in exchange for the place.

I can't believe this. I'm devastated. I ask Olivia why I can't go home with her. That swimming, lonely, despondent belly feeling overpowers my senses again. She says she has to finish school and she's working like crazy and the apartment is too small. I know this means I'm too difficult for her. I fucked that up by being a disobedient punk.

I cry violently. I feel absolutely alone. Olivia doesn't want me at her place, Edie is too fragile for me to stay with her, I'm not allowed to go to my house. Where the fuck is home? I feel like I'm floating in cold slime, immersed in a bath of silent solitude.

Why did no one intervene in this shit earlier? Why does no one want me? Where am I gonna go now?

I check in with my ma regularly, calling to say hi and tell her I'm okay. Mostly I get her answering machine, but occasionally she picks up. One morning I catch her, but her aggression makes me quiet. My strategy is to wait it out. I let her rant for a few minutes about how they shouldn't feed me shit, until she wears herself down, or gets bored, and says she has to go. I'm silent when we hang up, and I don't cry until I get back into my bed in the room with the blinds drawn and the door closed.

The summer is a tug of power between April and me. I obsessively worry about my ma, calling her every day when I wake up and when I go to sleep, checking that she's not freaking out. Of course I know she is and that there's nothing I can do about it, but I want to at least help scab that wound.

The loneliness is so thick it makes me feel sick. I have a gnawing fear of my pop not winning the case. I start to spin out on the wreckage of possible futures.

July is really touch and go. The city is lobbing all kinds of curve-balls at us. Olivia and Pop fight, Olivia and Edie get into it, Edie and I have it out. The stress of the whole thing makes everyone's threads come loose.

My aunt Alice ends up getting on the stand in early August, eight months pregnant, to do the craziest thing anyone has ever done for me. She knows, I know, we all know what my ma is like with loyalty. Once you cross her, you're dead to her, no matter who you are. So when Alice gets up there and says she thinks my ma is an unfit mother, she sacrifices her sister, banished forever to be a ghost pain in place of a life companion.

Olivia is struck by this show of loyalty to me. She and Alice, finding themselves in something of a refugee camp, called on to perform an impossibly painful act of duty, form a bond that will last many years to come.

To add to the misery of it all, my ma's "dark angel" reveals himself to be a piece of shit. He's an out-of-control drunk with a violent streak. I don't fully understand this at first, but pieces of stories she tells me about him are at odds with each other. She has never been known to lie to me, so I sense she is trying to protect me from something. I grow to hate him quickly. I so badly want him to have her back in this awful situation, to be a pillar for her, since I can't, but it looks like he just bleeds her of her last few dollars and calls her shitty names for not offering them more easily. They swing between marriage proposals and death threats with such regularity it dizzies me. By August first I have vowed to kill him.

There is no pervasive sense that everything will be okay; everything could go either way. I've never been in love, but I would guess that the desperate attachment I feel to my poppa would compare. When he comes around I become filled with light, smiling, giddy, joyous, a different person. I am crushed by him leaving, every single time he pulls away in a cab or walks off down the street. He is jovial and brings stories of great adventures he's been on and places he wants to take me, trying to keep my spirits up, but I'm too weighted by the gravity of the whole thing to fall for it completely. I am possessed by worry.

IT'S LATE on a Thursday afternoon in the middle of August. The phone rings through the entire house and the hair on the back of my neck stands up.

I pause my game of solitaire on April's computer and listen as Edie shuffles across the floor and picks up. I lean back in my chair, straining toward the open door.

It's muffled, but I can hear her having a short conversation with someone before she calls out in her pseudo-British accent.

"iO? It's for you!"

Adrenaline speeds through my system as I leap out of the chair, but I slow when I get to the top of the stairs. Something tells me that this is serious. Something tells me this is scary.

I take each step with consequence, holding the black painted railing in my left hand. I am aware of my heart in my chest. I am aware of my cargo shorts and my Jordans, and my Old Navy T-shirt.

The receiver is on its side on a slab marble end table, in front of a wall-sized mirror. The hold button blinks red. I look at it for a few seconds before I press it.

"Hello?"

"Bugsy! It's me! We did it! We won!"

Poppa's elation is so beautiful.

"Bugsy? Hello?"

"Hi. I'm here."

"We did it! You're officially legally in my custody, kiddo! Are you excited?!"

I genuinely thought that I would be, but I'm so worried about her.

"Is my ma okay?"

He sighs, pausing.

"She's okay. I think . . . you know . . . she left with her lawyer right away, so I didn't get a chance to talk to her . . . but I think she's okay."

What is "okay"? How could she be okay in a situation like this? She is a shell, a ruin. A ship wrecked on a solitary island, its beautiful bow smashed in with no one left alive to fix it.

This notion sends my belly into my feet. I have to sit down on the cold stone floor. Poppa says he's coming home to celebrate. When we hang up I put my face in my hands and start to cry.

Is this really what I wanted? Is my freedom worth this impossible cost? Did I really understand the weight of the planets I was shifting when I set this thing into motion? Certainly not.

Where does certainty come from in the face of such monumental, impossibly huge risk? How can one ever know that the leap they are taking is the right one until it has been taken? What compass guides you if not your gut instincts? How am I meant to process such an equation?

The only thing I have is my gut, and despite the tearing feeling it has now, it never wavered.

## Chapter 29

┄┄

# The Escape

*Karlsruhe, Germany, August 1998*

Late on the night of August 26 we take a taxi to JFK airport. I feel like James Bond, arriving at this late hour with everything I own in two army duffel bags. From the second we get out of the cab until the plane actually lifts off the ground, I can't help but glance over my shoulder every few minutes, expecting someone to intervene.

My father is calm, mellow in his laid-back way, shirt unbuttoned to the chest, skinny in his Levi's. He has a piece of red string on his wrist, left over from a tour through India, and he charms the pretty agent at the ticket counter with his intelligent humor. His passport is thick with visas and he knows his way around the airport by heart. He doesn't speak to me like a child, he treats me as an equal, just with a guiding hand. I'm nervous, but I try not to show it so he doesn't think of me as a little kid.

I'm turning thirteen in less than a week. My second godfather, Poppa's best friend of twenty years, rented a big villa outside of Rome, so after a few days in Germany we're going there to visit him and celebrate my birthday.

I'm asleep for my first drive through pop's German town, Karlsruhe. Poppa shakes my shoulder gently when we pull up at an ornate green metal gate and says we're home.

The sky is blue with a haze of white, bright with summer sun. Pop's girlfriend, Julia, waves from a small balcony at an upstairs window, then comes down to help us carry the luggage. She's sugar sweet, a ballerina from North Carolina with a high-pitched voice and a big smile. She sweeps me into a hug and tells me how happy she is that I made it. This feels nice.

The building smells like warmth. It's hard to describe, but it's a mixture of things that make up what I've always imagined a home to smell like—blankets and soup, flowers and soap, babies and hot porridge.

The apartment is trimmed with beautiful wood and flooded with sunlight. Immediately I think of my ma, how sun is all she ever wants in an apartment. I feel guilty that now I'll have it, and she's still there in the darkness. I push the thought away.

Julia is bubbling with excitement to give me a tour. Showing hospitality gives her joy.

The place never seems to end. She starts in the kitchen, tiled in white and black checkers, dishes clean and drying on a rack. I notice this with admiration. It smells like food is actually cooked here. There's a balcony in the back that looks out over a garden in which the downstairs neighbors have hung their laundry up on a line. Ma makes fun of things like this, domesticated paradises. I like it. The hanging laundry makes me feel soft like cotton inside.

The bathroom has a big wooden door and a tub of equal proportion. I think of Ma's incessant bathing and how much she would love a bath like this, sprawling and clean.

Their room is like every other bedroom Pop has ever had: a low bed surrounded by books and pretty objects. Art scattered around the walls and beautiful lamps he designed. I feel funny looking at the dresser. I fetishize such objects of organization. It almost feels weird to be standing so close to one.

The living room is the size of our whole apartment in New York. It's big and open, with almost no furniture in it. I ask if the TV sitting against one wall actually works. "Yeah!" Julia says. I ask if I'm allowed to watch it, and she says of course I am. My head starts to tingle.

Finally, the crown jewel—my room. I can barely believe the size of it. It's so big it has two doors, one to the main hallway and one to the living room. The ceilings are fifteen feet high, and it's as bright as a greenhouse.

"This is *my* room?"

"Yeah! Isn't it nice?"

Julia throws open the huge windows, letting a gust of crystal-clean air in. There's no bed, and the room is filled with their stuff, but she is quick to explain that the stuff is on its way out and that they're buying their friend Barbara's gorgeous, handmade, family heirloom bed frame. We can build a desk wherever I want. I feel so much gratitude I want to hug her and cry.

She tells me to hang out and get settled in as she closes the door behind her. I watch the handle twist as she pulls it shut, then listen to the sounds of her bare feet padding away down the hall.

I sit on a wooden stool and look around.

I feel like a pair of cymbals, one side freaked out and uncomfortable, the other explosively excited, my ears ringing from the collision.

My first instinct is to unpack. I place my shoes in a straight line by one wall and make neat piles of my new Old Navy gear, organized by type, on the clean wooden floor next to them. When I finish, I fold my duffels and sit back, looking at everything I own in the whole world, lined up in one little row like that. It makes me feel small, but fresh, like everything is new. The table is wiped clean, and now I get to start living the life I've always dreamed of, here, in this utopia, with my beloved poppa. I did it.

## Chapter 30

# Fork and Knife

*Ronciglione, Italy, August 1998*

THE GIRL IN THE POOL IS NAKED AND CHOKING. THIRTY minutes ago my father was commenting on how beautiful she was as she dipped in and out of the turquoise water in the dusk light. Now there's a chicken bone lodged in her throat.

Her boyfriend, bronzed, lanky, and goateed, who I was just thinking looked a lot like Jesus, lunges toward her. Arturo's handsome face struggles through a stoned haze to arrange itself into the grimace of panic and determination its owner feels is expected of him. To no avail. He is shirtless and helpless, and I stare at his body as he lifts hers into his arms, arguing in English with his friend while at the same time soothing her with an Italian that runs like caramel through her coughs and gags. Raised in New York, he knows how not to freak out, but he has no idea what to do.

He and his cohort lay the girl, his lover, on the bright blue tile that circles the Olympic-size swimming pool. His best friend runs to call an ambulance as the girl, Flavia, starts to chameleon to the tiles. Arturo is whispering to her in Italian as she chokes and convulses. His long fingertips, tender on her ribs, are tensed with fear.

My godfather pulls his sunglasses up onto his silver pompadour

and props himself up on one big arm on his lounge chair. He is annoyed at the disturbance. Kun, his dainty Japanese boyfriend, lifts
his eye mask, and both watch the couple with curiosity. Fear hasn't
wafted to that side of the pool yet.

Arturo lifts his girlfriend's naked body into his arms and carries
her out to the pebbled driveway flanked by tall cypresses. I clamber
after him to see. The fainted girl and the saintly boy make a beautiful
pair among the green trees and the dusty Italian clay earth.

Flavia spends the night in the hospital and the dinner table is
aflutter with gossip. "She was once pregnant with Arturo's baby."
"She loves him, but he'll cheat on her." "His mother wants her gone."
"He is a self-indulgent martyr, staying there all night." At the end
of the table, sitting in the center of a beautiful watercolor, I spot a
green-brown lump the size of a fist, enshrined like a meteorite. My
godfather or Kun occasionally saunters over to chip off a piece. When
I finally figure out what is going on I decide I need to talk to my pop,
as seriously as I ever have in my life. I take him by the hand into the
dark garden and walk in a circle around the fountain.

"Poppa, I want you to know that I will *never* do any kind of
drugs . . ."

It is our first night on the property.

The next day, at lunch, Flavia and Arturo make a triumphant return. The table is laid outside, under an olive tree, with a giant bowl
of salad, several bottles of wine, jugs of water, and fresh bread. My
godfather grunts with annoyance through Arturo's dramatic retelling
of the story of her rescue, while Flavia smokes a cigarette and giggles,
her nipples barely covered by a sundress.

Mariangela, the cook of the house, comes out carrying a bowl
of pasta three times the size of her head. Five foot one in platform
flip-flops, in her mid-seventies, she's wearing a red apron and a cigarette dangles from her wrinkled lips. Mariangela blasts techno all
day while she cooks, chain-smoking in the downstairs kitchen. She

doesn't speak a word of English, so she yells at Arturo to clear a space for the bowl, which he jumps up to take from her. She frowns and waves him away with her head, nodding at the table, commanding in Italian.

Mariangela uses a clawed ladle to serve out massive portions of spaghetti carbonara. I whisper to my pop that I only want a little, so he hands her my salad plate. She questions him sharply, to which he responds with something charming in Italian, nodding in my direction. She swings her head of white curls toward me and wrinkles her face further. She plants a dollop of pasta on the salad plate but is clearly upset about it.

Embarrassed by the attention, I keep my head down as I shovel up my pasta with my fork, which I hold in a balled fist. At the first bite, I know it's the best thing I have ever tasted.

Mariangela returns with a platter of breaded veal cutlets, which blows my mind, because how could anyone eat more than this pasta? She serves them, trading jokes with Arturo and my godfather, nodding with pleasure at the sight of everyone enjoying her food. She pats my portly godfather on the back and moves around the table.

I'm too busy concentrating on getting the delicious noodles into my mouth to notice what's coming until I feel her hands on my shoulders. She grips tight, like a bird, and shrieks something in Italian. Everyone at the table looks at me. She waves them off, makes a joke I can't understand, and they laugh and go back to their meal. But to my father, she directs a serious question. He looks at me, to my fork, then back to my eyes.

He says a few words to Mariangela in a tone that sounds like he's at a loss. I stare at him.

"She wants to know who taught you to hold a fork like that."

My hand feels foreign, hot with embarrassment. It drops the offending fork. What have I done wrong with this familiar object?

I look up at Mariangela's face, but grandmothers are no fools. She looks into my eyes and tells my father something in a quieter tone.

"She wants you to visit her in the kitchen."

"Okay . . . why?"

"You do know how to hold a fork, don't you?"

"Dad . . . of course I do! Jeez!"

THAT WEEK, Mariangela teaches me how to use a fork and knife properly for the first time. Every day I go to her for a lesson and come out covered in flour, stomach full of olives and fresh tomatoes, veal, pork chops, and chicken with fresh rosemary. She gathers basil from the garden and rubs hot toast with garlic. Truthfully, she is teaching me to eat.

She speaks to me in Italian and I gesticulate and smile a lot and run out to play in the sun and jump in the pool. Making her laugh is a personal victory. Mariangela quickly becomes my favorite person on the property.

She serves me a bowl of pasta on the third day, but when I can't finish it she goes off. She teaches me to pace myself, not to crouch over my bowl and inhale. Through her gestures I understand that she thinks I eat like I'm in prison. She tells me it's okay and shows me the gigantic vat of noodles and sauce, as if to say I don't have to stress, there's plenty more where that came from.

Each day, at mealtime, I sneak my bowl or plate into the kitchen and show her the evidence of my triumph. She claps and says something congratulatory that I can't understand, to which I pull up my shirt and pat my distended belly with glee. She makes an unintelligible crack, pulls on her Marlboro, and bounces on her two-inch-thick electric-pink flip-flops.

At the end of our five days, it's not the beautiful couple I will miss the most, nor my moody godfather who I barely know or the majestic landscape. The most important piece of that life-changing summer will forever be Mariangela, who taught me that food was something to be savored, enjoyed, and loved, not stabbed.

*Chapter 31*

# Karlsruhe

*Karlsruhe, Germany,*
*September 1998 through Christmas 1999*

KARLSRUHE IS A BITTERSWEET EXPERIENCE. THE TOWN IS quaint. It smells of concrete after a spring rain. Fresh, the smell of earth rising from unexpected places. But I miss my city. I'm an alien here. I wear my headphones at all times, bringing the beats that conjure home into this strange, pristine environment that is supposed to be my new world. Rap is the only thing that makes me feel grounded, like I come from somewhere with grit and fucked-up personality. The anger and rawness of it brings my ma to me in this distant place.

Everyone rides bikes along manicured cobblestone streets, with babies on board. I sit next to the crystal mountain river that runs through the town, sketching graffiti pieces, and watch them go by.

Pop has been amazing since I got here, exactly the best friend I wanted him to be, except that his job at the theater keeps him super busy all the time. We bike everywhere together, him on his sleek black racer, pointing out cool facts about the historic buildings in town. There's a cathedral here that took us an hour to walk to the top of, where he showed me graffiti from the fourteenth century—WILLIAM THE BOLD, 1392—chiseled into the stone. We went camping in the mountains of the Black Forest just outside of town, and he cooks for me a lot. If I could, I'd only eat food he cooks, partly because it's delicious, but mostly because he made it.

Julia is genuinely nice. She took me with her to rehearsal and introduced me to the dancers in her company. They're from all over the world, which makes talking to them an adventure in accents. They rehearse in a giant room at the top of the state theater with a wall of windows that looks out over the train tracks and the city.

Julia creates modern dance pieces that confound the audiences. She plucked my pop out of New York and asked him to travel with her and create the visual components of her work, and gave his boundless brain complete freedom and access within the well-funded theater. He made a stage set that consisted of a thirty-foot man made of wire that dancers moved in and around as it was slowly unfolded from the ground and pulled into the rafters.

The Germans stand around after performances trying to solve the riddle of "what the piece means," not getting the fact that it's not meant to mean anything, it's meant to be visually extraordinary and make you feel.

I only knew how to count to ten in German when I got here, which was just enough to buy candy at these things called kiosks, which I did as much as I could, simply because I'm free to.

I enrolled in a school that has a class for *Ausländer* (foreigners), that's specifically designed to teach us the language. The teacher is a serious guy with a potbelly and olive skin, who speaks to us only in German. I like him. At first I thought he wasn't that smart, but it turns out he's a brilliant teacher. He draws objects out in colored chalk and has us copy them in colored pencils. He says the colors are essential to remembering the vocabulary. He says this is the only class we'll ever take where we will walk straight outside and use what we're learning. He's right, on both counts, and I've picked up a lot in my first three weeks already.

The class is filled with kids from Turkey and Albania, rugged teenagers who've seen awful things. There are two Russian girls, Evita and Olga; a Greek girl and her brother; a French kid; and a beautiful boy from Brazil who makes me think of my own brother. His mom took him back to Brazil when she got divorced when I was eight and I haven't seen him since.

I don't get picked on by the Albanians who run the yard because they're impressed that I'm from New York. They want to know if I'm friends with Jay Z and Puff Daddy. Sure, I say, we hang. They flip out and ask me to translate lyrics for them. I tell them I will once I don't have to use sign language to explain myself.

This is all well and fun, but I know how brutal kids are, how quickly admiration turns to resentment, so I keep my interactions with them swift and minimal, ducking out to my bike the second school ends.

Pop has an art studio a few blocks away from our house, in a huge concrete room that was once a car repair shop. His friend Barbara, whose heirloom bed I sleep on, lives in a converted bunker next door with her six-year-old son, Leo.

Barbara is a deep hippie, the type who only eats vegetarian and organic, wears clothes made out of weird plants, and consults crystals about her health woes, which are abundant. She has a condition that makes her skin itchy and powdery, like leather that's been left out in the rain. This tortures and embarrasses her. She spends a lot of time concocting creams in her place, which is a makeshift house covered in colorful cloths, Hula-Hoops, beanbag chairs, exercise balls, and kids' toys.

Leo's father is way out of the picture, "a bastard" long gone. Leo is a blond dynamo with crystal-blue eyes and endless energy. Poppa says he will grow into a dictator and enslave the whole world, and often asks him to his face to think of him when he's the Führer and to spare him.

POPPA AND I HAVE TO GO BACK to New York twice in the fall for meetings with a counselor from the government. They want to check on how I'm doing. I'm scared of seeing my ma.

I've been calling her a ton to check in and let her know how awesome everything is, but she's hard to reach. Every time I get her, she tries to trick me into coming home. She tells me there are several incredible auditions for big movies that I can't miss, and then that she has a friend who's going to buy me a ticket to come home for them. When I find out that it's a one-way ticket I feel betrayed, like she doesn't hear me, or care, when I tell her how happy I am.

One day she tells me that something is wrong with her shoulder. She doesn't know what it is, some kind of growth. Could it be cancer? Nah, she says, probably not, it'll probably go away. Worried, I tell her that things don't just go away on their own, she should go see a doctor. She reminds me that she hates doctors and has no intention of finding one who would know what the fuck this thing is. I plead with her, to which she retorts that she'll only go see a doctor if I come home and take her.

That night there's a dinner with the entire dance company at a restaurant in town. I am so wracked with concern about my ma having cancer that I sob through the entire evening.

I use my poppa's reassurances as a crutch until we go back to New York in October. I meet my ma in the presence of a counselor, which is a humiliation to her. She shows up in her trench coat with a scarf wrapped around her head like a peasant woman, barely concealing a black eye. I'm already raw from weeks of fearing for her health, and now it's like I got punched in the eye, too. Seeing her like that, her proud back stooped, pulling envelopes covered in scribble out of her plastic bag purses, makes me want to throw up. It's all outside of me, but my body is trying to eject it from within.

The counselor can sense that I can't handle her, so he lets us go early.

I spend a month in Karlsruhe haunted by visions of Ma being hit by this character Gus. I imagine killing him in a multitude of ways. I try to call extra often to check on her, but she is even harder to get ahold of.

When we go back to New York in November, she is bleeding from the face like a religious icon. She shows up late, cupping a paper towel filled with ice over the other side of her face, blood streaming from her eye. She is carrying her head scarf and coat in the same hand as her plastic bags, trying to hold it together, but I've never seen her in so much pain. This time my stomach tries to claw its way out of my mouth.

I'm not supposed to talk to her, but I can't handle this. With a broken heart I run to her.

"Maaaa. What happened to your face?!"

"Nothing, my bud."

"What do you mean nothing? You're bleeding!"

She winces, taking a deep gulp of air. I realize she is trying not to throw up, too.

"Ma. Did Gus do this to you? Did he hit you in the face again?"

She turns sharply to me and in a pointedly loud whisper sternly says, "No! Nobody did shit to me."

Then, with a glance toward the counselor, who is nervously consulting someone out in the hall, she says, "You don't give these people any added reasons to go poking around in your shit, you hear me?"

She whispers something about Gus having thrown a belt across the room and the buckle having skewered her eyeball. I start to cry and my pop whisks me out of there. I scream in the hallway that I won't go unless they take her to a hospital. She comes out of the room, crying because I'm crying, and says she's going to go. I make her swear on everything we've ever held sacred, and will only get in the elevator once she does.

People are staring. My pop rubs my back and buys me a pack of M&M's while I sob on the steps of the court building, snot running out of my nose.

INSTEAD OF GOING BACK TO KARLSRUHE, we head south to São Paulo, to visit Elio, my little brother, a treacherous and exciting voyage. I'm thirteen and my brother is nine, but we've only ever met when he was a baby. I see photos of him all the time, but he doesn't speak English, so we can't talk on the phone.

São Paulo is massive and terrifying, which is bizarre, seeing as I'm from New York. But São Paulo is like five New Yorks, scrambled together with endless horizon after horizon of city. We pretend to belong at fancy hotels; my dad just waltzes in with us and asks for three towels, "two for my sons." We hit the roof pool and stay all day, laughing and swimming and scarfing down grilled meats and fresh fruit juices.

I'm starting to wear a T-shirt with my swimming trunks because something is beginning to sprout on my chest. Pools are a hazard now. The changing rooms are a minefield and my whole body just makes me uncomfortable. My shaved head signals a clear gender delineation for the rest of the world; the turmoil is inside me, and I'm increasingly afraid someone will figure me out.

I wonder what my brother thinks of his big sister, who is effectively a boy. Does it confuse him? Does he care? Is he embarrassed?

My brother is a delicate, beautiful boy. His skin is darker than mine; his hair and big eyes are brown. He is all bones but he's proportionately built, a healthy kid. He is quiet and loving, which makes me want to take him in my arms and protect him. We pantomime folding him into my suitcase many times.

Pop and Rita fight about everything. She is a tightly wound coil always finding a reason to have an outburst and direct her dragon breath at our pop. Elio and I walk ahead of them through the sweaty streets, my arm around his shoulder, his around my waist, saying the only words we mutually understand—*brother, sister*—and smiling at each other. I hug him a lot and pick him up as much as possible.

It's a weird thing, this idea of being a family suddenly, thrust together on a vacation when none of us really knows each other. Pop hasn't visited Elio since he was five, so they seem fairly disconnected, too, although Elio is ecstatic about the visit. Pop swings him around and entertains his mind with stories and drawing sessions, which my brother is particularly talented at. I know that feeling, kid, the blissful love you feel for this magical man. I know. I'm just sorry for the hole it's gonna create in you for the rest of your life.

POP AND I GO BACK to our quaint German town and by Christmas I'm fluent enough to correct his German, which I do eagerly. I like to show off.

We hang out in the theater a lot and he introduces me to the people in the makeup department, who I ask to make a goatee and mustache for me. They find a wig with hair a similar auburn color to mine and make my dream facial hair. They give me a tiny bottle of wig glue and I carefully apply it all in the theater bathroom.

Walking around as I want to be is almost too wonderful to handle. I wish so badly it was permanent.

Then the unexpected happens. I get blindsided by a feeling I've never had before. It burns, it tingles, it makes me sweat and feel weak in the knees. I get stupid, shy, unsure of my actions. I start bumbling, dropping things. I'm off my game in a major way. I get a crush, a huge one.

It's the Greek girl in my class, Vikki. She's sixteen, a Goth from Athens, with a sheet of straight black hair, skintight jeans, and black platform boots. I don't even see it coming, but suddenly I'm a mess when she comes into the room. I find myself wanting to sit closer to her to smell her shampoo.

Her family owns the Greek restaurant on the corner of our block, so I finally work up the gumption to offer to walk her home. I suggest that her brother come along, just in case she thinks it's weird. She is blasé about it, but she doesn't refuse. I regale them with my best New York stories all the way across town, and by the time we turn the corner to our street, I am hopelessly at the mercy of her every hair flip and blink. My heart beats to get that next tiny giggle out of her.

I'm red-faced, sweating and giddy when I get home. I burst in the door and Julia gets the brunt of my gush. She's thrilled. We sit at the kitchen table brainstorming on how to rope her in, although it will take me weeks to actually say the word *crush*.

It makes going to school thrilling. I put more effort into my homework so I can impress her with my brain, and all my jokes are for her benefit. What's going on soon becomes apparent, and some of the Albanian kids make cracks about it. This scares the shit out of me, because, I realize, if everyone finds out I'm a girl, Vikki might be disgusted, and the boys might kick my ass.

One day, I'm coming up the stairs from lunch headed back to class when I feel something wet hit the top of my inner thigh inside my boxers. I am horrified and confused.

Going to the bathroom is still a nightmare, but this is too urgent and weird not to just do it. I barge into a stall and pull my pants down and pee. The toilet fills with blood.

Holy shit! I didn't even think about that!

I sit there for a while, marinating in my discomfort with my own body. I have absolutely no relationship to it whatsoever, it's just a kind of inconvenient vessel for my thoughts and words. I get around in it, I play ball in it, I dance in it, but I don't feel particularly connected to it in any way. I don't think of myself as having a vagina, even though I know it's there, but now here we are and blood is coming out of it, and my throbbing little boobs are telling me I am most definitely, at least biologically, a girl. Ugh. I hate it.

Confused, I bolt straight out of the building into the brisk fall day without my coat and waddle home.

My pop is there, futzing around in the kitchen. I linger in the hallway, trying to figure out how to approach this.

He comes out holding a tea towel and sees me standing there, frozen.

"Hey. What're you doing home? You okay?"

"Uh . . . I don't really know how to tell you this . . ."

He looks at me with apprehensive confusion and waits. The silence dries the air out like hay.

"Um . . . I . . . got a visitor."

"You what?"

"I . . . well . . . . it's a girl thing."

"Oh! Oh shit! For the first time? Um . . . shit! Well . . . Jules has torpedoes in the bathroom . . ."

Torpedoes. Nice, Dad. I'm horrified. I waddle to the bathroom, leaving him blushing in the hall, and close the door. I kick off my shoes, get rid of my soiled pants and boxers and scrounge around the counter.

I find them stacked up in a glass. They're size Super Plus, whatever that means. They look massive.

I peel the plastic off one and, sitting on the side of the tub, try to ascertain where I'm supposed to stick it.

"Dad! I'm supposed to . . . put this thing inside of me?"

"Yep! That's the idea!"

At least I know we're both dying inside. I really need him to help me out right now, but I get the sense that this could be a woman-only thing, which might be the first time that line has ever been drawn in my head in my whole life.

"Where's Julia?"

"She's at work!"

I poke around with the tip, which comes up bloody, but nothing feels like an entryway that's going to open. There's one spot where it seems like maybe it could go, but it hurts like hell when I try to force it. Fuck. I need help.

I wrap a towel around my waist and go into the hall, careful to close the door behind me so he can't see the massacre that is my bottoms lying on the floor.

We are both too embarrassed to look at each other, so he yells from the kitchen: "Did you get it sorted?"

"Nope! What the hell do I do? Those torpedoes are *massive*."

"Ummm . . . have you thought about calling your mom? I think this might be more her arena."

Jesus, the thought never crossed my mind, but I guess that would be a good idea. I pick up the phone, one hand holding my towel, and dial her number. It's early enough that she'll be home. She picks up on the sixth ring.

"Hello??"

"Ma. It's me. I need your help."

"What's up, my bud?"

"I, uh . . . I got a new visitor."

"Huh? A visitor? From where?"

"From the land of being a girl?"

"What the fuck are you talking about, kitty?"

"I'm talking about . . . I'm saying . . . a monthly visitor . . ."

"What? Who is visiting you?"

"There's blood, Ma, in my pants, for chrissake."

"Ohhhhhh! Yeah . . . okay? So what?"

"So! I need your help!"

"With what?"

"I have no idea what to do, Ma! Pop said to use one of Julia's torpedoes, but they're insanely huge. It hurts to put them up there, I can't do that. What the fuck do I do?"

"Huh. Are those the only ones you got?"

"Yeah, I think so. They're the only ones I saw."

"Well, you go in the bathroom, you take some toilet paper, roll it up into a real tight little roll, and you shove it up there."

"Wha— For real?"

"Yeah. That's how yer ma has been doin' it for years!"

This doesn't work for shit. I try it, but first of all, it's hard to push around, second, it feels like it's leaking, and third, it's impossible to get out. So I go back to the mirror and contemplate the giant torpedoes. I've got to make this work.

I limp back to school with a crooked stranger inside my body, feeling like I've been microchipped by my womanhood. It's hard to sit, but I get through the day.

MY MOOD OUTSIDE THE CRUSH SHIFTS, becoming dark and angry. Pop is less patient in asking me to do my chores. I'm not cooperative with him and Julia. I don't feel that I should have to earn my right to a roof with my own father. He starts to think that I'm intentionally sabotaging their relationship, though it's not true, but when Julia starts bossing me around I lose my shit. I scream at her with a rage she didn't cause, telling her she's not my mother and not to get it fucking twisted.

Her face goes scarlet, holding in the furious storm of angry things she wants to say to me. She wants to call me ungrateful, a brat, an asshole. I want to tell them that this is my fucking birthright, to be with my fucking dad, in a safe, warm room, and I shouldn't have to do anything to earn it. Where the fuck were they when the fridge was turned off and I was stealing food to live?

The fights get more and more frequent, and Poppa's behavior gets more and more erratic. When the dancers come over for dinner parties, they all sit around the living room passing joints back and forth. I observe this and the change it produces in my poppa.

Some days he comes home from work elated and buzzing. I can hear him whistling as he rides up the street, locks his bike, and sails up the steps. He will burst in, singing about going to the circus the next day. I'll go with him on this trip, getting excited and making plans. He'll put on some music and clean the whole house, top to bottom. Then he'll lie down at eight o'clock and pass out until the morning.

The next day he'll have no memory of any plans for the circus and say I always accuse him of making false promises. I swear, up and down, but he says I'm crazy and to stop making up absolutes. This will drive me wild with frustration.

By the summer, Julia and I aren't talking. I've told Poppa I want him to stop smoking weed, but he just waves me off. The dream has collapsed with Pop and her. I thought I was finally coming into a family, a home where the love is unconditional. But something keeps my poppa and me divided, something intangible, and my disappointment in him taints all of our conversations. We can't discuss anything without it ending in my tears, built up over so many years of hoping.

Julia is caught in the middle, but instead of removing herself from a relationship I feel has nothing to do with her, she inserts her infuriating opinions in the moments I most want to be left alone.

This unfortunate brew leads to constant fighting, so I start to spend most of my time at Barbara's, hanging out with her and Leo, or down by the river, painting on legal graffiti walls. I sleep over at Barbara's often, and find it so weird when I wake up to no missed calls on my tiny Nokia, as though I am not missed or being kept track of. Things with Poppa are great when Julia's not around, and as long as we stay out of the house, so I guess it makes sense that he's not eager to get me back there. I know he loves me, it's just a real touchy situation.

Vikki and her brother come over to watch a movie one night when Poppa and Julia are out, but I am absolutely petrified of being too close to her. If she found out my secret she'd think I was a freak, so I sit on the other side of the couch, obsessing over what she'd say if somebody told her I was a girl. Would she think back on this as a super creepy date? Maybe her brother being there is a buffer for my shame.

I can't handle the stress, so I distance myself from her as the summer goes on, which teaches me a few things about ignoring girls and reverse psychology, but I start having an earth-shifting thought: When I switch schools in the fall, what if I tell them I'm a girl?

This sits in me like a brick for a few days. I've never lived a day since I was six years old without the perpetual hassle of gender discussion, so I can't even imagine what that would be like. Glorious relief, probably.

Biking home one day, I spontaneously decide to just do it. My pop comes around the corner, riding to work, like a sign that I need to affirm my decision out loud.

"Dad . . . I have something to tell you."

"Okay . . . What's up, bugs?"

"I think I want to be a girl again."

"Wow! Okay . . . cool!"

We both look at and through each other, lost in thinking about what that would actually mean.

"It's good timing, with switching schools and all that . . ."

"That's what I was thinking!"

"Yeah, seems smart."

"But, Pop, I want to grow my hair out before I start wearing girls' clothes. I don't want to look like a boy dressed as a girl."

He shakes his head back and forth like he's whipping water off his face, confused and amazed at the same time by what a weirdo I am. He loves it.

"Cool! Okay!"

"Can I just keep the front short like a boy while I grow out the back?"

He laughs.

"Boy in the front, girl in the back? No! That's just called a mullet."

"Ewwwww!"

We stand there, in the middle of the street, laughing.

"Wow. Are you gonna wear, like, skirts and stuff?"

"I dunno . . . sure, I guess."

"Wowwwww. That's gonna be crazy! Oh well, I'm not losing a son, I suppose, I'm gaining a daughter."

AND JUST LIKE THAT, it's done.

## Chapter 32

# Barbara's

*Karlsruhe, Germany, Christmas Eve 1998*

B ARBARA'S GOT TWO CATS. WHEN SHE LEAVES TOWN I GO over and feed them. She shows me a tiny room upstairs in her loft that's under the bottom corner of the slanted ceiling. There are no windows, it used to be a grow room for her friend's weed, so there's a little glass case and not much else. She says it can be my space if I want some privacy. I am deeply grateful.

I stick some books in there and a camping lamp. You can barely sit up at the highest point, and you have to crawl out through a hole in the drywall, but it's mine. There isn't a day I don't get into a fight with Pop or Julia, so Leo and I hang out and play, and when he's real well behaved he gets to come into my room with me and I'll read to him from my books.

Pop's weird weed highs have gotten more extreme as the weather has gotten colder. He's out of his gourd about the new piece they're working on at the theater, and he's got pretty much no time for me. He's made a billion drawings and they're all over the house and his studio.

We sit down to dinner in their living room on Christmas Eve. It's Pop, Julia, Barbara, Leo, and two of the dancers who are Julia's favorites.

Julia makes some comment about how I should be setting the table, which dampens my mood. I'm pissed she would come out of the gate like that, and I want to leave.

At some point in the night, I snap at her, which gets my poppa pissed off, so he tells me to cut the shit. This makes me feel betrayed, so I lay into him for being a shitty dad with no loyalty. This makes him stare at me like I'm the devil, his eyeballs bulging with exhaustion. Julia gets all fired up and can't stay in her seat. She stands next to the table and starts laying into me about what an ingrate I am, how unacceptable my behavior is, and how I need to learn some manners and to do what I'm told.

This is fucking embarrassing, so I scoot my chair back, tell her to go fuck herself, and storm into my room, slamming the door and locking it behind me. She starts banging on it, screaming about how I better open it up, how she doesn't want me locking the door in her house, how it's her fucking door. This makes me want to jump out the window. It's like my ma all over again. No locks, no closed doors. Fuck no. I'm not a child anymore. I'm fuckin' outta there.

I hear her stomping around to the other door, so I grab my coat and run out the first one, letting her chase her own tail, and bolt into the hall.

I hear her screaming behind me, and then my poppa yelling at her to leave it alone, which only makes her start crying and scream back at him that he's ganging up on her.

This must be some waiting room for hell. Out of the frying pan and into the seminormalized, everything-looks-fine-on-the-outside, inner circle of fireballs. Suburban domestic batshit.

I take the stairs two at a time and throw the door open to the snowy night, but Julia is hot on my heels, screeching at me to stop walking away from her, to have some respect. I spit nasty words at her over my shoulder, telling her to fuck off and leave me alone.

She makes a grab at my coat, but I wriggle out of it. I'm in the snow in my shirtsleeves and overalls, but the adrenaline of the situation has my blood running hot.

I bolt into the street, but before I can get all the way across, I feel her tug on the back of my overalls. Her nails scratch my back as she grabs me, and she throws me down on the hood of a parked car. She is a creature transformed by stress.

I yell at her to get the fuck off me, but she climbs on top of my body and puts her beet-red face in mine.

In a higher pitch than I've ever heard a human voice go, she screams at me that I better get my shit together and stop acting like an asshole. She's the only person who has ever really loved me, and she's the only person who ever will.

Then I know her marbles have scattered. I shove her shoulders and scream back at her to get the fuck off me or I'm gonna punch her in the fucking face. She taunts me back, and I realize she's nailing her own coffin. This shit is so bananas, there will be no way for her to save face with my pop now, and the dancers can all hear us through the windows. She's sealing her own deal.

"Fuck you," I spit. "You're a nasty person. Get the fuck off me."

Something in my tone registers, or maybe she realizes she's pinning a fourteen-year-old to the hood of an icy car on Christmas Eve, screaming two inches from her face, and she lets up just enough for me to wriggle out from under her.

TWO DAYS LATER, I call Barbara and ask her if, when I come to feed the cats, I can move into my little room permanently. Shit is too insane at Julia's place, and I need somewhere safe to be. I'll trade babysitting Leo every day for rent, because I've got no money. She says sure, and that's it, I pack my duffels, fold up my mattress, and drag them over to her place.

When I slide the bed in through the door and unfold it, it touches the walls on all four sides, that's how small the room is, but once I lay my clothes out on the incubator, stack my books on it, and tack up my Aaliyah and Faith Evans posters, I put on my headphones and fall into a deep sleep, knowing that I'm finally safe.

# PART II

·  ⊩ ⊩

# Agency

*Chapter 33*

# The Boot

*Karlsruhe, Germany, and southern England, May 1999*

P OP AND I ARE SITTING ON THE FLOOR OF HIS STUDIO EAT-
ing Chinese noodles when he introduces the idea. He starts
reminiscing about the boarding school he went to, and how fun it was to
run around the English countryside, free from parents and rules, smoking weed in the trees and making friends independently. It was the seventies, I point out, bored, but he's insistent on the magic of the experience
being one of the pillars around which his personality has been built.

I ask him, flat out, what he's getting at. He explains that, well, seeing as I'm having such a hard time with the rules at my new school,
since the strict German system seems to not be the best fit for me, and
I've essentially run away and am living in a cubicle at Barbara's, maybe
we should be thinking about going to a live-away school as an option.

Gendered uniform. Skirts. Rules. Headmasters. HORROR.

I become emotional instantly. The hot mozzarella ball that precedes
tears coagulates in my chest.

Why would he want to send me away? I already live at Barbara's
house and require almost nothing of him—he barely ever knows where
I am. I get myself up for school, take myself there, eat dinner with Barbara, cover my own rent by babysitting Leo; and I only just got to Germany last year.

He confides that he and Julia are on the rocks, and he's thinking of moving into his studio. He says I obviously can't discuss this with anyone or it could complicate a delicate process, but once he moves into his studio he might also have some money problems for a while, because if she won't let him work for the company anymore then he'll have no salary and he won't be able to take care of me.

The wreckage of my future whips itself quickly into a frenzy, like a storm wind, burning my cheeks. This is not my problem. He needs to figure that out. He is my father. I already rely so little on him, I don't think this is a legitimate enough reason to get rid of me. My ma and I didn't have any money, but she never sent me away.

"I kind of put the word out, to see if anyone knew of any good places, and my friend told me about what sounds like a really amazing school in England that—"

"*England?* You're sending *me* to England?"

My insides are at gale force now. If we were on a ship the sky would have gone black and he'd be shouting at me over the howl of my anger, squinting against giant raindrops of my disappointment pelting his face.

"Well, I'm not shipping you off. It actually sounds like a really cool place. It was founded by an Indian philosopher and there are no uniforms. I went to a school very much like it and it saved my life, besides being the best experience I ever had and my first taste of real freedom."

The ocean breathes, deciding whether to toss the ship, and he steadies himself on the rickety guardrail of my brief hesitation.

" . . . They don't have rules?"

This thought hooks itself around my hysteria's neck and drags it down slowly into the general murk of confusion about my future. Images of my dad in bell-bottoms, smoking weed in lush trees, laughing with his friends, overlay grainy, colorless images of what would surely be three more years of brutal clashes with the German school system. Pop's face looks so much like mine that the image starts to melt my resolve. I'm willing to test the waters.

We fly into Heathrow from Frankfurt and take a car from there.

You're in the country pretty quickly from the suburbs of London. I roll the car window down to look at the bright green fields that smell like cow shit and chimney smoke.

The driver hurtles along macadam tentacles laid out in the mud. Signs warn of ELDERLY PEOPLE CROSSING and FARM TRAFFIC, the latter with illustrations of tractors. We pass blustery men whose rotund bodies look more like gristle around their bones than soft flesh.

Everyone is dressed in shades of earth, grass, and wood. The people are oddly pink, their jackets green, their corduroys brown. It's Ichabod Crane's world. The trees carry spirits in them.

We drive down the wrong side of a narrow country road, flanked by high hedges and pastures filled with sheep, arriving at a mansionlike white house with deep green lawns stretching from it in all directions.

As soon as we step in the door we are enfolded in a rich, complex smell, of earth and coziness, of radiators and toast, black tea, oiled wood, and wool sweaters; it smells like a place where people take their shoes off to respect the carpets and speak in quiet tones to respect each other.

There is so much silence. Silence to allow for the silence of others that blankets all your movements in a kind of slow, deliberate feeling. I notice this as we move down a long, narrow corridor with a low ceiling to check in.

For my preliminary week, I'll be staying in a room with two other girls, a Brit and a Greek, at the tippy-top attic of the east wing of the main building.

When I was first brought up and introduced, they were polite but confused. They took the staff member out into the hall and asked her why a boy prospective was being housed in their room. I could hear through the thin door as she explained: "No, iO is a girl, she just looks like a boy." That was awkward, but once they adjusted they were super nice. I was nervous to be away from my pop, but the girls plopped right down on the floor and started asking me questions about my life.

Fuck if it isn't isolated here. Sheep field on sheep field on meadow on sheep field. At first it's cramped and scary, every new face is a threat, but the rooms kind of expand as you fill them with life. The whole place starts to slide into being an oasis—a place of calm and stability with a ton of smiling, sweet new playmates from all over the world.

There are fifty-three kids from twenty-six different countries, so everyone has a hybrid accent—their native speech mixed with a pseudo-British twang. Kids are scattered around, killing time. Phones are not allowed, and the only Internet is dial-up on four old PCs in the computer room in the basement. Everyone reads, plays the guitar, journals, hangs out with each other, goes for walks. Kids run and play soccer in the icy air, which makes me think they're insane.

The school kitchen is vegetarian, and twice a day meals are set out in vats. Everyone serves themselves on steel dishes and sits at long wooden tables in the bright dining room together to eat.

No one knows if I'm a boy or a girl. For the first few days I see kids staring and talking about me. But I sit with my roommates and Malia, a gregarious Syrian girl from Paris. Even if they're curious about what I am, everyone seems open and nice.

I'm trying to adjust to getting up for "Morning Meeting." I've never woken up at six forty-five in my life. Eighty people gather together and sit in absolute silence. You can hear every creaking shift of weight in the room. I don't really get the point, so I use the time to scan people's faces and imagine what their stories are.

At seven thirty the green ground is covered in a layer of silvery frost. Like the earth is an aging punk whose green hair is coming up salt and spirulina. The first morning the sky is streaked with blue and pink. It's so beautiful it stops people as they walk, but by the afternoon it's hazed over into a dense purplish gray.

Poppa only stays for half the week. The day before he goes, I see him in the common area and he beckons me to follow him. He leads me into his little room and points to a white plastic bag on his bed. It's a chocolate cake. I want to hug him, I'm so grateful. He tells me he made a friend he wants me to meet, an older student he caught smoking on the path out of here, a beautiful German girl he thinks I'll like.

That evening, I'm sitting on the steps in the main hallway when the door opens and a blond girl comes in wearing a white sweater. She's not tall, but she has a commanding walk.

She looks at me with huge brown eyes, not smiling, but not not smiling. It's weird. She reeks of misbehavior. She says her name is Nikita, that we were supposed to meet.

I pop off a few things in German slang I shouldn't know, in the ridiculous southern German accent that I've picked up, and she gives me a laugh in return. It's a short exchange, but it's troublemaker to troublemaker.

Nikita comes over that night. I tell her made-up stories in funny accents, and we giggle for hours. She ends up giving me a massage long after bedtime, even though being out of your own room that late is strictly forbidden.

WHEN MY WEEK IS UP, I have three pages of phone numbers and addresses, and people actually cry when I hug them good-bye. By the time I think of writing them letters, though, I've already been accepted into the school, and my plane tickets have been booked to go back.

My heart has swung the other way now, and I can't wait to go to boarding school.

Packing up my life in Karlsruhe is easy. All my clothes go back into my two duffel bags, plus I take the CD player, my music collection, my kicks, and my marble notebooks. Done. Good riddance to this place.

ON SEPTEMBER 6, 2000, wearing crispy gray cargo sweatpants (left leg rolled up because that's how the drug dealers do it), black Timberlands, a navy blue sweater, and a gray bandanna keeping my fresh cornrows tight to my head, I perch myself in my new bedroom window right over the main entrance, crank my boom box as loud as it will go, and blast Biggie into the dewy British country silence.

My roommate is a tiny English hippie with pearlescent skin, who doesn't care what bunk I take and doesn't mind my music. She sits down to apply glittery nail polish to her fingers and starts asking questions. Questions I realize I don't have the answers to. Questions that lead to my own questions. Questions like what the fuck happened? How did I go from my great New York jailbreak plan with my pop, to this? How the fuck did I end up here?

## Chapter 34

# Give Me Life

*Southern England, September and October 2000*

I HAVE NO IDEA WHERE TO SIT OR WHAT TO DO, BUT NIKITA appears across the serving tray at my first meal. She smiles a smirking half smile, asks me when I arrived, says it's nice to see me, and saunters off to the farthest-back table to sit with the older students. If I were older, maybe I'd read it as something else, but all I grasp is that she sees me. Her nineteen to my fifteen gives her a vocabulary I don't have yet.

The first few days I don't know what to do with all my free time. During the day we have activities, wash dishes together, meditate, weird shit like that. There's no tour or orientation at any point, you just kind of fall in step and figure it out by watching people.

Classes are somewhat optional. You have to take a certain number to keep the government happy, but the school approves of independent studies and long walks to "reflect" on your inner workings.

Nobody seems bothered by the cold here. Boys are on the soccer field panting white clouds in the nippy freeze while I'm bundled up in a hoodie and a scarf. Kids just saunter out onto the lawn and drape themselves onto the damp grass.

In the evening, students gather in the sitting room, playing songs, chitchatting, learning games. I'm disappointed to find that Nikita is never there. She's holed up in her garden room, depressed because she misses her boyfriend who graduated last year.

I want her to come out. I want to play with her. I wish she were there. There's an emotional current already running under my skin, and close quarters turns up the voltage. Eventually it gives me the juice to go knock on her door.

"Yeah!" she calls out after a few knocks. I open the door timidly and offer a sheepish smile. She's in her bathroom, pinning her hair up. She smiles at me in that way of hers, so easy to misread.

We start to hang out a lot. I'll drop by, and she'll come back to have tea with me. Every time I make her laugh it's a victory. Something swells in me when we end up on the big blue canvas couches in the sitting room, probing each other about our lives. My jokes put her in stitches. But then she says, "Okayyy," with a little sigh, stretching, "it's time to go," and she retreats back to her room off the garden.

When she doesn't appear at meals, I bring her food. She pretends not to want it, but when I come back for the plates she's nibbled at it.

The whole school gathers once a week in the atrium to share feelings and thoughts about the place. Nikita is always late, and she always leaves early. As soon as she's gone a part of me leaves with her.

Something is building. We hang out every minute we're not in classes. In the evenings I make her laugh so much we both feel nervous, and we tell each other as much. We start to tickle and wrestle with each other to blow some of the steam off. At first it's gentle, but it gets rougher and rougher. Soon we're teasing and pinching and head-locking each other until we're both red in the face and her barrettes have come out.

Her smile has changed now. There's something animal in her eyes. Boys sit with acoustic guitars on the chairs behind us and pluck out old Beatles songs while we tumble all over the place, crashing into the furniture.

A few times I fake an accident to get her to slow down and be tender with me. Once, I say I think she's broken my finger, and we get Jacques, the school nurse, to take us into town to have it x-rayed. The concern she shows is so genuine. In the car, she puts her hand on my head and when her fingers drift to my neck something electric happens and I jerk away. She looks at me with urgency. She feels it, too.

My finger is fine, of course, but my old trick pays off. That I might have been injured, that I needed her, has released something in her now and she can't hide it, even from herself.

That night, after bedtime, when everyone is in their respective rooms, there's a soft knock on my door. Nikita has snuck across the entire school, at risk of a serious reprimanding, to see me.

"Do you mind that I'm here?"

She says this in her low, throaty voice, her eyes wise pools of amber. I see their depth for the first time.

My roommate is an enthusiast, and is excited by Nikita's appearance. It's actually a kind of honor to have a fourth year in the room.

Nikita simply asks which bed is mine and then climbs in. She looks at me as if to say, "Aren't you getting in?" This makes me giddy, almost dizzy, but I climb in beside her. She drapes an arm over me and asks me to tell her a story. I lie there grinning, high on the transgression and excitement.

Examining the bottom of my roommate's bunk above me, I make up a story about a baby elephant and a cloud that weaves itself into a braid and drops down from the sky so the elephant can climb up and hop from cloud to cloud and explore the world. He travels the globe and makes all kinds of new friends, the descriptions of which each come with a new accent, which makes Nikita giggle.

She asks me where the talent comes from, and I tell her that I've been acting since I was two. She wants to know more. That eventually leads to Ma and my life in New York. I keep talking until our eyes close.

When I wake up in the morning, Nikita is gone, but her ring, a naked silver woman, is on my bedside table. At morning meeting she enters from the garden side, as usual, and no one is the wiser. We smirk at each other.

Afterward, I fold the ring up into a note with a bad drawing of an elephant and tack it to the board with her name on it. The day goes by and I don't see her much, but later there's a note with my name on it.

*I miss you.*
—*N.*

I don't know what to do. I don't want to leave her hanging, I don't want her to have to miss me, and the feeling of being missed is intoxicating stuff, but I absolutely do not want her to stop missing me, so I put up a note that says:

*So come find me.*
—*Eye-oh*

Malia, my rambunctious Syrian friend, can see that we want to hang out and gives us her room for the night. She says she can sleep at a friend's.

We stay up till dawn, me whispering stories about my life in New York. At one point I look over and she's crying.

"Are you okay?"

"It's just . . . so heavy. I'm so sorry you had to live through that."

Confusion persists.

"What do you mean?"

The wooden bed frame creaks as I roll over to face her, growing bold and wiping a tear from her cheek.

"I just have never met someone who has dealt with so much and is so . . . normal."

I'm normal?

She lifts her soft hand up, cupping my cheek, and, ever so softly, leans in and kisses me.

It's warm, the softest thing I've ever felt, and absolutely terrifying. What do I do? How do I kiss back? I've never been kissed before.

She pulls back and looks at me, checking if I'm okay. I am far too nervous to make eye contact, but I smile shyly.

"Why are you getting so shy?"

"I don't know."

I'm starting to blush. So is she. I can see confusion in her face. I think she has surprised herself, but at least she's kissed before. In spite of her hesitation she looks at me and says, "Can I do that once more?"

"Yup."

It happens again, this magical envelopment of my lips in the pud-dinglike pillows attached to her angelic face. Her hand is so soft on my cheek, gently guiding, then pulling me in to her. Something loosens in me, like an electrical wire burst from its bundle.

She pulls back and looks at me for a second and whispers, "iO . . . I think I know why we cannot leave each other to go to class."

"Why, Nikita?"

"Because we are in love."

All the air in me goes. It doesn't even whoosh, it's just gone. My eyebrows sail up. Can she be serious? I only just switched back to being a girl again, and now this?

"Wow."

"What do you feel about that?"

"Well, yeah, I mean . . . um . . . well, Nikita, I'm not gay."

"I know. Neither am I. But you feel that thing, right?"

It takes me a minute, eventually nodding my head. I touch her torso, by her solar plexus.

"In here, right?"

She bursts into a wide, glittery-eyed smile.

"Yes. Right there."

I'm quiet for a long time. All I can do is breathe, and it's even a challenge to keep that going. If I stop concentrating it will certainly stop.

So many thoughts are happening, but also none at all. It feels like my universe is realigning itself around this person. This person who has ceased to be a human and instead has dissolved her edges out and bled into a ball of energy, magnetic, electric, on fire, blurry, and yet totally in focus.

Time has changed. I have a vague awareness of the sunlight crawling across the carpet, but I feel no fatigue. I feel like I could play a basketball game . . . as long as she's watching. And the thought comes over me that I would do anything as long as she is watching. I would go anywhere with her. In fact, I don't want to go anywhere without her.

I realize that I'm not in control of any of this. She's simply pointing out something that already is, not something that could be. No matter what I say right now, it won't change the fact that it already is.

No fear comes from her, just this calm. She doesn't pull her eyes away like I do, she looks straight inside of me, with her unreadable smile, the way she always does, waiting for me to answer.

I'm afraid. I'm afraid of being gay with her. Of everyone knowing I'm a girl and then knowing that I've got this thing with her.

But why would they have to know?

Because we are in this tiny school, in the middle of sheep fields, in the middle of nowhere in England, and everybody knows everybody else's everything. Plus, this is *big*. What is happening here, this cartoonish explosion in our chests—this thing that grows arms that tickle the inside of my body each time we hug, like some alien was split in half and we each swallowed one side and every time it senses the other it becomes electrified—that thing is big, and I don't know if I can keep it hidden.

But I'm an actor . . .

They'll judge us, surely. They'll think we're weird. No, we can't tell anyone. They'll shun us. It was already such a huge hurdle getting people to understand why I'm in the girls' dorms, looking and dressing like a boy; now they'll think I'm a pariah. It's different for Nikita because she's got her own room in the garden where she's isolated, but I'm up in the thick of it with all these girls. They can't know, they'll think I'm a pervert.

Then she touches me and my brain shuts up.

She laces her fingers into mine and it's all I can do to stay on earth. She pulls our hands up and puts them between our chests, right between the alien halves, and I realize the creature is writhing to get at itself.

She scoots closer to me and hooks her finger under my chin, pulling my face and my eyes up to meet hers. I say, "I don't know what to do . . ."

"You don't have to do anything if you don't want to . . ."

"But I do."

There is no world in this galaxy in which I'd have the balls to kiss her again, but I've decided that I really want her to do it.

"You do?"

In the tiniest voice in which I've probably ever said anything, I tell her I want her to kiss me again.

When she leans in, she pauses, barely a centimeter from my face. I can smell her nice moisturizer and the breath coming out of her nose. My own is suddenly a deep exhale. I've never wanted anything so badly. It's like I'm hungry for her mouth, but I can't move. I let her hover there, hesitating, in her own mental circus of second thoughts, probably; I'm unable to because I haven't got the first clue how to do this without being a total creep. But the longer she stays there, the crazier it makes me, the more I want to bite her face off in the sweetest way possible.

I look up and see that she's staring at my mouth and her breathing is labored. This makes my head tingle and I start to feel crazy.

Finally, finally, finally, finally she puts her lips on mine, and the whole world stops.

I have been hurled into something, the entirety of my being reduced to the trembling of a leaf. I am no longer my own master. An unknown rider has taken the reins. I am suddenly aware of a madness that took hold of me weeks ago.

I love her. Profoundly.

When our tongues touch, we begin to speak a new language, one spoken by no one else on the planet but us two. The air is suddenly thick, like we are breathing honey. It's so hard to breathe like this, dangerous and sweet, but I'd rather drown than take my mouth away.

Her hand wraps around the back of my neck and she pulls me toward her, our tongues twirling around each other, and my whole body is enflamed.

I have absolutely no fucking clue what I'm doing, and my worst nightmare would be to get this far and turn out to be a bad kisser.

Tock, tock, tock.

Three soft knocks and the door creaks open. In pokes Malia's majestic head of curls, cringing at the sound of the old hinges, scared of waking our floor person who lives on the other side of the wall.

I'm frozen, face burning, a puddle in my underwear. I'm so embarrassed and so excited. I try to act natural, but all I can do is grin. Malia looks at me and cracks up laughing, but Nikita rolls over to face her and says, with nonchalant but commanding authority, "What, Malia? We were just talking."

I chime in, "Literally all night long, dude. It's nuts. We haven't slept."

Malia shrugs and says, "Nikita, you better go. It's almost seven. You've got to get out of the wing before everybody wakes up."

Nikita turns and looks at me over her shoulder. She smiles a calm smile, and under Malia's beautiful Syrian quilt she squeezes my hand. I smile back, trying desperately to play it cool like she is, and she gets up and goes, patting Malia's hair and kissing her on the forehead on the way out.

## Chapter 35

# The First Time

*Southern England, October and November 2000*

THE SCHOOL BECOMES A MAZE OF HIDING SPOTS. TRAILS that were just for jogs become a snarl of secret paths to secret bushes, logs turned to benches, leaves turned to blankets. But for every hiding spot, there's a curious human out for a stroll, eager to bust you.

This tango teems with excitement. We greet it with the nimble feet of teenagers in love, lightning in our heels and blaze in our hearts, for each moment we can sneak is a universe of new feelings.

I start to lose track of how much I've learned. Like an astronaut catapulting through galaxies, unable to soak in the details of each passing planet, I can gather only that this thing is infinitely bigger than me. I open my arms to it and fall chest forward, smile on my face, thrilled that I have been chosen by whatever gods of love have bestowed this blessing on me.

I have no need for sleep, I have been awake for a week straight, and I show no signs of slowing. Every minute of the day is spent thinking of her: if I'm stuck in a classroom, I'm daydreaming of her lips, doodling poems for her; if I'm free, I'm running to her. If she's busy, I make her something.

There's a long weekend and all the British kids go home. On the last night, six of the remainder gather in Nikita's room and we play spin the bottle, truth or dare, and strip poker. Anya, a girl from New York, ends up in nothing but her underwear, holding her cards in her mouth for modesty's sake. Thomas, a French boy, apparently wants to kiss me. I'm willing to do it, in the interest of a cover, but when he probes my mouth with his tongue, I can't help but recoil. It makes me want to kiss Nikita so much I can't speak.

Nikita and I are dared to kiss three times, and the boys jeer at us to "snog," so we try to do it without letting on that our brains are fusing. I wonder if they can feel my body temperature shoot through the roof when I pull back from her, but no one seems to suspect anything.

Finally, after three hours, everyone leaves. I tell them I'll be right there, and stay behind. Nikita and I sit on the bed and stare at each other for what feels like an hour, smiling, never breaking eye contact, feeling the surges of something foreign in our bellies.

My tongue becomes hypersensitive. Every time I run it over my lips, my breathing gets heavier. It's like I want to eat her. I want her to be inside of my skin; nothing less than that could bring us closer.

I can smell everything, and I am acutely aware of my palms. It's as if I have heat vision. She is the only thing my senses can detect, just her outline. I feel a pull, from my center outward.

Slowly she crawls across the bed and kisses me. A bullet fired in a pool, a slow surge, spiraling in.

Her hand wraps around the back of my head and I start to feel myself invert, my insides fold out, my edges defined by her touch.

Breathing so deeply makes me feel like I am a body electric, my skin a blanket of nerve endings firing all at once.

When our tongues meet, I groan involuntarily. The feeling overwhelms my body, my stomach drops out, and my hands reach for her, pulling her toward me by the small of her back.

Frustrated by the boundaries of our shapes, she grinds down into me so hard our hipbones bruise each other. A bruise never felt so good.

I have to bite my own lip to contain my heat.

Our faces press into each other, taking in smells, desperate to inhale each other. When her fingers interlace with mine, I feel like my head might burst. I can only stare at her.

She looks back into my eyes as her mouth moves down my stomach. Slowly she pulls my sweats down. I am so scared I stop moving altogether. I don't want to do anything wrong. Gently, she puts her hand on me, and I realize there's been a flood. Her fingers inch their way down me and I stop being able to breathe. Then she puts her tongue inside me. My eyes roll back in my head and my brain explodes.

Time melts away as my fingertips become supernaturally sensitive and my mind bends into and out of itself, as I learn what it is to become one with another person, riding her wave with the entirety of myself.

If she never stops, my happiness would never stop. If I die right now, I have lived enough.

## Chapter 36

# Feral

*Southern England, November 2000*

I FEEL CONFUSED. WANDERING. I FEEL PROTECTED. THIS part is disorienting.

Nikita's beautiful hand rests over mine, gliding a razor up my calf. We're in the bathtub in the east wing. She plugged her speakers and CD player into the blow dryer outlet and they're sitting on the closed toilet, Erykah Badu singing softly to us. A candle burning on the sink is the only light in the room. The mirror is fogged with steam.

I have never shaved my legs before and the hairs are fine and dark brown, about a quarter inch long. Piled in the sink are a bag of cotton swabs, some hair bands, bottles of Weleda face wash and moisturizer, a pair of tweezers, a set of nail clippers, and a stick of deodorant. Self-care school.

I watch Nikita's strong forearm in the flickering light, resting on top of mine as she guides my hand. My toes, bearing freshly clipped nails, are pressed against the tiled wall. That happened right after Nikita taught me how to put my hair in a ponytail for the first time.

This all started with a shirt. Nikita asked to borrow something to wear after we fucked straight through sports class, but when I gave her a T-shirt she smelled the pits and made a foul face.

"Okay, iO. What's going on with you and deodorant?"

Embarrassed, I shriveled up into the blanket.

"What kind are you using??"

" . . . I don't."

"What?!"

"I thought you were supposed to use a pumice stone, but it doesn't work. So . . . I just don't use anything."

"A pumice stone?"

I was so confused and embarrassed I wanted to cry. I felt ashamed of myself, and there is nothing worse than feeling ashamed about your hygiene.

She looked at me with thoughts behind her eyes before asking me slowly, "Have you shaved your legs before?"

I wanted to die. I couldn't even look at her. Staring at the blanket, I shook my head. She took my chin in her hand.

"Hey . . . baby . . . it's okay. Do you want me to show you how?"

Shame spilled through my body. She put her arms around me and kissed my face.

The appropriate words were unavailable to me to explain my sense of inadequacy, my alienation, my desperation to feel like a real girl, like I belong. The language didn't come to describe the fear and loneliness that came from realizing my ma isn't good for any practical lessons, from the realization, as I moved further out into the real world, that she is kind of crazy. That I'm on my own. I can't go to her for advice, for structure, for rules, for tips on how to be alive and functional.

I'm unaccustomed to feeling things like that. I bury such feelings under projects and arguments and weed. The feelings overcame me and I wept into Nikita's shoulder. She wrapped her arms around me only tighter, gently telling me it was okay, I was going to be okay, she would help me be okay.

## Chapter 37

— —

# Out

*Southern England, December 2000*

PHONES DON'T RING THE SAME WAY IN GERMANY. IT'S LIKE a drawn-out beep. It's more clinical, more official, more daunting. I'm nervous as the third beep drags.

I don't usually call my pop, so he picks up a bit confused.

"Hello?"

"Poppa, it's me."

"Hey, squirt! How are you?"

"Good! How are you?"

"Great! Getting ready for the premiere of the new piece. Working insane days, into nights, into more days."

"Yeah? Is it looking good?"

I'm stalling.

"Yeah! I think so . . . We'll see. You never know."

"Oh, Pop, I'm sure it's gonna be beautiful, as usual."

"Ha. I hope so, kiddo. What's going on with you?"

"Well . . . I wanted to tell you something."

"Yeah?"

"Well . . ."

I think of that moment on the street, on our bikes, and how he re-acted when I told him I wanted to be a girl again. How could this really be more shocking than that, right? My belly is a little tight, but Nikita puts her hand on my thigh and it softens.

"You know that girl you wanted me to meet when you were here? The German girl?"

"Nikita. Yeah?"

"Well . . . she's my girlfriend now."

"Ha . . . no shit!? Wow. She's gorgeous, I. Lucky you!"

"Dad!"

He laughs from his gut, as if he's relieved that that's what my news was. I'm smiling in the phone booth. I give Nikita a thumbs-up.

"No, really, I, that's wonderful news. Are you happy?"

"Yeah . . . I'm in love, Dad."

"Yeah? *Wow*. That's powerful stuff. Does she feel the same way?"

I glance at the beauty watching me from the corner and smile.

"Yeah. I don't really know how that happened, but she does."

"Psh. You're a catch. That's how."

My tension has released. I feel so relieved to have just gotten this over with and been forthcoming. Now I have an ally in the most insane experience of my life.

When we hang up, I dial my ma's number. I am sure she will be just as easy.

"Hello?"

"Ma."

"My bud!"

"Heyyyy, Ma. How are you?"

"Ah. You know . . . How are you?"

"I'm good. I, uhm, I want to tell you something."

"Oh god, you're pregnant."

"No, Ma! Jesus."

"I've been waiting for you to get knocked up since you were thir-teen!"

"What the fuck, Ma?!"

"You're built for it."

"Wow. Well . . . no, it's kinda the opposite news, actually."

"Oh?"

"Well, I, uhm . . . I fell in love with a girl, Ma."

There's a thick silence between our continents.

"Ma?"

"Yeah."

"Well . . . ? Can you say something?"

"I . . . uh . . . well . . . Are you a dyke now?"

"No! I'm just in love with a person, Ma."

"Uh-huh . . ."

"Ma, for chrissake . . ."

I am blindsided by her coldness. Coming off the high of my pop's warmth, I thought that for sure she would match his enthusiasm.

"Ma, what's your problem?"

"I just . . . I really wanted grandkids . . ."

"You're still gonna have grandkids, Ma! Of course I'm gonna have kids! You can still have kids with two women, for God's sake."

"Oh . . . well, then, it's fine."

I start laughing just to let the tension out. This is so ridiculous.

"You sure?"

"Yeah! As long as I get grandbabies."

"Jesus, Ma, you sound like a yuppie."

"I know. Hey, I'm happy for you. I gotta go. I love you, my bud. Sooner."

"Sooner, Ma."

## Chapter 38

# Too Soon

*New York City and southern Germany, Summer 2001*

L OVE FRIED MY BRAIN. ITS HAZY OPTIMISM MADE ME THINK it would be a romantic move to take Nikita to stay at my ma's house for the summer. She'd never been to New York, and I figured maybe I could brave the madhouse if she was my buffer. It would be a nice graduation present for her. Fuck was I wrong.

Ma is thrilled about the idea on the phone. She tells me about the weed plants she's been growing on the fire escape for her new business venture as a drug dealer. Our first night there she pulls out an Altoids box with four nugs in it and tells us that growing weed was too much work, so we should smoke the remnants of her abandoned career.

She carves out enough floor space in my old bedroom to put down a futon for us. It pulls at my heart to realize that she's washed the sheets, for probably the first time since I left three years ago, and put a candle down to make us feel welcome.

We are jet-lagged, so we pass out early, and wake up to her talking to herself in the darkness. I get up and go into the kitchen to see what's going on.

Ma's eyes are red and glazed over. She is smiling, but there is a wickedness to her face that wasn't there earlier. Her words are slurring together and her pants are unbuttoned. She stumbles around the house, limping brutally, talking about shooting yuppies and fluorescent lights descending like a toxic umbrella over the whole city.

Bending from the waist, she leans over and cranks her radio up, blasting Chopin through the house. I ask her to turn it down in various tones, but it's as if she can't hear me. She just keeps rambling, her lips pursed forward, eyebrows arched in disdain, lurching around, shedding her clothes.

I plead with her, telling her we are exhausted, at the very least for Nikita's sake, but Ma just lopes into the bathroom and plops down on the toilet, her run-on sentence unbroken.

Standing there in my underwear and T-shirt, ears burning with upset, I remember what it's like to feel invisible. I remember what it's like to feel lost, alone with a shell of your mother. I slam the door to the bedroom, crawl under the covers, and bite my fist, unsuccessfully trying not to sob.

Nikita is afraid of the way I change as the days go on. She says I am retreating into myself, that I am hardening, that she doesn't know this person, that I can be mean and cutting. I apologize, pretending I don't know what she's talking about.

The third night, the buzzer rings at three A.M. Ma doesn't get it, so it rings a second time, and a third. By the fourth ring I jump up and storm to the front door.

"What the fuck! Who is it?"

"It's Gus! Let me in, baby!"

"Ma! It's your fucking boyfriend. What do you want me to do?"

Like a dispatch from the grave, she grumbles, "Let him in, of course!"

I buzz him in, prop the door open, and go back to my room and try to sleep.

Five minutes later, crashing noises announce fuckhead's arrival. I clench my jaw, trying not to feel anything and failing. He groans loudly, whimpering in pain, as if trying to get my ma up out of bed to come check on him. At full volume he yells, "Baby! I hurt myself. Come here, baby. Come help me."

My ma doesn't respond, but he keeps going.

"My love, come and help your man. I'm hurting here! I fell into the door. Come on, woman, come help your fucking man!"

That's more than I can handle. I feel skeeved out just hearing him call her baby. I get up and go out into the foyer.

"Get the fuck up off the floor and keep your fucking voice down. People are sleeping in this house."

"Oh, shit. It's you. The bad seed returned."

"Listen to me, motherfucker, this is my house. Don't call me names. I'll fucking kill you."

"Oh, you'll kill me, huh?"

"Get the fuck outta my house."

"Rhonna! Baby! Your daughter is threatening me!"

"You fucking pussy."

I grab him by the back of his jacket and drag him toward the door. I'm considerably smaller than him, and my bare feet and legs are exposed, but I feel no fear. Adrenaline surges through me, rage surfing its volatile crest. I throw open the apartment door and push him out with my foot. He's too drunk to resist.

"You're a fucking bitch! A fucked-up bitch!"

"Get the fuck out of my house, you pathetic piece of shit."

"Rhonna!"

"Shut the fuck up!"

I slam the door and stomp back toward my room. My ma scares the life out of me, standing at the door to her room, stark naked, glaring at me. She hisses, "You threw my man out?"

"He was wasted and screaming, Ma. He's an asshole."

"This is *my house*!"

"He has no respect for you, Ma!"

She lopes toward the apartment door, berating me for being such a mean bitch, throwing it open and calling his name. He is gone. She starts to cry.

"And? What if he never comes back now? What now? Because of *you*! You're gonna take your little girlfriend and go back to fancy-ass Europe with your fancy-ass *father* and leave me here again, with no boyfriend now, because you fuck everything up for me."

My feet feel like lead. Betrayal surges through me like a snake with a razor spine. I feel crushed by her words.

Only when I hear Nikita's voice do I snap out of this. I turn and go into our room, slamming the door as hard as I can. With every ounce of my body, I scream at the door, "FUCK YOOOOOU!"

I collapse into the bed, weeping uncontrollably. Nikita is stunned by the scene. She detests my rage so much she almost can't console me, but the crying is too painful for her and she takes me into her arms. We make a pact to leave as soon as we can.

We go back to her parents' house in Germany, where I stare at the boxes of all her things, her whole room, packed up on her floor, labeled and stored away, to be divvied up into her new life, wherever that will happen. She is done with our school.

We start to talk about what is to come. The directors are threatening to kick me out for having an illegal sexual relationship, and generally being mouthy and averse to authority, but after an extensive round of begging and pleading, they have decided I can come back. I am going back to Highland and Nikita is staying home for the foreseeable future. The idea of losing her makes me feel nauseous, but I'm yearning to experience other things. A part of me thinks I wouldn't make it through the entire year without kissing anyone, and I never want to lie to her, so, in a grab at maturity we aren't ready for, we decide to try and have an open relationship until we can be in the same place again.

The impending separation weighs heavily on me, and days are overcome with tears, big discussions in the forest. Sticky days are spent staring out from her balcony, worrying that I am fucking up the one good thing I've ever had. But I don't want to lie. She says she understands, that I am gonna be sixteen and I need to experience as much as I can.

I tell her my love for her is the most significant thing I've ever experienced. That she taught me how to feel like I am a part of the world, which is an indescribable gift. I tell her that she is my family, no matter what.

She sits on her bed and gives me a tiny white box. Inside is a replica of the ring she wears perpetually, a naked woman's body wrapped around her finger. The gesture makes me cry. I swear I will wear the ring every day until my finger falls off. She laughs and says she hopes that never happens, my fingers are way too precious. We kiss, and she shows me exactly why my fingers are treasures to her.

When the time comes to leave, I feel like I am leaving my soul mate, my other half, my puzzle piece. I know I will be back with her soon, but the act of leaving is awful. We hold each other on the train platform in the hazy dusk light for a long time, crying and kissing, promising each other forever.

As the train pulls away, I watch her sweet blond head shrink into the distance. I can see the embers of her cigarette long after I can see her, and I cry, burying my face in her scarf, smelling her hair. I sigh, long and hard, from a deeply tired place within myself, and turn over in my bunk, knowing I am returning to where I came from before all this magic overtook me. That place where I am alone with it all.

## Chapter 39

# The Second Round

*Southern England, fall 2001*

YEAR TWO OF BOARDING SCHOOL IS A GRIND. I PUT MY head down, headphones on, and try to learn to navigate this place alone.

The first week back I fall into bed with a British waif named Alexandra, one of the cool fashion clique who never seemed to know I existed before. She's striking, though shy. Olive skinned, tall, draped in bright fabrics and things she sewed herself, she has a quiet, intelligent presence. She carries pain in the hunch of her bony shoulders.

I compartmentalize my affections. I have a new sensation of being desirable to others, but my love is off limits. I belong to Nikita, and we speak every few days. She's heartbroken and lethargic at her parents' house in rural Bavaria, and she wants me to talk to her more. This makes me feel suffocated.

I can see beyond myself for the first time. I notice that everyone has perfectly clear skin from drinking nothing but water and tea.

If you sleep through dinner here you might starve, but that's all I want to do. The cold makes me want to snuggle, a pillow or a girl. Maybe it's the poor nutrition, or the damp, but people have started to piss me off. I'm better at managing my anger by now, but not perfect. Sometimes I punch walls, and that gets me a talking-to from the higher-ups.

Without real rules I have nothing to bounce back against. The foundation of my character is the dance of continually regaining my balance from slamming into rules. Here, you sign agreements, you commit to acting a certain respectful way, and you know that everyone here has done the same. When you break the agreements you're not a rebel getting one over on the system, you're just an asshole.

I get along well with the students, but the staff are wary of my volatility. I switch my tactic to charm, but these people seem to want to erase the impact of personality. Too bad that's the only currency I've ever been taught to value.

It's hard for me to sleep. I hate being confined to my room. Once the doors have all been closed and silence has been called, I grow despondent in my cell. The endless silences, meditations, and whispers in this place are smothering me. I can't even hear myself. I have nightmares where everything shrinks to ungraspable size or swells beyond measure, where I lose all ability to control anything. I wake up sweating and gasping, filled with baseless terror that won't subside for hours.

I am so very trapped here. The nearest town is a forty-five-minute walk, and it's a pub and a gas station at a single stoplight. More people live in my building in New York than attend and staff this entire school, so sometimes I have to sneak out and go for a walk.

When the conversation turns to what I'll be doing for the winter break I get quiet and embarrassed. That is very much not my way, but I know everyone else is traveling to exotic places with their loving families.

By this point, my poppa lives in his studio. He left Julia the summer I went to school and fell in love with a German girl less than half his age, a friend of Barbara's named Nina. He's made it clear that having me live there, the three of us in a single room where he actually has no right to live at all, would never do. He's says my "odd aggression," my "desire to blow it all up" and get him to live with me alone somewhere else, in our own apartment, has no basis in reality, even if I can't believe that. What would we live on? he asks me. He says he is on fragile ground, that he is determined to change his life, to remake it entirely, to save himself from something terrible, but I have no idea from what. And what could take precedence over his own kid? How he could he possibly expose me again to all that I escaped from?

I've worn out my welcome with Barbara, and my mom's is a disaster, so yeah, I don't really know what to say when these kids complain about having to visit Mom in France and then fly all the way to the Maldives for the second month of break. I go home to New York and sleep on my aunt Olivia's floor.

By spring break the staff are warning me that they're considering not inviting me back to school again, and send me "home" to contemplate the situation.

I turn up in Karlsruhe a self-righteous mess. Barbara is out of town, so I get to stay in my old attic room. Poppa stays in bed in his studio the whole week I'm there. He says he's sick, but I don't understand why. He doesn't have a cold or anything visibly wrong with him. He says it's on the inside. I ask him if it's got anything to do with his weed smoking.

Every inch of his studio is covered in charcoal and pastel drawings, about ten of them taller than me, all in different stages of completion, hallucinations of saints engaged in unsaintly activities, botanical or geometric shapes, trees, clouds, hands, feet, drapery, and flowers, like medieval dreams or maybe nightmares. The floor is covered with the inspirations for these drawings: pictures ripped from books, photos of friends, dancers, explosions, landscapes, and body parts.

I'm standing next to the plywood sleeping platform he has built, a kind of Elizabethan affair with a huge bed high off the ground encircled by black velvet curtains that keep what little warmth his oil heater generates inside the makeshift room.

He's scrawny in a T-shirt, wrapped in a black duvet. He looks at me with a new clarity in his eyes. He says, "iO . . . it's not weed."

"What do you mean?"

"It's not weed I've been smoking all this time . . . as a matter of fact I never smoke weed. I hate it. Makes me psycho."

I don't know how I know, I've never met this devil before, but something in me just does.

"It's heroin."

He looks ashamed. He asks me if I knew the whole time. Miraculously, I had no clue. I never guessed. I've never seen somebody on heroin before, as far as I know, and I never could have imagined that my dad was a junkie. That's why he was so up and down, why he'd pass out so hard, why he'd never remember our plans in the morning.

"Holy shit. For how long, Pop?"

"Umm . . . since just before Elio was born."

"Since I was four?!"

"Yup. Since you were four. The fight of my life. A lot of people I knew and who knew you are no longer with us. I, on the other hand, intend to make it. And I am going to make it."

This leaves me reeling. My head feels light and heavy at the same time. I feel angry, I feel sad, I feel confused. I think of every junkie I've seen throughout my life, collapsed on stairwells, needles in their arms, mumbling bullshit gibberish, passed out standing up on my block. Poppa has never been like that, but isn't that what junkies are?

I feel bad that he's sick. I want to know what it means. I just feel so . . . fucking . . . alone. Fuck you, dude. Fuck. You. Way to show up for your fucking kid, man. Great job. Go fuck yourself. But are you gonna be okay?

I GO BACK TO SCHOOL like a lit flare. I climb the biggest tree on the property and pretend to fall seventeen feet out of it to the ground. I wander inside and act confused. I make my eyeballs shake back and forth, and I pretend to have amnesia.

Jacques, the school nurse, is fatigued by my shenanigans, but he can't afford not to take me seriously, no matter how implausible. He drives me to the hospital in town and lets my New Yorker friend Anya come along to keep me company. I am burrowed into the act so deeply I almost believe it myself.

I feel pathetic and childish for regressing like this, but also dark and sad. I want someone to care. I want people to worry about me. I feel dangerous, like I might harm myself, but I care too much about how that would hurt my ma, so I'm trying to warn people by acting out.

They keep me overnight, in a hospital bed, on watch. Anya is down when she leaves, and her worry makes me feel a little bit better. Jacques is over it. He sees through me.

I spend three days in bed, shaking my eyeballs back and forth whenever someone comes into my room, pretending that my memory is returning slowly. I get offended when people suggest I'm faking it, but the whispers build.

When I "recover," Anya and I take to smoking joints in the sheep fields. We got a brick of hash from a kid on a yellow bicycle in Southampton, the nearest big city, which is an hour away by bus, and roll joints so strong we get jelly knees. They'd kick us out on the spot if they caught us doing drugs, which terrifies me. I become consumed with paranoia about it, because, despite my disdain for so many things here, this has become the only home I've got. My room is a sanctuary, a bed I can rely on.

Somewhere during the course of this I decide that it's time for me to lose my virginity in the technical sense. Nikita has certainly demolished whatever barrier there was between me and proverbial adulthood, but I want to know what a boy feels like.

This, of course, is completely forbidden, which means it will involve a fair bit of planning. The process of choosing which boy it will be is a bit like selecting which cow you will slaughter—which one has the most meat on it, and which one is most likely to be led away peacefully.

Rumor has it that the size of the boy's endowment is crucial to the girl's enjoyment of the act. I do a little snooping and find that there's a boy from California who is supposed to be qualified; he's also built like a rugby player and doesn't offer much in the way of intellect. Perfect. The hurdle is that a friend of mine has a crush on him. I tell myself that because I merely want to have a strictly one-time, almost technical exchange with him, it shouldn't cross any boundaries.

One night, a bunch of us sneak away to the tree house and play spin the bottle. The boy is there. Truthfully, I haven't the faintest idea how to flirt with men, but I do my best to let him know that the tide of something within me has shifted in his favor. I do this by sitting close to him and selecting him to kiss during truth or dare. At one point, after what I think is a particularly successful make-out, I sit between his legs, leaning my weight back against his broad chest.

At the end of the night, when everyone is making their way back to the main house in the glistening, frosty moonlight, I pull him by the hand. We fall behind enough that by the time I pull him off through a field to the left, they're all so far ahead that no one notices.

I practically drag the boy to a dilapidated shed in the center of a distant field. In all my romantic wisdom, I think that this abandoned hut, dubbed "the shag shed" by the older kids, would be the perfect place for him to deflower me. Surrounded by discarded boards and dead leaves, under a collapsed roof, is a broken red velvet couch.

To his credit, the boy is willing, enthusiastic even. We make an awkward pair. I lie down and shimmy my jeans off, looking at him expectantly in the darkness. He pulls his pants to his knees and gets on top of me.

Behind his formidable head, I can see stars in the English night sky.

He asks if I have a condom, but I tell him as long as he doesn't have any diseases, it doesn't matter. He laughs nervously and tries to kiss me. This amounts to him stabbing my mouth with his tongue, so I position my face away from his, guiding his hips to get the act done.

In the half-light, I can see that his dick is massive and thick. I'm scared as he brings it toward my body and tries a half dozen times to get it inside me. When he finally does, it feels like I've sat on a lamppost.

I try to find something to like about the experience, but my body is in full revolt. I don't want this person inside me. I want the softness of a girl. I want my girl. I want Nikita. My thoughts drift to my friend who has a crush on this boy and guilt overtakes me. I feel sick.

Abruptly, I push him away, yank up my jeans, and take off running for the main house. It's nearly three in the morning, so I sprint as quietly as I can up the stairs and into my room. I feel filthy, like my entire body is covered in bugs. I don't want to get in my bed like this, I have to wash it off.

I go to the private bathroom and run the shower as hot as I can stand it. I sit in the tub and cry, scrubbing myself until my skin is raw. I feel violated, like I invited a stranger to invade my body. I did.

Why did I do that? What am I trying to prove?

When I'm done, I go down and crawl into Anya's bed, whimpering, and wrap myself around her warm body.

Word seems to spread through the school quickly, and that whole group of girls, including the friend who had a crush, drops me like so much rancid cheese. I'm dead to them.

ASIDE FROM THE WEED and the social rejection I start doing super well, but then a beautiful black boy comes for a prospective week. He's tall and graceful, gentle and soft spoken. He's read the books the school is built around, and he believes in the philosophies. He is an asset to a soccer team, and he dances at the talent show.

Once he's gone the school tells us that they've decided not to allow him to attend. They "would have to ask him to cut off his dreadlocks because visitors might interpret them as a religious statement," and they don't want to ask him to do that. This enrages me, and I lead a charge taking the directorship to the mat about it. I have no problem calling it what it is outright: racism and hypocrisy. They don't respond well to that.

I want to stay here, but I'm disillusioned with the bullshit hippie diatribe. Spare me. I'm the only kid who's had a lover of the same gender who's open about it, and there's no one darker than Indian, which seems sanctioned only because they have some kind of spiritual hall pass.

At the next school assembly I propose, with lengthy justifying leadup, that we abolish the fourteen agreements that make up the structural backbone of the school and start over. I suggest that since we'd been adding on to the agreements as needed over the years, we should be able to hit the reset button now that they've gotten out of control. I'm sure, I say, that no one here intends to be racist or exclusive, so let's enact some proof of that.

This lands in the room like a big fart. First it's funny, kids snicker, then the seriousness of it hits and people are silent, repulsed or not, moved and alert, curious to see how the powers that be will react.

It sparks a big discussion, which I am perhaps too vocal in, but by the end of the melee I'm still standing, holding my moral sword, covered in my own blood, and a few of the more patient of my peers have begun to see my side of things. They liked the prospective student, too, and equally don't buy the bullshit excuse offered for his rejection.

Over the next few weeks, the topic comes up again and again and again, with my tiny army growing glacially but steadily, despite the squirming and sighing of the less rebellious students.

I get wind of the increased likelihood of my expulsion, so I kick my campaign to stay into overdrive. I ask every staff member who will listen to have tea with me, and I bombard them with horror stories of my other options. I tell them that this has become my home, that perhaps I'm poor at expressing it, but I cherish this place. If they kick me out, I'll have to go and live with my ravaged mother and her abusive boyfriend in a hoarder house in New York.

My instincts tell me that it's a long shot, but I am too desperate to listen.

I'm on my best behavior when the entire school is assigned their end-of-year jobs, scrubbing the laundry room until it's unrecognizable. I pack up my room, just in case, but I refuse to say good-bye to everyone. I tell them I'll see them in the fall and then I fly to New York.

*Chapter 40*

# Homecoming

E VERYONE HATES TO SUFFER. THEY'LL DO ANYTHING TO avoid it. Not my ma. She lives within pain like the war-torn overcoat of a Bosnian.

Her scars form a moat dividing her from the rest of society, from those who have never experienced emotional dismemberment. Her stories are not about life's pokes and pricks and sticky problems she had to solve. Her stories are tragic, Gothic, Civil War splatter flicks of amputation without anesthesia. Awful in the grand sense.

She plows into pain, through it, with it inside her. Sometimes there's the question of whether or not it's possible to go on, but never of whether or not one should. You just find a way. This is life. No matter how heavy the blows.

My mother is not of this world. In a city full of puffed-up, politically correct yuppies and gluttonous, self-centered adult children bursting with stories of that one time they volunteered to serve a meal to the homeless, my ma operates by a different code. For all her failings, for all her faults, she would curl up in a damp sheet in the cold of winter before she would ever take a blanket off me. She would go to sleep hungry if she ever thought I needed her portion of food.

When she was under attack, accused of neglecting her most treasured baby child, she still never publicly shamed my father for his addiction. She never threw him under the bus, though she could have taken that cheap shot a thousand times. She knew I treasured him, and they had a deal.

She worked several jobs with a brutal hip injury to keep us from starvation, for years, but she never touched the money I made as a child actor. She never stole, she didn't lie, she never intentionally hurt anyone. She made do with what she had, and she gave the bigger portion of all she had to me.

She is an eccentric in a world where eccentrics often live out their lives as untouchables; that is, until they die and are lionized as brilliant. When they overdose at twenty-seven we put their faces on T-shirts and call them "Bright comets" or "flares extinguished before their time." We celebrate their art, their music, their performances. We love and exploit the products of those very peculiarities, but try growing up with them as your only guiding lights. Try having such an "eccentric" as a parent, your primary guide through the world.

I've been home for a few weeks and I've been witness to a transformed person. My ma, who was once my superhero, my stalwart warrior queen, has been broken. It took several blows before the snap, but I know my being taken away was the ultimate wound, and the guilt of it is with me constantly.

The severity of her hip pain has crippled her proud posture. Unable to overcome it with willpower, she has been worn down by the frustration of crappy health care provided to the impoverished: the endless runarounds, unmotivated doctors, interminable waits, cold-blooded refusals, and profound humiliations. She can't have her hip replaced on Medicaid in any way that will be safe, but to get better insurance, she will need to put up thousands of dollars she could never earn. So she's stuck.

She won't discuss Gus with me, but I see her thrashing in it, overwhelmed by the cruel joke of being in love with a man who batters her. It gives her a commonality with countless women, but she will never seek a community or support. She'll just *tsk* and nod and shed a tear or two when she sees another in such pain, but validation from them would do nothing to soothe her. She is isolated in time's relentless forward march.

The apartment is like I've never seen it. She has always hoarded useless shit, fragments of all the beautiful eras she sees being whitewashed and plowed over by this antiseptic new world. But now it's hard to move through the place. A pile of empty jumbo olive oil cans takes up the center of my old room, something she claims to be saving for an art piece. There are pieces of furniture far outsized for the house and sacks of envelopes, each written on in her distinctive scrawl. I pick one up and read a dark poem about Gus, his betrayals, her misery. How she'd cut his back open in the night with a box cutter when he told her he had cheated with a woman who might have HIV.

She has kept every single thing I have ever made, including a four-foot easel I built in wood shop when I was eight, a stack of cardboard castles I made in the second grade, and my entire autograph collection, gathered over my whole life, including Puff Daddy, Isaac Hayes, and James Brown. There are bags of my old clothes, my scarves, my baby shoes, my socks. It's insanity.

She thinks of all things I've touched as treasures. I am the exalted one, but it's as if this distinction is reserved for the memory of me. In person, she can barely bring herself to be warm, she has so much to be angry about.

A thick shell of emotions encloses her, feelings hardened into tangled armors of resentment, fear, love, fury, and responsibility. She has become a kind of giant tortoise, majestic, slow moving, unreachable. Everything vulnerable has been pulled inside. When I look at her a chasm opens within me and I long to fill it with maternal care, a space that hasn't been filled since I was seven or eight. Since her eyes started to go dark. Since the visitor started to take her over. I want to mend her, fix her body, wrap her fingers in mine and protect her bones. I long for her to caress my head. When she offers to massage my back at night, I jump at the chance. But I know it won't last. Her moods are fickle and her turns are violent. I carry apprehension like a shield into every interaction with her, but my affection weakens it and this angers me. My wounded hope for a true mother is scabbed over by disappointment.

I love her. When people watch her jump the turnstile with judgment in their eyes, I want to cut them. I want to push them onto the tracks. What do they know about being a widow? What do they know about being a single mom, scraping together enough money to feed your fifth grader, trying to keep a kid's mind stimulated by sneaking them into the second half of Broadway shows when you're under threat of eviction? What do they know about surviving on ten dollars a day? Would they support their child if they decided they were really a boy? Would they wash the sheets to welcome her and her girlfriend when she came home as a lesbian teenager? Could they even begin to imagine what it's like to carry a torch for a man who's been dead for twenty years?

Her greatest love was sundered by the horror of murder, but my ma goes on, left behind in a world too banal to understand her, an inverse ghost, too alive in a soulless void, wandering the wrong purgatory.

IT'S SUMMER IN THE city. Nikita hasn't given up, or so she says. The open relationship thing is a challenge, but she's still mine. Am I still hers? I wonder this as I sit in Washington Square Park watching the freaks mill around in circles, enfeebled by the heat.

The air steams off the pavement like a mirage, the sunlight blinding white. A giant gushing fountain is the center point of a thousand people forced from their homes by the weather.

I got the e-mail from the boarding school directors shortly after I arrived in New York. It went something like this:

Dear iO,

It is with regret that we must inform you that you will not be invited to the Highland School for a third year. We fear that if you stay, you may incite a revolution amongst the student body.

On behalf of the entire staff, we wish you all the best in your endeavors, and we are confident that you will find the perfect place for yourself and for the furthering of your education.

This is the perfect place for me: three crackheads trying to lure a squirrel out of a bush with a filthy tissue; an old man's broken lope wobbling to the beat in my headphones; a woman in a wheelchair with one leg pointed out in front of her, zooming determinedly across the circle; a pair of punks with two sets of fishnets, to better display the rips in them; the Rastafarian with dreads down to his ass, mumbling "smoke, smoke, smoke" as you walk by.

This is it. This is home. The buck stops at Ma's house. For all her crazy, she's always had a roof to put over my head.

Anya and I spend our days and nights together, smoking joints and walking around, counting down the summer. She will go back to Highland in a month and I will be very much alone. I have the phone numbers of two old friends, but really I don't know anyone here anymore.

A cigarette dangles from my fingertips as I spot Anya moving toward me now. She stops to ask a guy for a light. The way she leans down to him clearly piques his interest. He is sitting on a skateboard. His shoulders are broad and he has a clipped afro. She says something and points at me. He looks from my bathing suit top to my miniskirt to my skateboard and says something to her. She waves me over.

He's a cheeseball, an athlete hunk with washboard abs and reflective sunglasses. I almost don't believe him when he says his name is Chico. He's an import from Indiana, half black, half Vietnamese. His interest in my body makes me feel sexy in a way I haven't before. He's over six feet tall and his muscles push back against his T-shirt. This is what I'm supposed to be into as a female: a beefcake.

The three of us spend the afternoon under a tree smoking cigarettes and talking about skating. Anya has to go back to Queens to have dinner with her family, so Chico asks if I want to get dinner with him.

We skate up Sixth Avenue and stop to get takeout, where I let him know he's eight years older than me. He feigns shock, but he still brings me upstairs to "watch a movie." He says he's in between apartments right now, his new one is being renovated. I smell bullshit but I don't really care. This is an exchange. I judge him silently, because he's twenty-four and wants to fuck a teenager, but it makes me feel wanted in the way that I long for.

Maybe I watched too many LL Cool J videos, but Chico's raw, lip-licking rapper sex energy turns me on. He tells me about the girls he fucks, basically copping to being a sex addict. He shows me pictures of them, and they're hot women in their twenties.

The night air is sticky, with the city noise just outside the window. I'm so excited by the fact that this man wants to fuck me, but it hurts when it happens. We do it doggy style on the couch. My body is stiff and uncomfortable and he says he's fine to go slow this time, but one day "we're gonna really fuck."

I leave as soon as it's over and skate the forty blocks home in the muggy night air. The wind is nice in my hair, and my body feels different as I move. I can smell Chico on my skin. I played it cool but I'm intoxicated by the fact that he wants to do it again.

For the next six months we will use each other, me just as much as him. I'll drop by his place on my way to a movie or dinner, play with him, let him go down on me until he can't stand it anymore and needs to fuck. I'm into it for the first few minutes but then I start to zone out and encourage him to get it over with so I can go. I never spend the night. Neither does he.

Chico is the first in a series of attempts to prove something to myself.

THE FALL COMES AND takes Anya. I turn seventeen without much fanfare and start at my new high school, a public school on the West Side that is half classes and half internships. It's a hustler's heaven, a bizarre intersection of young overachievers and intellectually challenged twenty-two-year-olds who repeatedly flunked the twelfth grade.

My homeroom heartthrob is a Puerto Rican hip-hop dancer with eyes like a doe, who makes a pit stop in my bed. I miss ten minutes of a movie to find out looks don't make a lover.

I'm up in Harlem doing a short film when I meet Jae, a six-foot-four drug dealer who carries his weed in a special hand-sewn pocket between his shoulder blades. He's saccharine, and a great kisser, but one day he refers to his dick as "the purple-headed yogurt slinger" and I get so nauseous I can't ever touch him again.

All the while I'm talking to Nikita every day. I put her to bed in my afternoon and wake up to her calls, the random boys conveniently couched in the period when she's asleep. She knows about all of them, but they're irrelevant. It turns out that our love is strong. I actually talk to her, vulnerability made easy by the relative solitude of the phone. I tell her how lonely I feel, how doubtful I am that I am attractive, how the house is so crammed with shit you have to shuffle sideways to get to the bedroom, and how Gus goes the other way if he sees me on the street.

In November, a thirty-six-year-old guy invites me out. I met him rubbernecking a bar fight at three A.M. I figure he's good for a few free drinks and I'll go home. When I arrive for our date, he's wearing ostrich-skin pants. He smells clean and speaks softly. He tells me he does the soundtracks for animated movies, and buys me cocktails. We're at the birthday party of one of his best friends, and he says I remind him of someone from his hometown who's also there, Francesca. He pulls me over to her.

She's my height, nearly six foot, with big brown eyes and pouting lips, shoulder-length brown hair, and a pretty face. Her big tits spill out of her shirt and she smells good when she leans over to talk to me, several bracelets clanking on her wrist. She's got a roughness to her, a tomboyish straightforwardness that I like. She puts an elbow on the bar and we bullshit until she asks how old I am.

"Twenty-four. You?"

"Me, too!"

"Wow . . . how old are you really?"

" . . . Seventeen. What about you?"

"Me, too!"

We laugh, sizing each other up. I like her.

She tells me she's majoring in fragrance marketing at FIT, whatever the fuck that is. She says she got early admission to get out of her hometown as fast as she could. She lives in the dorms on Seventeenth Street and Seventh Avenue. We agree that we should hang out.

I don't see her again until New Year's Day. She is brash and unconventional enough that I feel like she won't judge me on the house or my insane mother. Somehow I know she'll just work around it, so I invite her over.

She's unfazed by the chaos. She comes in with bags of groceries, cracking jokes and chugging beers, laughing so loud the neighbors can hear. She manages to cook a feast in our excuse for a kitchen, careening around like a puppy with paws too big for its body, dropping things and scooping them back into the pan. We smoke joints and talk until we pass out.

It's two in the morning when a pot starts slamming into the kitchen counter. Francesca shoots straight up in the bed when my ma screams, *"Fuuuuuuuuck!"*

"Don't worry. It's just my mom. She's harmless."

"Holy shit, dude. Is she gonna hurt us?"

"No. Don't worry. She'll calm down eventually."

She doesn't. The screaming goes on for so long that Francesca starts shaking. She tells me her dad was abusive like this and it's freaking her out, so I go into the kitchen and tell my ma to cut the shit. I'm scarlet with embarrassment. Ma is mad because we didn't do the dishes and now there's no cup for her to drink her tea out of. She doesn't look at me when she screams, "What is this, a fucking hotel?"

We go back and forth for a few minutes, and ultimately I swear I'll do the dishes first thing in the morning if she will just shut up and let us sleep.

Francesca and I become inseparable. She is gregarious and charming and I am enamored. I love that her nickname is Frankie although she's such a girl. She doesn't judge the situation or even think my ma is that weird; she makes light of everything. Her father is a famous musician, so music pours out of her. The piano is an extension of her body, and she's teaching herself the guitar. All she wants to do is hang out, smoke weed, and write songs.

She teaches me how to do my makeup and lends me clothes to dress up when we go out. She introduces me to the world of nightclubs because she knows some promoters. We make out and occasionally fuck when we're wasted, at the end of a long night. For a few months we both wonder if we're in love, but ultimately, my heart is saved for Nikita. I want to end up in Europe, with her, having a family. Francesca is straight anyway, so we start to go boy hunting together. Sooner or later, she introduces me to hard drugs.

THE FIRST TIME I do cocaine I ask how I'm gonna feel. Frankie says, "Like a supermodel!"

We're at some loft in Chinatown with the guy who introduced us. The bed sits isolated in the center of a tacky room. I stare at the raw beams holding up the high ceiling as the guy cuts lines on a mirror. This is like a scene from a shitty movie, where the rich older dude lures the two underage girls to his circular bed with a tray of drugs and tries to fuck them both. He alternates making out with each of us while flattening coke nuggets with his Platinum MasterCard. It's a joke.

I do the tiniest rail and I can't feel my teeth. Supermodel my ass.

A week later, we're out at a cheesy club and I'm bored, so I do it again, and again for the same reason the week after. It's not a habit, and certainly not a problem.

Then it's a couple of times a week.

Then there's a six- or seven-week stretch where we're doing it regularly. We get all amped, have this incredible night, and go to bed feeling sexy and sexed and smiling. I wake up the next day feeling pretty all right even though I spent hours walking around in the dead winter freeze wearing nothing but a vest. Supermodel maybe.

By month three we've lost ten or fifteen pounds and all the bouncers and bartenders know our names. I think I look great (skeletal is hot, right?), but my throat is starting to burn from the constant coke drip down the back of it. My nostrils are numb, so I'm constantly rubbing my face and I'm starting to wonder if people are noticing. At school? At my lame part-time job?

Then the worst part is, I do a bump—off a key in a bathroom, off the tip of a credit card—and the high only lasts twenty minutes. I have this arc, of not even feeling amazing, just okay, vaguely normal for a short stretch, then there's fifteen minutes spent worrying about coming down, ten minutes of actually coming down, and it's back to the hunt, eyes scanning, fingers tapping, lips sucking vodka straws. Over and over, all night long.

Getting out of bed in the morning starts to really suck. My body feels like garbage and the subway ride to my gig stuffing envelopes for ten bucks an hour is a test of endurance.

If I'm not high, I'm cranky, pissed off, uncomfortable, and guess what: I'm seventeen and I've bunked off work in a coke haze so much that I've gone broke, so when I feel like too much dog shit to go out to a club, there isn't the option of calling a dealer or a delivery service to help with the fact that I've developed one of the most expensive habits there is.

So I throw on a dirty hoodie and begrudgingly end up at the corner deli scouring the shelves for something with caffeine in it to make myself feel better. My eyes land on the diet pills on the counter, right next to the horny goat weed. That shit gets you high, right? I spend the dollar and eat a handful of Stacker 3s and I'm up for the next four days, hands shaking, craving beer or something vaguely digestible that will fit into my shrunken stomach.

Then I get sick. Real sick. My tonsils gets so swollen I can't even swallow water and my ma has to take me to the emergency room in the middle of the night, two nights in a row.

The first time, she holds my hand and coos when I cry because they have to stick a six-inch needle into my infected tonsil and pull the pus out. She fills the prescription and pays for my antibiotics, even though she can't afford to, and makes me take them even though she thinks they're evil. She wants me to gargle tea tree oil, but she knows I'm beyond homeopathic remedies.

The second time, she bundles me into a cab that she pays for with her food money, because I was crying out in my sleep. The pain was too intense and breathing was becoming difficult. She is patient and kind when I try to apologize for us having to go back, and she rubs my head when I whimper in the waiting room. She out and out cries when I do, tears rolling down both our faces, while the same young doctor holds my jaw open and slices my tonsil with a scalpel to relieve the pressure.

Two days later I show up at the neighborhood Medicaid clinic, in size zero stretch jeans that are hanging off me, and pass out in the middle of the hallway trying to make the four-step walk to the bathroom to throw up. They pump me full of a bunch of drugs, feed me intravenously, and tell me they're going to have to operate.

My ma looks pale under the bright fluorescent lights, holding my hand, face crinkled in concern. My eyes can't focus as I dip in and out of consciousness, but when I come to, I use her as my stabilizing horizon. I wonder what I'm doing here. This feels like somebody else's soap opera.

My nostrils are filled with the sterile stench of hospital anti-air; thoughts of all the addicts in my family float through my consciousness, and I wonder if it's hereditary. Even with this garbled brain, I know that beating the genetic imperative is a lot more interesting than being a teenage fuck-up.

I am propelled by something much stronger, much bigger than a desire to destroy myself. I want to leave something good behind, something better than a sob story, a warning to other kids, something that helps people. Even if I don't make it past thirty-five, I want to be sure that my death is at least a loss.

I don't want to wear my tragedies on my skin, in my teeth, in my walk. I want something different than what I'm inheriting, but I'm going to have to make that happen for myself, and it's not gonna be like this.

It's time to get my shit together.

*Chapter 41*

# The Hospital Incident

*New York City, April 2003*

FRANCESCA HAS FOUND HERSELF A BOYFRIEND FROM THE projects on First Avenue named Victor. He's a handsome Dominican guy with a sharp business sense and a soft demeanor. He drives a nice car and pays his mother's rent. Victor wears a uniform of gray sweatpants, wifebeater, and classic fitted Yankees cap, with a tire of paunch around his middle. He rolls with a posse of no fewer than three guys at all times. Frankie loves the bad-boy thing. We got tight, Victor and I, as my throat healed up while I lay on his new couch playing video games with him.

He has a partnership with an Armenian kid he grew up with, Lance. Lance lives in a place his parents left him on the East River, and he has a taste for downers. The first time we're introduced we all end up at a twenty-four-hour diner in Hell's Kitchen after the clubs. Lance tells the waitress to go into the fridge, take his steak out, put it on a plate, and serve it to him just like that. He wants it completely raw, and he'll tip her twenty bucks for the health code breach.

Lance and Victor hired me to run weed and coke for them because they figured a white girl on a skateboard was less likely to get pulled over by the cops. At first I found the idea charming and exciting, but I quickly

discovered the unseemly reality of seeing respectable people at their ug-
liest. Friends turned to customers would relentlessly beg for deals and
freebies until I stopped answering their calls. Then my voice mail filled
with frantic pleas at all hours of the night, so I shut it off. Seeing the great
equalizer morph normal people into amped-up freaks has been good for
my need to be doing less blow. I'm starting to think it's gross.

School is a no-brainer. A lab rat could do it. My history teacher is a
fifty-year-old black guy who dresses like a marine who became a tennis
coach. He can't pronounce Saddam Hussein's name, and he says "nucu-
lar" instead of "nuclear." One day it comes out that I was in school in
Europe, and after that he defers all questions he can't answer to me. It's
embarrassing.

I told the school that my abundance of *physik* credits on my old report
cards from Germany meant I'd studied physics, even though it means
physical education, so I got out of science forever, but I can't weasel away
from the final exams. It's been weeks of studying and research on all
kinds of shit I've never taken a class in, so I'm nervous. If I flunk the tests
I can't graduate. If I pass, I can take off for Europe right away. I'm desperate to see Nikita and get as far from all this shit as possible.

I've been spending time with Naima, my old friend Mira's best
friend since they were five. She's a tiny half-black, half–Puerto Rican
poet whose formidable vocabulary cuts the world into shapes I can
comprehend. We smoke blunts and talk about things that matter, and
being around her helps me to not get back on the yay. She keeps me
calm and centered while I'm trying to ground myself before the tests.

Ma and I have been getting along decently since I had my tonsils
removed, but I'm wary of getting too close during an upswing, so I've
been staying out of her way. My exams happen to fall on her forty-sixth
birthday. I haven't made any specific plans, but if we manage to stay decent with each other, I'll take her out to dinner. Maybe Indian at Panna,
our old haunt on Sixth Street, for nostalgia's sake.

The night before the big day, Naima and I are up talking. It's late,
she tells me; it's time to sleep so I don't fuck up on my tests. She's sleep-

ing over, like a boxing coach the night before a big fight. I turn out the light and we lay down on my futon.

It seems like the second I close my eyes my ma starts screaming. I have no idea how long Naima and I here been asleep, but we both jolt alert.

Naima is nervous. I tell her not to worry. Ma is obliterated, wasted. I am calm, just sleepy and annoyed. Tomorrow is important, and I wish she wouldn't pull this tonight of all nights. I go into the kitchen, where she is teetering by the telephone, and ask her to please stop. She doesn't seem to hear me.

I don't want to yell at her because it will scare Naima, but she's unreachable. Finally, I grab her by the shoulders and pull her to face me. Her eyes are red and swollen. She's not even in there. It's the visitor.

"You don't care that it's my *birthday* tomorrow. What kind of child are *you*? It's my birthday, and you haven't even seen me in days!"

"Ma. It's your birthday *tomorrow*. I'm gonna take you out to dinner."

"You don't even care about me! You only care about yourself. You don't even have the decency to make plans with your own *mother* on her *birthday*. Psssh. Godddd."

There is a sound she makes only when she's drunk. It's like a teeth-sucking, attitude-giving noise. It lets me know she is on the other side of rationale. When she makes this noise, I shut down. I stop trying to reason with her. She wriggles out of my grasp and turns toward the bathroom, staring at nothing.

"Ma, I need you to be quiet. My final exams at school are in the morning, and I need you to keep it down so I can sleep. I will take you out to dinner tomorrow. I promise."

"You don't even care about your own mother! What happened to real children who treat their parents with some kinda respect!"

She's beyond my reach. I turn and go into my room, closing the door.

"Open that fucking door!"

I rip it back open.

"Ma! Shut the fuck up! Naima is in here asleep and you're scaring the shit out of her. Stop fucking screaming at me."

"Open that fucking door, iO. I don't want closed doors in my house."

"I'm gonna close the door, Ma. I need to sleep."

"Open the door!"

I close it and lock it behind me, apologizing to Naima. My ma tries the handle but I push my back against it to be sure she can't get in.

"I'm sorry. She'll pass out soon."

"Don't worry, boo. It's all good."

Naima is being a good sport, but I can see that this is making her uncomfortable. As I get back into the bed something crashes into my door. Naima jumps. This is exhausting. Opera starts blasting from the next room, and there are more crashing noises through the wall.

When I pull the door open, I see that my ma has thrown a guitar case and a giant metal frame at it. I can hear her sobbing. I don't understand what the fuck is going on. This is madness.

Ma is on the floor in the small room, one leg bent up under her at a strange angle, trying to tie her sneakers. She hisses at me and calls me a liar. She says I'm vile and a poor excuse for a daughter.

"Ma, listen, your birthday isn't until tomorrow. You need to calm down. I'm gonna take you out, I promise."

I am embarrassed that Naima is witnessing this psychosis.

"Ma, where are you trying to go?"

"I'm gonna leave this civilization."

"What are you talking about?"

"I'm gonna take the train to the end of the line . . ."

"Okay . . . why? Then what?"

"Then I'm gonna get out and *walk*."

If she means this metaphorically, she's seriously considering offing herself. If she means this literally, she'll end up deep in the Bronx at four A.M. and her metaphor will become reality. Either way, this is a problem.

In my bed, Naima has turned on the light. I sit down and we discuss our options. She calls a friend who is a social worker, apologizing profusely for waking him, and explains the situation. He recommends calling an ambulance to prevent my ma from hurting herself. He explains that the police have something called "AOB," which means that if there is alcohol on your breath and you're threatening to harm yourself or anyone else, they have to detain you for the night.

The idea of calling 911 on my ma, the night before her birthday, finally kicks fear into me, but what option do I have? Naima and I whisper to each other in stressed tones. This is the last thing I want to do, but the only conclusion is that Ma has to be restrained or she might hurt herself. So, with regret, I call.

Ten minutes later, there's a knock on the door. Ma is still struggling with her laces as I pass her to let in four cops and two ambulance attendants. I'm shaking. I explain the situation to them and ask them to please be as gentle with her as they can. They agree, but just the squawking of their radios gives me nerves.

I can't watch as they enter the little room and start badgering my ma with questions. I stand in the hall for the five minutes it takes them to determine that she has AOB and needs to be taken in. The sound of their radios echoes through the entire building. I imagine the neighbors are being woken by this drama.

I turn away as they bring her out of the apartment, an attendant holding each arm. She hisses at me that I'm a traitor, and I catch a second of her imploring, horrified look as they pass. I feel party to a witch hunt. This pulls at my stomach like a claw.

I ask the cop I'm standing with if it's okay for me to go and explain to her what's happening, just to calm her down and so she's not alone. He says sure.

I'm in my pajama pants, T-shirt, and socks.

In the ambulance I find that they've strapped her into a chair by the waist and wrists. Her veins are distended from struggling against the restraints. I feel sick knowing that I did this to her. Naima stands outside listening as I try to explain to my mother why this is just for her own safety. Within seconds we are screaming at each other.

The female attendant, callous and exhausted, looks at me strangely and says, "Are you also inebriated?"

"What? No."

"Your pupils are dilated."

"I was just in bed."

"Then why are your pupils dilated like that?"

"Oh, I don't fucking know, maybe because I'm seventeen and it's four in the morning and my mother is screaming, wasted, and strapped into an ambulance getting taken to the loony bin?"

"That's it. You're intoxicated. You're coming with us."

Blam. She reaches over and slams a belt across my waist. I start yelling at her, but she shuts off. She doesn't even register that I'm calling her a stupid bitch and warning her that if they leave us in the same place my ma is gonna rip me apart, that she's not herself right now. My ma is calling me a piece of shit, a pathetic excuse for a child, evil, a traitor, possessed.

Poor Naima jumps into the ambulance at the last second before we drive off, confused and scared.

At the hospital they separate us. Ma is so livid and dangerous looking they put her in a room by herself. I get handcuffed to a chair in the waiting area. I tell Naima she should go home. This is insanity and she doesn't have to stay for it. There's nothing she can do anyway. She asks me if I'm sure and I tell her to please make a break for it before they decide she's "inebriated," too. She says to *please* call her tomorrow and leaves.

A young black guy in a security uniform comes in with the same attendant. I spit at her. I tell her she is awful at her job and she should lose it. That she just locked up the child of a drunk having a psychotic break, because she was scared.

"My pupils were dilated in fucking *fear*, you get that? Good fucking job!"

She ignores me and the guard unlocks my cuffs, steering me by the shoulder into a locked room. Panic is surging into my throat. I'm not concerned with being in this place, I'm concerned that if they keep us both here until my ma sobers up and let us out at the same time, she will go ballistic on me in the street. Having her locked up is a breach I don't know how she will respond to. I don't know what she's capable of.

I pace the room trying to figure a way out. I try the door, quietly, but it's bolted. I see the guard through the window. He's just a kid himself. He doesn't give a shit about all this. He's got no flag to fly for justice or whatever, he's just stamping a time card. I smile at him. He half smiles back and turns away.

I knock on the glass. He comes to the window and looks into my face. I smile, doing my best to show him I'm not a threat or losing my mind.

"Hey. Listen. I know you're just doing your job, but do you think I could go to the bathroom? I swear, I just need to pee. I'll come right back. I'm not drunk or anything, I just got roped into this shit because of my mom. I'm not psycho. Please?"

He looks into my eyes for a minute, then around the hallway. It's deserted. No one cares if I pee. I can feel him conceding.

"I really appreciate it, man. It's just so nasty in here."

He turns the lock. I smile at him huge as I pass, my heart thumping with fear. He points me down the hall and tells me to come right back. I tell him I will and start walking, slowly, so I have time to figure out what to do. Glancing over my shoulder, I see that he has sat back down; he's not even watching me.

Just before the bathroom, a hall cuts down to my left and I see a red EXIT sign. Without thinking, I start sprinting toward it, my socks padding against the blue linoleum floor. Fear tearing down my spine and tightening my asshole, I slide to the beige door, bound down three flights of metal stairs, and explode onto the street.

I'm bolting down Twelfth Street toward Sixth Avenue in the dawn light, leaping over a pile of discarded syringes on Tenth Street, making my way east toward St. Marks. I send Nikita a text message, something of an SOS, to call me urgently. I tell her what happened as I make my way down Second Avenue in my socks, the sun fully up, terror coursing through me about what will happen when they cut my ma loose

The fear in Nikita's voice takes mine away, and now it's me who's calming her. I tell her I'll be okay, to just please stay on the phone with me. My socks are caked in filth by the time I sprint up the stairs to our apartment.

Half convinced Ma will already be there, I push the door open silently and check for noise. The opera record is skipping and the lights are on in the kitchen, but no one is home. The air is tense, electric. Clearly something happened here that was interrupted. It's creepy. I move nimbly to my bedroom and lock the door.

I curl up with the blanket pulled over my head, cell phone pressed to my ear.

"I think I've probably got a few hours before she gets out and makes her way home."

"Why can't you leave?"

"I've got nowhere else to go right now . . . I just want to sleep, so bad. If I can get an hour in, it'll be early enough to go to school and wait it out there."

"Okay . . . I'm going to stay on the phone until you're asleep, just in case."

SLEEP VEILS ITSELF like a thin film over my nervousness and I jolt awake when the apartment door flies open, slamming into the wall, the doorbell dinging from the impact. She screams my name, calls me an expletive. Nikita, still on the other end of the line, starts freaking out, demanding to know what's happening. I whisper, "Shhh. I can't talk or she'll know I'm here."

The doorknob wiggles and she throws her body weight against the frame, screaming from her guts that I'm a disgusting piece of shit traitor and that I don't deserve to be in her house and "Fuck you, you evil bitch" and so on. I pull the pillow tighter over my head, staring out the window at the brick wall across from us. I wish I were a bird on the tree just past the glass. I pray that the lock will hold.

The sound of wood smashing on wood. She's hitting my door with a baseball bat, screaming as loud as she can, crying. I imagine her body, enflamed and erupting with rage, hurt, confused, like an animal, thrashing in the forest. I can hear the door bending concave from the beating, but it doesn't give in. Nikita is sobbing in Berlin. I tell her it's okay. It's gonna be okay.

Ma passes out before she can break through. I can't sleep, so I lie there under the blanket for an hour until I'm sure she's down for the count, then I grab my backpack and sneak out past her. She looks so harmless, asleep like that. She's beautiful still, like Annie Lennox if she served in Sarajevo for a couple of years. Watching her, I wonder if our relationship will ever be the same.

I'm sorry, I think, I'm sorry that whatever is haunting you is so savage. I'm sorry you're more often this horrible creature than the other one that I love. I'm sorry I hate you more often than I love you now.

I'm not taking you out to dinner anymore. I can't bring myself to do it.

Happy birthday, Ma.

## Chapter 42

# Good-bye, My Friend

### New York City, May 2003

I'M BEING SMOTHERED BY EVERYTHING I'VE EVER FEARED. IT was an epic mistake to think that any one person could salve all the loneliness. I was stupid to have trusted her, the biggest fool on earth.

How could Nikita want to be done with me when she's the very air I breathe?

Lovers share one pair of eyes. We guide each other when we cannot see. Now it's as if I'm blind. I sit on a pile of dirty clothes and records that hides the armchair in the living room, which has become my mother's bedroom. I feel like my bones are melting out through my skin.

Ma is on the toilet behind me, in discomfort, listening to me weep, fidgeting and murmuring to herself, helpless. This is a woman who lost the love of her life in one shattering evening and roared back in the face of agony like a lioness. She took the blow, went through unimaginable pain, and conquered it with willpower. She knows only the searing extremes, not the equanimity needed to comfort her child's broken heart.

I am despondent. When everything was collapsing around me, the one thing I was sure of was Nikita, my one hope for escape. The walls used to be transparent, something that couldn't hold me. Now I'm trapped, grounded in hell. I can't see my way out.

She says I'm too young. She's too far away. She met a boy.

I think about that boy. Some guy she met through someone I introduced her to when I was in Berlin. Some party king with awesome friends and a cool house who plugged her in to ecstasy and house music. Fuck them both.

Berlin has a club scene beyond anything I've ever known, windowless halls so you never know when it's time to go home, entire compounds filled with throbbing masses, faces and bare chests upturned toward a guy in a booth sweating and sucking on cigarettes, fist pumping at himself. A pill to pull you up, a joint to level you out, a drink to calm the edge, a line to get you psyched again. Fuck that. Fuck all of them.

Her tiny hands. Her bird bones entwined in mine. She made me feel strong, like I was worth something. Like I had a place in this world, because we were building a world together.

The stack of tires that we fucked on down the path from school. The secret world we existed in. Her ankle, encircled by the bracelet I gave her. The hundreds of letters we wrote. Countless mornings spent wrapped around her throaty voice on the other end of my phone. Her guidance through my roughest moments. The ripping high that just didn't end, of falling in love. Feeling like somebody beautiful, who I respected saw me, felt me, heard me—cared.

My mother whimpers, sympathetic and impotent. Across the vast gulf of the kitchen she feels my pain like a twin. I don't have to turn around to see her, pants around her ankles, eyebrows pulled together, fiddling with a piece of toilet paper. She doesn't care about the pee drying on her, the appointment she's missing, or the people she might be standing up. She feels like murder, but she doesn't know where to put it.

Chinese people are whining opera songs and I scream at the radio.

Ma stops moaning, out of respect for the mourning.

I dip into a hopelessness I had never imagined was possible. I stand still because the idea of walking feels too big. The world has so many rules, customs, social graces that I don't understand. I am a wolf child, but Nikita was my guide. Without her it feels insurmountable.

I take to my bed and don't get up for three months. I don't know how I am supposed to survive. Ma comes in with water and strange teas sometimes, but I don't touch them. She sits at the end of the bed and caresses my foot under the blanket.

I don't have a home. That's all I can think about. I built my home in Nikita, and that was a mistake. I cannot grasp how that could have been a mistake, but it was.

No one will love me like that ever again. How could they? That love was essential. I have ghost pains where she used to be.

Closing my eyes hurts. Getting through a few minutes exhausts me.

I wither. Weight vaporizes from my bones as if it were being pulled into the air. Food repels me. Water is disgusting.

Ma futzes around in the kitchen, making teas and soups, mumbling and humming along to jazz standards on the radio. The radio stays on, as always. No catastrophe can move that rock. Some nights I cry out in the darkness and Ma comes and sleeps next to me in the bed. One night I roll over and put my arm around her and she gently removes it because she's not who my dreaming mind wishes she was.

Why bathe? Ma doesn't care, and I'm not trying to impress anyone. Who else would ever care what I smell like? And as a matter of fact I kind of like it. It reminds me that I'm alive.

Some nights I wake up and Ma is gone. She comes back possessed. She puts on a pot of rice to boil and goes to take a bath. I fall asleep again to the sound of the water running and am awakened by the smoke alarm bleeping and a black cloud seeping under my door. The sound hammers at my eyelids until I slouch into the kitchen on autopilot, clutching my ears, climb on a chair and rip it out of the ceiling. Turning the stove off I see that the rice is burnt black, and tiny craters have bored into the bottom of the pan.

I open all the windows, leaning over the plants that crowd the sills, and wave giant charcoal drawings of my mother's face back and forth to clear the air, as I have done countless times before. Ma has curled her entire length into the tiny bathtub. She is naked in the drained basin, mascara cascading down her cheeks, hands draped across her belly, asleep. When I yell her name or kick the cabinet in anger she opens her crystal-blue eyes and purses her lips as she looks at me. Her look tells me she thinks I'm ridiculous.

"Get up, Ma."

"Pssshhh."

"Ma! Get up! Get out of the fucking tub."

"Mmm . . . Leave me alone."

"You almost burnt the fucking house down! get the fuck up out of the fucking tub!"

*"Wwaaaaahhhhh! Go cry to your fucking frieeeendddss!"*

Like a demon has snapped a rubber band on her spine, she arches upward and spews this at me violently.

Some nights I scream, too, other times I go back to waving the drawings around, trying to clear the noxious chemicals from the air before we both lie down to sleep in it.

The lower half of the saucepan is caked in black from this ritual.

In the morning she will shuffle in with tea, wearing her broken gold-glitter flip-flops. Mascara will be hardened in the ridges on the outside of her eyes, her wifebeater ripped into a V at the chest. I won't roll over. She'll sit on the edge of the bed and tell me a story about something that happened on the train or at dance class yesterday and I will want to jump out the window, but I won't say anything. She doesn't remember.

Three months in, I get the craving for a FrozFruit. It is the first desire I've had for anything other than Nikita in so long that I pull myself to my feet. In sweatpants and a hoodie pulled low over my face, I drag myself to the corner deli to get it.

As I am handing Abdullah my dollar, the headline of the newspaper catches my eye: WOMAN'S LEGS MANGLED IN HORRIFIC SUBWAY ACCIDENT. I stand there, feeling sorry for myself in my depression suit, and then something tingles in my brain. Some deep-seated notion that what I've got isn't as bad as getting your legs ripped off by the R train.

When I get upstairs, I look at myself in the seven-foot mirror I've been watching myself grow in since I was born. Pulling off my hoodie, holding the green FrozFruit between my lips, I see a skeleton. I take off my sweatpants and see that they were hiding two sticks. My long hair is matted and electrified, haloing my face.

Something pounds its fist on my insides, reminding me that I'm still here. Seventeen years of bone and flesh and thought and dreams and love and screaming and joy stare back at me.

Somebody else will think I'm cute.

*Chapter 43*

# Finding the Answer

*New York City, August and September 2003*

I T'S SKATING THAT FINALLY PROPELS ME FROM THE SHEETS.
It's the furnace of summer, the apartment is too sweltering to
sit around in, and I crave the feeling of throwing my board down and
launching into the breeze. It's like flying, speeding through the city, on
display but invisible at the same time, moving too fast for anyone to really take you in or talk to you.

I put music on at top volume, R&B and hip-hop, anything I can buy
bootleg on Canal Street. I ride with no destination, coasting through
parks and up the sides of the island, just to be outside. My body is drained
from being in a slump, but I work my way back to my normal strength in
a few weeks.

I fill my days with this solitary ritual, falling in love with my city,
trying to fall back in love with myself. I wander through areas I haven't
seen since I was a kid, skating from Battery Park to the tippy top of
Harlem. It bodes well for my job as a drug runner, which I return to
with a new vigor. Lance is thrilled that I can do twice as many deliver-
ies in the same four-hour period. I blitz around downtown, my backpack laden with felonies, headphones shielding me from interacting
with anyone except an occasional shitty driver.

One day I'm sitting at a table at Mamoun's falafel in the Village when a guy in a long leather coat comes in. He stops at my elbow and says, "You like desserts?"

"Fuck off, dude."

"No, I'm serious. Do you like desserts?"

"What are you talking about, creep?"

"Do you like sweets??"

"Yeah . . . so?"

"Here, you can have this."

He sets a tinfoil-wrapped square on the table.

"Like I'm fucking born yesterday, man. I'm not gonna eat that."

He smiles at me and continues to the counter. The boys who work there greet him with fist bumps and grins, and trade him two falafels for an identical tinfoil square. I consider his offering anew. Fuck it, if the boys are doing it, I might as well try it. I unwrap the small brownie and pop it in my mouth.

An hour later I'm skating into oncoming traffic on Sixth Avenue and Forty-second Street. I have no idea how I got there, or why I'm going up when I should be going across town to the east. Everything is wobbling, and by the time I find Lance's apartment, the TV is melting into itself. I'm supposed to be re-upping my supply for my coke runs, but I'm too fucked up, so I fall asleep on his couch.

In the morning, I have an audition for *Sex and the City*. I've been praying for something like this for so long, but when I wake up, I realize I'm still off my face. Too bad. The show must go on.

I arrive at the audition a disheveled mess. I walk into a room with a big table and seven people behind it, four producers and three directors. I almost barf with nerves.

"Good morning, iO!" one says cheerily. The others just stare at the papers in front of them.

"Good morning!"

"How're you today?"

"I'm great! Fantastic. Just great . . ."

They all look up.

"Wow. Good! Good for you!"

Oh god.

"So, today we're going to have you read for the role of a perfume salesperson at Macy's, who is trying to sell Charlotte some perfume. Okay? Whenever you're ready, you can just improvise."

Oh, I'm improvising? No problem! I got this. Easy. Everything is sparkling and in Technicolor, and I swear I can smell the perfume I'm spraying on this imaginary woman.

They seem impressed.

"Wow. That was really good. Let's try another character. Now you're working at a McDonald's, and Sarah Jessica Parker comes in with her new lover. She's in a ball gown and he's in a tux. You're really thrown off by them, in their fancy outfits in your McDonald's, and you give them kind of . . . a look . . ."

"Like this?"

"That's *perfect*. Oh wow. So great. I think that's all we need from you today, iO. Great job. We'll be in touch."

I bumble my way through Queens to the train, miraculously make it home, and spend thirty-six hours asleep. My manager wakes me up two days later with a phone call to tell me the news: I got the job. It boggles me how, but I booked the McDonald's worker.

Frankie is sleeping in the little bedroom. She broke up with Victor and I caught her wandering on the street with a bottle of Jim Beam, on her way to some guy's house in Brooklyn. She said she was couch hopping and depressed because she had nowhere to make music, so I pulled her upstairs, took away the booze, and moved her into the small room in our house. She's been here for three months. Her room is a Zen zone, filled with candles and perfumes and bras and scarves draped over the harsh lamps. Mine looks like her teenage brother's boy hole by comparison.

My ma went to Puerto Rico, on her first trip out of the city since we went to Europe when I was little, so there's a new sense of calm in the house. Lately, every time Ma goes out, Frankie and I try to do a little cleaning. It's risky, because when Ma comes home, if she notices that we moved anything she'll lose her mind, screaming and throwing things, until we bring all her stuff back and put it where it was. Today, however, I give no fucks at all; I want to make some headway with the piles of trash lying all over the floor.

I go into Frankie's room and lie down in her bed. She's topless, fallen asleep with her laptop on her stomach while watching porn, hand in her thong. I close the computer and put it away.

"Frankie. Wake up. Let's clean this bitch."

She groans and reaches for her bong. Clearing her throat, my friend rolls over and takes a huge rip before getting up, rubbing her gigantic tits together and dropping them up and down a few times.

Both of us in nothing but our underwear, we survey the house. Every room needs help, but since my ma is out of town, we take the opportunity to deal with her area. She has a soft spot for Frankie and her beautifying ways, so I'm not as scared to do it if Frankie is involved. Frankie also has a patience for my ma's lunacy that I don't. She moves things delicately and remembers where she put them in case there's a frantic need to return them. I just want to throw everything into the trash and gut the place. The grime of it makes my skin crawl.

We start by separating out the things that can be tossed and the things that absolutely have to be saved, then we try to find a place for those things that's not on the floor. Then we sweep. To really get all the filth up, we have to get under my ma's mattress, so we lift it off the ground.

There, underneath her bed, I see an orange pill bottle.

I pick it up.

It's a nearly empty prescription for something called Desoxyn.

My stomach falls out. My intuition tingles, telling me this is big.

Frankie carries on, unfazed.

"What is it? Something fun?"

My voice sounds muffled to my own ears. Far away. I'm doing that thing I did as a kid; I'm leaving my own body. I almost feel nothing. Frankie has no idea that anything is wrong, that just here on the other side of my thin skin is an emotional riot. My intuition is urgently begging me not to sit at the computer and google Desoxyn. But I do.

> Desoxyn is a central nervous system stimulant. The exact way
> it works is unknown. It controls the release of certain chemicals in the brain that affect mood, behavior, and appetite.

Okay. That's not much.

> Desoxyn® (methamphetamine hydrochloride tablets, USP),
> chemically known as (S)-N,α-dimethylbenzeneethanamine
> hydrochloride, is a member of the amphetamine group of sympathomimetic amines.

Wait. What? Like Meth?

> METHAMPHETAMINE HAS A HIGH POTENTIAL FOR ABUSE. IT
> SHOULD THUS BE TRIED ONLY IN WEIGHT REDUCTION PRO-
> GRAMS FOR PATIENTS IN WHOM ALTERNATIVE THERAPY HAS
> BEEN INEFFECTIVE. ADMINISTRATION OF METHAMPHETAMINE
> FOR PROLONGED PERIODS OF TIME IN OBESITY MAY LEAD TO
> DRUG DEPENDENCE AND MUST BE AVOIDED. PARTICULAR AT-
> TENTION SHOULD BE PAID TO THE POSSIBILITY OF SUBJECTS
> OBTAINING METHAMPHETAMINE FOR NON-THERAPEUTIC USE
> OR DISTRIBUTION TO OTHERS, AND THE DRUG SHOULD BE
> PRESCRIBED OR DISPENSED SPARINGLY. MISUSE OF METHAM-
> PHETAMINE MAY CAUSE SUDDEN DEATH AND SERIOUS CARDIO-
> VASCULAR ADVERSE EVENTS.

No. Like prescription speed . . .

> Desoxyn has a high risk for abuse. Long-term use of Desoxyn
> may lead to dependence. Use Desoxyn only as prescribed and
> do not share it with others.

Oh God. My skin cools. I'm trembling. My innards are separating. Frankie is singing along with the radio, dancing, stoned. I want her to know. I want to cry. But nothing happens. The only thing that moves is my mouse finger and a part of my brain that tells me to search for the side effects of mixing Desoxyn and alcohol. And then there it is . . . in plain, clinical English:

> Side effects from combining Desoxyn with alcohol include psychotic behavior.

So . . . my mother isn't insane . . . ?

Jesus. Blurry images rush into focus: the years of yelling into my mother's blank stares and her looking through me, all the times I've agonized over why my pain meant so little to her, why she would go on drinking in the face of our ruin, the insane hoarding, the manic mumbling, the twitches and sleeplessness, the endless walking, never knowing which version of her will come home at night, why she's gutted me repeatedly with vicious verbal attacks, with her glassy black eyes and twisted lips, and why she remembers nothing after. Why there is now an impenetrable wall between us. Because it was never us, because it was never her. There it is. In the bottle in my hand. The visitor.

Darkness pushes into my field of vision, blanketing, suffocating my thoughts and feelings. I push it away by spinning around and shouting to Frankie, "It's speed. Should we try one?"

"You're shitting me. Okay, yeah!"

We sweat for four hours, amped up like lunatics, scrubbing the place from top to bottom. Frankie pulls down a trunk from on top of the fridge and a shower of cockroach carcasses falls over her face. I stay low, scrubbing furiously. Anything not to think.

When my ma comes back from Puerto Rico, the house is cleaner than it ever has been. I send Frankie out to greet her and tell her where all her precious treasures are. I don't want to see her. All her freak-outs and lunacy. It's all bullshit. The psychosis of a crankhead. She doesn't need any of this shit. She isn't getting better. She doesn't even see me. I want her to be dead to me, but I love her too much. I can't look at her.

A VAST DISAPPOINTMENT SETTLES IN, one that I can't describe in words. I don't have a mother. She is gone. I have a child, another immature kid in distress. I don't have a caretaker, I have a charge. I don't have a home, I have a hovel. There has never been any room for me in this show, and now I finally know why.

This breaks me all over again, profoundly. I'm disoriented and sluggish. I start to separate from myself on a daily basis. It lasts weeks, which seep into months. I stop seeing things in linear order. I spend my nights out of the house, experimenting with a stream of psychedelics that give me a way to address myself, a portal into feelings I can't access without them. I feel homeless, more alone than I ever have, swimming in a city so much bigger than me. I taste a new kind of depression, and I finally understand why my ma stayed in bed for those months when we moved back to Third Street. It's like a wave of sadness has broken over me and drowned my whole world. Every time I find a dry patch to plant roots in, the ground is soaked through.

If the night ends alone, it ends in tears, knuckles swollen from beating on mailboxes and phone booths. I'm desperate to get it out, this tension and pressure in my chest, and the pain in my body forces a release.

If I could only pin my hopelessness on a single cause. It would be easy to blame my ma for all of it, but I can't. She is just trying to make it through her own graveyard of fantasy lives. Shattered dreams splinter into the sharpest shards, littering her forever.

When I get angry with her, Billy floats into my mind, visions of them together, running the streets in the seventies, him in leather, her in sequins. I feel the tenderness in her voice when she would tell me about their adventures, driving up to Boston for Christmas in a Camaro with no floor, snow and ice blasting up her skirt, her loving each second of it. She loved his every breath, how he shoveled snow in front of their storefront on St. Marks wearing nothing but biker boots. I imagine them performing together, him playing piano standing up, singing his heart out. I imagine her caressing the sutures where his collarbones once were, her favorite part of his body, while he lay unconscious, handcuffed to a hospital bed, his voice forever gone because they shot him in the throat. This was his drug, not hers. Her taking it was a way to remember him, before it made her forget everything else.

How can I hate her?

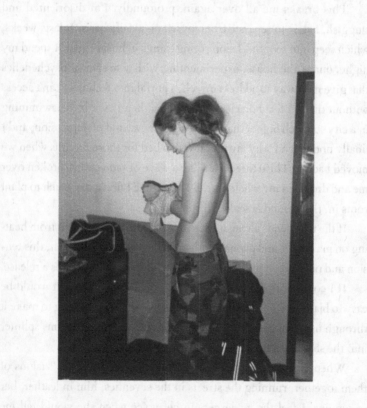

Chapter 44

# Black Eye

*New York City, November 2003 through October 2004*

POPPA HAS COME HOME TO STAY FOR THE FIRST TIME SINCE I was six. Grandma Edie is getting too frail to care for herself and Pop's job was coming to an end, so he moved into the top floor of the house where he was born, to take care of her.

His twenty-three-year-old German love, Nina, has come with him. They married so she could have citizenship. He bought rings from a gumball machine in Chinatown and asked me to be the witness. I was thrilled to oblige. On the way to City Hall we stopped to pick lilies from a tree pit on Park Avenue for her. He grabbed my elbow and whispered, "I'm not only marrying her for papers . . . I really love her."

He was blushing and cute, like a teenager in love. I smiled and put my hands through his handsome hair. I'm happy for him.

I'm burnt out on the skeeviness of the coke business and I don't want to get arrested, so I'm taking odd jobs doing videography stuff, filing negatives for photographers, stuffing envelopes, trying to act.

It's coming up on Thanksgiving and I get offered a gig filming backstage at a fashion show in a church on the Lower East Side. I'm there before anyone else, poking around, observing, pointing my camera at anything interesting.

Models start to saunter in like baby giraffes, beautiful but in an alien way, mostly from other countries, asking directions and instructions in broken English.

They are predominantly teenagers, younger than me, with not much to say. They wait for someone to tell them what to do. Hair takes a frantic hour, makeup thirty minutes, dressing ten, then they sit around dangling cigarettes from endless fingers for two or three hours, listening to music, chattering away on cell phones.

They fascinate me. I've always been taught to idolize these creatures, serenaded since I was tiny with glory stories of my ma's days modeling for Vidal Sassoon, ordering a bowl of pure hot sauce at a table with Andy Warhol, walking the catwalk for God knows who in the seventies; but the truth is, these kids just look bored. And boring. Their conversations are mundane, debating whether tomatoes have calories, laughing thinly at bad jokes, telling stories of boyfriends who sound like meatheads. But I can't deny the allure. There's something magnetic about them, because the world lauds their beauty.

The male models have it the worst. They don't have hair to do, so they have to wait for almost five hours. One boy in particular fascinates me. He's wearing a baseball hat with metal clips on the bill, his skinny arms covered in tattoos, with a fat chain tight around his neck, cinched with a padlock. He has too much energy for the room and no interest in the gossip or the girls, keeping his earbuds in and air-drumming through the tedium. I can tell he's listening to punk or something heavy by the way he pounds the air and bounces his scrawny body.

We catch each other's eye, and I work up the guts to approach him. Improvising, I tell him I'm thinking about making a documentary about the reality of being a model versus what society idealizes it to be, and would he be interested in being in it. He's nice, speaking slowly and clearly but with intelligence. He smiles at me, tells me his name is Jonathan. He shakes my hand like a gentleman. When I ask him for his number he rips a page out of his ninety-nine-cent composition notebook and writes down his landline, explaining that he doesn't have a cell phone. I feel a flutter.

It takes several weeks for me to realize how beautiful he is. I do a two-hour interview with him on my roof about his life and his dreams, then I follow him around one of his shows, sneaking a peek as he changes clothes, ribs jutting sideways as he slips out of pretentious designer jeans into his baggy shorts and Chucks.

It happens gradually, over five or six hangs, but the day we lope down Twenty-second Street and discover an abandoned pier on the Hudson River, I start to realize I can't get away from him. I love his dazzling California smile, his laid-back gait, the stories he tells about birds and the desert and the coast off Big Sur, adventures he's taken down Route 1.

I love that he wakes up early and rides his bike everywhere, that he lives in his head, that he stays quiet at parties and observes people. I love that he will vanish into the evening to wander alone, because parties cloud his conversation with himself. He goes out into the streets of New York to clear the signal.

As I swing my body around a barbed-wire fence, following his six-foot-four frame into the darkness; as he sits looking out over Jersey, watching helicopters carrying rich people lift off from the West Side, I stare at the back of his head, his shoulders, his calves, and I realize I want him. I want him in a way I've never wanted a boy before. His pillow lips and big dark eyes, his perfect hairline. I want to kiss him and fall into him. I want to be his. Not just as an escape from shitty things I feel, but in a real way. As I look at his silhouette, I realize he is my match, my other half.

I put a camera between us as much as I can, hiding my interest behind something vaguely professional, but the pretense of the documentary quickly gives way to best friendship. We spend every other day together, wandering the city, going to castings, watching movies, going to music shows, doing psychedelics and graffiti. He comes up with a tag, a simple, cursive I LOVE YOU, that lights up the town. People write articles about it and put it in movies. His noble approach pushes my crush into love.

He says he wants to screen print, so I take him up to Edie's and show him the family business. My pop teaches Jonathan how to make screens, how to hand-pull stripes, how to get a good layer of color, how to treat the fabric. I learn, too. He is ecstatic and impressed.

Jonathan has a girlfriend, a model. She's a six-foot bleach blonde who wears high heels every day. She's a hippie from a commune in California. He says she's "crazy" and "hot" and desperate to have his babies, which is nuts since they're both only twenty-one. She was away for the first month Jonathan and I knew each other, and it was a big problem when she came back. She didn't understand our friendship and got catty about us hanging out so much, always wanting to come along.

When he tells me they fucked on the balcony of our secret pier, I want to throw up. Finally, I crystallize what I want: I want to be his girl. I wanted to fuck on that balcony when we were there, but he's not interested in me. I'm awkward and weird, I'm scrawny and don't wear thongs. I wear hoodies and sneakers. I skate. I'm one of the boys, even with hair down to my ass. I don't register on his radar.

He breaks up with the model a few months later because she's pressuring him to "put a baby in her." He gets into being single until he falls into it with a woman who is fifteen years older than him and even more desperate for a baby.

He lives in a fifth-floor walk-up with three other guys in Chinatown. They turned the place into an art den, covering the walls in collages of bits of mirror, silver paint, and pull-up bars. I go there and sit on the couch, awkwardly, drawing and writing and waiting for Jon. They start a band, which is terrible, but I go to every show.

I think I do a pretty decent job of hiding it, but he must know that I'm in love with him. He must.

We are out tagging one night when the cops roll up on us in SoHo. I'm in charge of keeping watch, and out of nowhere, an unmarked car speeds up the wrong way and jumps the curb, and three dudes start chasing us. I manage to shake them, but they all pile on Jonathan, bearing down on his lanky gait with their brawn and guns, tackling him and dragging him to the Tombs. I'm up all night, worried, waiting for him to call, but he doesn't get in touch until the following evening. When he does, he says he got out that morning, called his new girlfriend, and went to her house to shower and sleep it off. I feel dumb, helpless, like a fish with a hook in my cheek.

A year goes by like this, hoping, wanting, yearning for this boy.

In the meantime, I've turned nineteen. I made a new friend, a Russian girl I call KGB, who looks like a buxom Kate Moss. She works at a bar two blocks from my house and we start doing psychedelics together at least twice a week. The rest of the nights, I go there and she serves me free drinks. When she gets off, at four thirty in the morning, we take a cab to her house and make out and roll around, only to wake up in the morning and act like it never happened. She has watched me openly sob in the streets because Jonathan went home with a girl or just went home without me. I spend her shift at the bar, writing stories on cocktail napkins, observing how every guy who comes in tries to hit on her and how she ices them out with a bitchy Russian wisecrack.

A month in, she confesses that the first night we hung out she took her boyfriend into the back of the bar and broke up with him on the spot, telling him she wanted to explore being with me. That confuses the shit out of me, but gets me interested enough to lend her my drunken body whenever she wants it.

Frankie and I are both still living at my ma's house. Ma started dating a reggae singer who I suspect is a piece of shit. He's got my ma convinced that he's a star in Jamaica, and he's always in the recording studio, but no one has ever heard of him and the Internet turns up nothing except a feeble Myspace page with some pictures of him in cheap sunglasses with some diamonds Photoshopped in. But my ma is in love, and she's never home, which gives us free run of the place.

Frankie started bartending, which is bad for her boozing, but I got all her friends together and we got her a new computer for her twenty-first birthday, so she can record her music again. She's getting really good and labels are starting to pay attention. I hope she blows up and gets a big place so we can get the fuck out of here.

Frankie left early for the bar tonight, to have dinner with a co-

worker, and I was alone in the apartment. I hadn't seen my ma for a
week, easy, which has been good. We're toxic when we're around each
other lately, unable to keep from fighting like cats, so this reggae shithead is a blessing. I was naked under a towel, walking from my room to
the shower, when the door flew open and she marched in. She seemed
lucid enough, not drunk, probably just hopped up on her pills, which,
I've learned, gives her sharpness a particular flavor.

Her hip has been really bad and she can barely walk. She told me
she has something called necrosis, which corrodes the cartilage in your
joints, and hers is completely gone in her hip, so it's bone on bone. She
says it probably started when I was nine.

As she limped into the house, swinging her body from doorframe
to doorframe, I realized that pain and difficulty with basic function are
making her frustrated and angry. I had a moment of sympathy for her
until she turned around and spat, "Where the fuck is my shit?"

"What shit?"

"My fucking glass bottles that were right here!"

The violence in her voice, the aggression she brought to the equation, precocked, meant that this interaction was not gonna end well. My
resentment for a laundry list of her failures, her exhaustion from trying
to grapple with that, plus the pain of her body was like a bunch of M-80s
stuffed into a shoebox. It took five minutes for the whole thing to blow.

In no time I was screaming at her, desperately begging her to shut
up and stop screaming at me, that I didn't fucking do anything, that I
didn't know where her stupid bottles were, and maybe she should just
go buy some legit speed. That sent her into the disrespect routine and
she went off on that for a while.

Finally I told her to go fuck herself when she called me an evil piece
of shit, and she got in my face. I actually thought about decking her, and
pushed her shoulders. She picked up the mop that Frankie bought and
briefly brandished it at me. I snapped, screaming at her, taunting her to
hit me, to hit her own child, about what a pathetic bullshit excuse for a
mother she'd have to be to do that. She told me I was a pathetic excuse

for a child. That I was a bourgeois spoiled brat little yuppie with nothing to offer the world except my talent, which I'm apparently wasting.

She smacked the mop handle onto the ground and caught my foot, causing me to yelp and lose my mind. Dropping the towel, I wrested the stick out of her clenched fist and smashed it against the wall, again and again, until it shattered into splinters. Screaming "Fuck you," I dropped it and went into my room, throwing on my clothes and storming out into the night.

I got into the cab I'm in now and told the driver to head to Twenty-third Street and Eighth Avenue, where I'm supposed to meet Jonathan for a beer picnic on our pier. I'm staring out the window as the city creeps by, feeling like I swallowed a cup of glass shards.

I put my forehead on the window, wishing to God I were any one of those people out there who look so happy and functional, free of this darkness, living real lives without all this violence.

My face scrunches into itself and I start to cry. Big, heaving, snotty sobs come out of me, which I do my best to hide from the driver by scooting out of his line of sight. I feel so much pain, like a balloon in my chest area, like something I wish would just burst and kill me.

I'm clenching my fists in my lap, squeezing them so tightly my nails are digging bruises into my palms. I wish my bones would break so I could have something to show for the massacre inside me. What will I tell Jonathan, I wonder, how will I explain the gravity of what just happened? How will I move through this feeling to be present with him?

Once, we sat in a cab for forty minutes without saying a single word to each other. He told me he thought that was the definition of love, two people who don't need to fill silence. Maybe he'll be okay if I don't talk too much tonight.

I feel an epic aloneness, a sense that I will never be understood, no one will ever know this damage, nor will they understand how much work it is every day to pretend I understand how people deal with each other, what's expected of me, to perpetually be learning on the fly and feeling like an alien child. I feel so hopeless that anyone will ever truly love me, because no one will ever get it. I think of Jonathan's sweet smile and I lose it.

With my right fist I take a whack at my temple, to shut myself up, to stop the stream of thoughts, to calm the anarchy in my mind, stop the tears. It isn't hard enough, so I take another, with a bigger swing. Checking the mirror to make sure the driver can't see me, I start pounding myself on the right eye, over and over again until it welts up almost an inch off my face. The sudden stinging stops the tears and I am lost in the pelting sound of my fist on my own cheekbone, disfiguring the flesh around my eye socket.

I'll tell him she hit me in the face with the mop handle. Then he'll understand.

## Chapter 45

# The Piece of Shit
# at the Center of the Universe

*Upper East Side, New York City, December 2004*

I CAME UP TO POPPA AND NINA'S HOUSE AFTER THE BRUTAL fight with my ma. They wanted to go visit Nina's family the second her travel papers came through, and somebody needed to look after Edie, so it all worked out. I'm sleeping in the master bed while they're gone, giving Edie her pills every day. I go to the fancy grocery store and buy her sandwiches and preroasted chickens that come in nice white boxes, with money she gives me from her little purse.

When they come home I'll be back to sleeping on the couch in the hallway, but I'm hoping that if I play my cards right, Pop will invite me to stay. For now, it's my palace to play in. It's so nice to be able to see the floor, to have some sunlight in the mornings, clean fluffy towels, and a set of huge brass keys.

I'm having fewer rage blackouts and crying fits, except if I'm really drunk, when I might punch something, but being up here is doing wonders for my calm. I want to be good to Edie, make sure she feels comfortable.

I'm in the hot shower now, scalding myself, admiring the tile, thinking about how to get them to ask me to move in for good. I brought the girl I've been fucking to sleep over. I'm going to take her out for a dinner I can't afford once I wash her smell off me.

The bathroom door is open and I can see the living room reflected in the steamy mirror. The girl is wandering naked around the living room looking at my pop's beautiful books and art scattered everywhere. She's tall and slender, with a sharp black bob. Her jaw is refined, like an Egyptian statue. She's an Italian beauty from Staten Island.

I met her while she was go-go dancing at a party. I was dancing with a huge black man in angel wings when she waved me over to her. Wearing nothing but pasties and underwear, she shooed away the boys flanking her, pulled me down on top of her, and kissed me. She said she'd almost forgotten how good it felt to kiss girls.

That night I took her back to my house and we fucked until the sun came up, shaking the walls of the building. I was conflicted when I saw her in the daylight, in her fluorescent leg warmers and Burning Man Hula-Hooper getup, but neither of us could stay away from each other. It's been a couple of months and we've exchanged outsize words neither of us can commit to.

The bedroom door slams suddenly, making me jump. Confused, senses heightened, I call her name. Tension is in the air and I can tell something has gone very wrong. Straining to see around the steam patches, I can make out the shape of a book on the table where she was standing. I realize it's my journal. I realize it's probably open to the page where I'm talking about how I don't actually think I'm gay, nor do I want to be, and how I miss dick. It's a page full of lies, lies I have been telling myself regularly, but lies that I cling to. The shittiness of hurting someone brings the untruth of these pages into focus and I throw open the shower door, calling her name.

Frantically toweling my body, I stumble into the hallway and push open the door to the bedroom. She's half dressed, fuming, stuffing her belongings into her orange backpack.

"Baby . . . what's going on?"

"Fuck you."

"What? Why?"

It's easier to play dumb than to try to explain.

"Where are you going?"

"Home."

"Home? It's ten o'clock at night. You can't go home right now."

She stops speaking, slamming each of her crystals and bracelets into the bag. She's older than me, and has suspected me of being a mess for a while now. She has no idea.

I chase her around the room until I realize she's serious about leaving, at which point I jump into my jeans, which I have a hard time peeling up my wet skin.

"Baby . . . let's talk about this."

*"Fuck you!"*

There's a violence to her words that makes the hair on my arms stand up. I understand where she's coming from. I'd be livid, too. I feel a breeze come through the window, a chill floating on the summer night, and it brings a fear with it, a sense that if she leaves I'll be all alone, scared. An instinct propels me toward her.

She stomps out of the room and down the stairs, likely waking my sleeping grandmother. I hiss at her to be quiet and she gives me the finger. I can't find my shoes, so I chase after her without them, struggling to run down the stairs and get a wifebeater on at the same time.

Barefoot, I chase her down the cold sidewalk, trying to coax her into at least speaking to me. She is crying. This is awful. I try to touch her, but she will have none of it. She waves her big Italian bones at me and swats me aside like a fly.

I chase her three blocks down Lexington Avenue like an insane person, begging now for her to at least look at me. I don't know where the hysteria or the urgency comes from, it's certainly not being in love, but something in me is frantic about her leaving.

I chase her into the subway station, where she blazes through the turnstile without glancing back. Pockets empty, I leap over. The soles of my feet are black with filth, and the idea of that coming home with me is nasty.

On the platform, trapped, she slaps me. She tells me I'm a lying piece of shit, that I never should have told her I loved her. She's right. But I tell her she's wrong. That I do. I need her to love me and the only way to have that is to love her. So I act as if.

This is my life, always acting as if: as if I understand why people do the things they do, why they say the things they say to each other; acting as if I have any understanding of how to take care of myself, like I know what's important; acting as if I'm not a complete fucking alien on this planet, learning its social customs at a scramble.

It takes twenty minutes for the train to finally come, during which she ignores my pleas to speak to me. The riders are unabashed about giving me side-eye because I'm barefoot. I sit next to the now weeping girl and implore her to give me another chance. I beg and beg until I realize that it's hopeless. This is the end of this one. I fucked it up.

In a last stab at chivalry, I walk her from the train to the ferry station in silence and watch her board without turning around. She doesn't say good-bye.

It's almost midnight as I watch the boat pull away into the night waters, carrying her back to her island, away from my excuses. She saw through me, she saw my garbled intentions. She didn't want to be a human towel to stop my bleeding. Good for her.

Chapter 46

# Sleep Is My Cocoon

New York City, 2005 through 2006

SLEEP IS MY COCOON. SLEEP IS MY SAFE SPACE WHERE I GO to be sad. Sleep is a slippery bath of no feeling, where I go when my heart feels heavy. Heartache is confusing for me. Emotions are confusing for me.

I am the fixer. Ma goes up in flames, I put them out. She sets a bomb, I diffuse it.

Ma doesn't believe in emotions. She never has. She believes in heart and soul but as objects, as actions, not as fragile, amorphous states in flux. When I get a pang of something, it overwhelms me. I shut it out. I grit my teeth and tighten my grip on the bow, braced for a tossing.

I rail against it with the full force of my body, I smash my bones into hard surfaces, trying to slam the bad feeling out like a coconut from a tree. My knuckles are flat and my heart is no less confused.

My mind is becoming a circus, a constant roiling of ten acts at once, some in the spotlight, but six always in preparation. I am preoccupied when I talk to people, trying to ensure that my tightrope walkers don't fall and the trapeze swings just right for the handoff. It makes me flighty and a little distant. Charm is never the issue. I can make them smile. But I can't connect. To connect would require me to stop, to sit still, to just be here, to be comfortable. I am profoundly uncomfortable. All the time.

But I have no words for this. That is not a sensation that has ever been allowed. I don't even know what it is. I just get angry.

Love becomes a salve. A girl who will listen to all the different acts, who will hold me, who will tell me that she thinks I'm brilliant when I tell her of the jugglers and acrobats and sword swallowers.

Inevitably, the carnies get fucked up to blow off steam, they get aggressive and mean, they use my brain as a punching bag; my head becomes a battered crash pad with a dilapidated couch and broken windows. I try to tape them up with caffeine and an alarm clock, to battle the chaos with an attempt at order.

My list of New Year's resolutions is long and strong. But every year it has the same shit on it. I can't get a jump start on progress because when I get close to a shift, the carnies start shouting at me about how shit is going. They tell me people are whispering about me; they tell me I don't have a home, that I'm alone in the world; they tell me I'm a fraud, that all I know how to do is be a hustler.

At first they use the cover of darkness. They come in at night when it's all quiet except for sirens, when I know I can't call somebody. These fucks don't need long to kick up their filthy feet and get comfortable. They perch like mangy gargoyles behind my eyeballs, gatekeepers to my thoughts, filtering what information I get and how I get it. They tell me what's worthwhile, and the only things worthwhile to them are the things that cause sharp sensations: love, pain, alcohol, heartbreak, coke, fucking.

It's not long before I find myself in a deli, staring at a fridge door, desperate for a drink, but unable to move my arm to open it. I'm shaking, quaking from the inside. I can only shuffle myself to a seat and whimper to my mother that I need some water. I recognize how bad it has gotten that I'm asking my ma to accompany me on a walk. Years later someone will tell me this is a massive panic attack. Years after that I'll figure out I am having daily and nightly panic attacks, but it won't be for a long time. For now, the carny gargoyles run this show. And it's a cruel set list.

I have absolutely no tools to deal with any such things. I have been raised like a gladiator, to fight and be strong, to weather storms and survive onslaughts. But I was never taught to be fragile. I was never taught that you are born fragile. I think of it as a failure. This is my failure.

Carnies hate one thing more than any other: to be ignored. Oh no, you must dance with them, listen to their song, clap along, scream when they frighten you, or else they'll dig their fucking claws in and shred you. So I become more and more occupied with trying to appease them. It makes me do shitty things to other people, people I love. I find myself neglecting them, not seeing needs that are plainly in front of me. I reach for salve anywhere I can get it.

Oh, you think I'm beautiful? Great. Let's fuck. It's okay. We don't have to tell my girlfriend because that's love, and this is just for the gargoyles. Just to keep them quiet.

I don't tell anyone anything except my journals.

The pain numbs me. My heartache spreads from the chest out like novocaine. The numbness is frightening, tense; it shortens my breath.

Anything to feel something. A cigarette to feel my lungs. A shot to feel my throat. Punch a wall to feel my nerves. Six coffees to feel my brain, my eye sockets. Coke to feel my heart beat. Scream to feel myself, buried in there. Music so loud my ears hum.

I go to dance class late at night. I stand at the front and let the music pulse through my whole body, throwing my bones around to heavy hip-hop beats in a dark room filled with sweating people. I give it my all. I dance like I'm never gonna move again. I lose myself in it. I throw all my rage into movement and I hope it turns into something good.

I don't want to break my hands. I don't want to get pregnant. I'm not an addict.

Tears come out of me in convulsions at the end of long nights pouring toxic shit down my throat, pining over people who don't want me. I black out and fuck people in stairwells and backseats, not because I have to, but because I don't want to wake up with them. I leave the cute Rollerblader boy in his bed, the R&B singer gets an hour, the photographer leaves before breakfast because he knows what's up.

I'm trying to prove to myself that they think I'm sexy. I dance my soul out on club floors and let them come to me. I never believe that they will, but when you have low standards inevitably someone will answer that question for you. Easy sees easy. Desperate sees desperate.

I don't want to be gay. I don't want to let go of the fantasy of myself as normal. I can't deal with how much I feel when I'm with women. I want them to sweep me up and protect me and promise me forever. Dudes feel so wrong, but maybe that's what it's supposed to be? Fleeting? No. I know this.

*Chapter 47*

# Blue Pea Dies

*New York City, January 2007*

P OP WOULD NEVER LET ME LIVE WITH THEM. HE SAID THE vibe in the house was "too fragile," what with Edie needing quiet. We were prone to huge, door-slamming fights and he said he didn't know where he'd put me, which was baffling. Apparently, I'm "a big personality" and there wasn't room for that up there. We fought bitterly because of it. Eventually we compromised with my setting up an office on the ground floor.

My high school had offered a free class per semester, so I had taken a couple at New School University, but they ultimately felt like a waste of time when I could be learning on the job, so I opted out of college and started a magazine about street art instead. It was growing and needed a home.

I've dated some people, curated some art shows, and I'm starting to find a community in the art world. I've even got ten people working for me who are all older than me, but no matter what I do, I can't shake my love for Jonathan, which has dragged on for nearly three and a half years now. I'm twenty-one.

Finally, this past Christmas, I did what any smart girl would have done years ago: I brought another boy home.

I threw my annual Wayward Kids Christmas Party at Edie's house, with Jonathan, Frankie, Naima, KGB, our new friend Devin—a Canadian import dipped in tattoos—and twenty other Jews, Muslims, Europeans, and orphans. We cooked a feast and danced the night away.

I spent most of it making out, very publicly, with a boy named Max, a painter living in Barcelona, home for the holidays. Eighteen people slept over, three to a bed, and in the morning I made them all blueberry pancakes and espresso. When we walked through Central Park to go ice skating, I was sure to hold Max's hand. I should have known . . .

Two weeks later Jonathan's best friend sat me down and told me he was pretty sure things were about to change, that I was about to get some good news. All of our friends are painfully aware of my love for Jon. Some of them think we're Romeo and Juliet, some of them think I'm stupid and idealistic; either way, they just want it to happen already so I'll stop pining.

Jon called me from California, his voice soft. He flirted with me, painting sunsets with his deep baritone. He told me he missed me and was eager to see me, flooding my system with endorphins.

When he got back, our posse went to a bar near my house. My chest was tight with nerves, so I sat by myself and drew a portrait of his back on a cocktail napkin as he talked to someone else. I took in his tanned skin, how he'd let his curls grow out an inch, how his eyes crinkled at the sides when he smiled.

I sat next to him, finally, and he rested his leg against mine, warming my whole body. We talked about records and whiskey and the glory of psychedelics. He was flirting with me and it was making my head feel like a balloon.

Frankie saw it and cornered me in the bathroom, hands fluttering and shrieking with excitement. She clomped around, daubing on lipstick and pissing with the door open.

I left the bar early, but offered for him to stay at my place that night if he didn't want to bike home drunk. He smiled. I couldn't look him in the eye for fear he'd see straight through me to the bottom of my heart and get freaked out by my enthusiasm. He said he'd call when they were done, for sure.

I went home and cleaned my room, slowly but with conviction. I stacked my notebooks, straightened my shelf of clothes, put my sneakers in a straight row. I lit a candle and put on some underwear I felt sexy in.

An hour later, my dream lover was in my bed. In the darkness, I could see the outline of his bony frame as he positioned himself above me and put his mouth on mine. I almost cried when I felt his scruff against my face. I had been waiting so long for this, I couldn't believe it was happening.

It was tender and sweet. He was just as nervous as I was, and our bones tangled together awkwardly. We were graceless but hungry for each other, determined to figure it out.

In the morning we got coffees from the deli and sat on the stoop, smiling sheepishly, my legs draped over his. He kissed me when he left, and I watched him ride away on his bicycle, heart thumping in my chest.

A few days later we met up at Edie's and he drove me downtown in his friend's Porsche. We drove through Times Square with the top down and I watched the fluorescent lights twinkling in the dusk, feeling hard pressed to imagine something more romantic.

He took my hand in his rough fingers and told me he was feeling torn; he had made plans to go on a trip around the world, starting in Mali and on to Asia. I asked him why that made him feel conflicted. He said because he also wanted to stay and be with me. I was calm.

"Jonathan, I've been waiting for this for four years. You think I'm gonna disappear in six months while you're on the trip of a lifetime?"

He looked at me with something I'd never seen before—relief, respect, admiration, gratitude. I told him to go, by all means, to do what he needed to, just if he fucked any girls to please double bag it. He squeezed my hand tighter and leaned over the gear stick and kissed me.

We packed up his apartment in Red Hook, a tiny place overlooking the bay, and rode our bikes back to the city.

He has two pet finches he keeps in a wrought-iron cage, which he's been teaching to say "I love you." When he leaves the house he puts a tape on repeat that says it over and over. I think it just makes them crazy. One is blue and one is green, Blue Pea and Green Pea, and he loves those fucking birds. I can't stand them. I can't stand any birds. I have a legitimate phobia and it even extends to his tiny creatures.

He asked me to take care of them while he's gone, and I regretfully told him he was dreaming. I'd never be able to come close enough to the cage to feed them, so he asked my ma, which I thought was a bold move. Jon's become a part of our family over the years, so she agreed, but the whole thing makes me nervous.

Jonathan left on his tour of the world, but something happens when you cut people loose—they want to be near you. He e-mailed me from Mali and told me he would come join me in Paris for Valentine's Day. I'm doing a play and we'll be rehearsing there for all of February. He's been gone for three weeks already. By the time I see him, it will have been five.

I'm living on a cloud. I feel like I've finally accomplished something I've been waiting my whole life for: I have a man, a beautiful, kind, wild one. I use any excuse to show people photos of him, to mention "my boyfriend." It feels weird to be on the right side of normal, to be just another straight girl, but my gay side keeps me comfortably couched in weirdness, even if it's hidden for now.

I'M SITTING AT A beautiful marble table in a room filled with interns on the ground floor of Edie's house when the sleek black phone rings.

"*Overspray* magazine."

"My bud."

"Yo, Ma, what's up."

"My bud . . . I gotta tell you something about Blue Pea . . ."

"Oh God . . . What happened, Ma?"

"I don't fuckin' know!"

"Is she okay?"

"Well, no. She's dead."

"What?!"

"She's fuckin' dead! Little sweet creature. I came in and I looked in the cage and Blue Pea was just tottering, like she was fainting, and I saw that the food dish was empty and I says, 'Oh my GOD,' and I ran down the street to find a pet store. I found one on Second Street, and it was one of Rafik's brothers, because you know, they have a syndicate, hahaha, and I got the bird food and ran back. As I'm running to the window to the birdcage, the little bird keels over and falls face-first into the food dish, which is empty. So I put the food in the dish, and put his face right in the food. But it was too late. But the other little bird—and those two birds were in love! They would clean each other all day, and feed each other from the, you know, how they have the food in the throat thing, and um, they were just completely in love. They were lovebirds—and when the other bird just fell flat over, and the food came to the dish, the other little lovebird pushed him aside, even though the other little bird is fucking dead, and started eating the food. You know, like that's cold-ass nature right there. It was over. And she pushed the other bird aside and started eating the fucking food and that's it. And went on, ya know?"

"Ma! Blue Pea is fuckin' dead?!"

"Yeah! Yeah! I took the other little dead bird and I says, 'What the fuck? Oh my God,' you know, it was just too much that I'm in charge of the bird and the bird just fucking died. And Jonathan is in *love* with his two birds, Blue Pea and Green Pea, and I says, 'Oh, what the fuck am I gonna do? Let me go and see if I can find another bird that looks exactly like this.' So I put the bird in a plastic bag

and I went to Petco, on the upper side of the Fourteenth Street park.
And I walked in and the kid that works there, you know, the little
Puerto Rican teenage boy who works there, says, I opened the plastic
bag and showed him the bird and I says, 'Do you have a bird with
this exact coloring? That looks exactly like this?' He says, 'Mmm, I
don't think so. Go look over there.' I says, 'When you getting in more
birds?' He says, 'In two weeks.' I says, 'Oh shit, that's too late.' And I
went and I put the bird in the freezer, in the plastic bag, so I could go
to another pet store the next day."

I'm dying of laughter at this point, tears coming out of my eyes.
I've put her on speakerphone, and the editorial staff is gathered around
the phone. It's not funny, but she took the carcass to the pet store in a
plastic fucking bag?!

"Wait, Ma, when did this happen??"

"A few days ago."

"A few days ago? And you're only telling me now?"

"Yeah."

Tears are streaming down my face. I can't stop laughing. She starts
giggling, too.

"Stop fuckin' laughing, iO! It's not funny!"

"I'm sorry. I'm sorry. So then what?"

"The next day, I put the bird in my bag and during the day sometime I went to [sneezes] Fourteenth Street and Avenue C, there's another
pet, whatever it's called, Petland. And I go in the back where the para-
keets are. And I show the kid that's working there the bird and ask if
he's got a bird that looks like this, and he says, 'Mm, there's something
close like that. Go over there and take a look.' And there was one that
was the right color, it was the blue one, but it had the wrong pattern,
like the black edging. Cuz Blue Pea had, like, white and black edging,
and it goes in little scallops on the edge of the feather. But this one had,
like, just black edging in perfect scallops, and Blue Pea had a variation on the tips of his feathers, with black and white, and maybe a little

yellow or cream in there, on the very tips of the feathers. You know the edging, like scallop kind of thing. And so I was like, oh God, you know, so I'm calling you."

It's impossible to breathe, I'm in stitches.

"Stop fuckin' laughing! This is horrible! You can't tell Jon!"

"Okay, Ma. I won't."

"Also the kid, the Fourteenth Street kid, he told me, 'Well, if you get another bird for the mate, the bird that's left alive, they're gonna fight the other bird. So you have to keep the new bird in a cage next to the first bird for like two fucking months, so that they get used to each other's presence, otherwise the first bird is gonna fight the new bird and kill it, if it just comes into the cage. You don't do it like that. You have to get them acclimatized by being in two separate cages next to each other.' So I says, 'Two fucking months! I don't have that kinda time.'"

"No. We have to do something before then, Ma. You have to tell Jon."

"No! I feel terrible!"

"Okay, Ma, okay."

"He'll never speak to me again! Or he'll try to kill me or something. I killed his beloved bird. Fuck."

"Don't worry, Ma. I'll handle it."

"Okay . . . Also, my bud, I'm competing in the Mister Lower East Side Pageant at the Bowery Poetry Club tonight. I want you to come."

"The *Mister* Lower East Side pageant?"

"Yeah! These fuckin' yuppie fucks around here don't know dick about the Lower East Side! I'm the realest fuckin' deal there is around here, and I'm gonna fuckin' show 'em! So what!"

I can't hold it together to speak, I'm laughing too hard.

"All right? And if you got a problem with that, you can take it to the fuckin' mayor kiss-ass himself. I'll see you there, okay? Bye."

She hangs up and I collapse onto my desk, dying, the entire office belly laughing at the absurdity of the bird corpse in the bag.

THAT NIGHT, FRANKIE AND I arrive to find the Bowery Poetry Club miraculously sold out. It's a local mainstay for disgruntled loners and frustrated poets. I explain that one of the performers is my mother, and they let us squeeze onto the stage.

The pageant is broken down into three categories: talent, swimwear, and eveningwear. We sip cheap beers as a parade of men come out, doing everything from the expected juggling or singing bullshit, to the weirdly unexpected, like the old man whose talent is to appear buck naked, bend over, and show the audience the inside of his asshole. The only other woman in competition also comes out naked, and fills a jug with her piss. Cheap. Then comes my ma, introduced as "Esqueleto!"

She appears from backstage holding Frankie's fold-up keyboard table, wearing her full-length black trench coat, Ali G goggles up on her head, and a do-rag. Two pieces of black tape cover her nipples, and she's wearing basketball shorts, flip-flops, and a belt with a giant sparkling weed leaf buckle. On the table are miscellaneous tools and a mannequin head that's been in my room for several years, that's now been painted blue and given a brown wig.

Frankie and I stare, jaws slack with awe.

Ma limps to the front of the stage, lowers the goggles onto her eyes and barks into the darkness, "Hit it!"

Aggressive *oontz-oontz* pours from the speakers, and she starts humping the air. We watch, thrilled, as she lifts a cone made out of a sheet of paper to her lips and lights it, causing an eruption I worry will singe her eyelashes off. She blows it out casually, keeping the comical "joint" in her mouth. She continues to air thrust as she sheds the coat, revealing a tool belt atop the knee-length basketball shorts, with the oddest assortment of things dangling from it: a bottle of Windex, a hammer, some yellow tape.

Then, she reaches down into her shorts and produces the coup de grâce: a long Italian sausage, which she positions just so, so it won't fall out, as she grabs the mannequin and makes it give her head to the beat.

Frankie and I completely lose our shit, screaming and clapping and falling over each other with laughter. Even the MC of the show, who has surgically implanted elf ears, is amazed. I lean over and tap her on the shoulder.

"Hey. You wanna know something crazy? That's my *mother*."

## Chapter 48

# Skeletons

*Paris and Los Angeles, February through May 2007*

JONATHAN CAME TO PARIS. HE FUCKED UP HIS DATES AND arrived the day after Valentine's Day, but I didn't care. I was so smitten it was like Cupid held the date for us. All the restaurants were empty the next night, so it worked out.

Jon wrote me before he came and said he needed to get laid, letting me know that he hadn't fucked anybody else while he was gone. Neither had I, and it made it all feel more legitimized. I was nervous though. Could I have sex with a boy regularly and enjoy it? Would it hurt? What if I couldn't go there, even with him?

I drove myself into a worried frenzy the night before he arrived. Malia, my old Syrian friend from boarding school, lives in Paris, so she came over and we smoked Gauloises and drank cheap red wine, which, in France, is still quality.

Malia, it turns out, had started dating girls, partially inspired by Nikita and I, so she had all kinds of insight into the realities of sleeping with men while thinking about women. Something about being Jonathan's girl, though, fulfilled a sense of correctness in me. I felt like I belonged in the world in some sick way.

After she left, I took a long shower in the gorgeous slate bathroom and thought about why I cared so much that he was a man. I felt like I'd been fighting to get over something since I was fourteen, to turn myself into something that a man would want—not just any man, but a man every girl wants—and now I'd achieved that.

I pushed aside my instinctive sense that love is organic, that it doesn't come from a place of what should be or a strategic move toward social normalcy, and focused on what it would be like to fuck him in that shower. The idea of it was so hot that I went upstairs, smoked a joint, and passed out, letting go of my concerns completely.

I dreamt of what it would be like to be his girl, to finally be wifey to him. He wanted to buy a farm one day and live off the land, and I painted myself into that picture.

When he showed up we kissed tenderly. He towered over me, but we landed in the bed quickly, and we're all equal when we're horizontal. It didn't hurt. It even felt good. We enjoyed the shower, as planned, went out for dinner, came back, and did it all over again.

Lying naked in bed, under the slanted roof, in a postcoital haze, my lover said to me, "There's something I need to tell you."

"Oh?"

"Yeah . . . if we're gonna do this, for real, I don't want there to be any skeletons in our closets."

Fear dripped into my perfect picture.

"Okay . . . well, I don't have any skeletons, but please go ahead."

"Well . . . I slept with KGB. Twice."

It was a cold tingling that started at the top of my head and spread down through my body, like he had poured liquid nitrogen into my brain. I couldn't speak. I was stunned.

Staring at my feet, I couldn't escape the visuals of one of my best friends, my part-time lover, who picked me up, sobbing, off the ground in my devastation over this boy, and my love, fucking. She is so much more woman than me, tits three times the size of mine, a face like a page in *Maxim*. Why wouldn't I have assumed that they would fuck?

"iO?"

"Twice?"

"Yeah."

"When?"

"Halloween and—"

"Halloween?! I was with you guys that night."

"Yeah. After you left, she invited me over to her place."

Her deceit was like a siren in my ears.

"And in November it happened again. Some random night. We were both wasted, both times. I'm sorry. I know she's your super close friend. I just don't want us to have any secrets."

I felt disoriented, my world a lazy Susan my lover had spun. Where was my point of entry back into normal functioning? Who did I trust? Who was I mad at? Where did I place these feelings?

Blame ended up landing with her. He knew I was in love with him, but he wasn't committed to me. It was her I was angry with. She knew how much her sleeping with him would devastate me, she'd seen it. She was so hot, she could literally get any dude she wanted, so why did she need him?

I pulled the blanket over my suddenly uncomfortable nudity and recoiled into myself.

"I get it if you don't want to be with me anymore, but I felt like you needed to be able to make that decision with a full deck of cards. You needed all the information."

"It's okay. She's hot. I get it."

"iO . . ."

"I . . . I just need a minute, okay?"

He nodded, folding his long body out of the bed. He went to the hatch window and propped it open, lit a cigarette, and blew smoke out over the Parisian rooftops, leaning on one elbow the way I'd admired thousands of times. I could see the sky past him and my eyes traveled to his ass. Here was the man I had spent so long pining after, the man I'd built a fantasy future with, the dock I'd hooked all my dreamboats to.

I watched his tattooed arm bring the burning stick to his mouth and I knew I loved him, no matter if he had been a selfish prick. The way his tanned skin spread over his collarbones, I knew I wasn't done with him, but something had shattered. Glass castles are made of particularly thin panes.

I WANTED TO FORGIVE HIM so badly that I forced myself through it. He booked two big modeling gigs and bailed on his world tour early, saying he wanted to come home to New York with me. We went back to my ma's house and shacked up in my room together.

He was supposed to find an apartment for himself, but in the meantime he was there, on my bed in his yoga pants when I came home from work every day. Frankie spent most nights at her boyfriend's place, and my ma was basically living with the "reggae star," but still, it was a full house. I grew irritated with the situation.

I spent nights out of the house again, on dance floors with girlfriends. Then one of them kissed me and started an avalanche. She knew Jon, and I was friends with her boyfriend. We all had a kind of unspoken agreement that this was okay, but it made me realize I missed the softness of a girl's mouth so much. I started hanging out with her on a weekly basis, going to parties and making out everywhere. Jon knew and was fine with it, but when he'd come meet up with us he'd be cold toward me.

Not eight weeks into being back, I skated home one night to find him sitting on my stoop looking sad. I sat down next to my dream boy and asked him what was wrong.

"I can't do this, iO. It doesn't feel right."

"You can't do this?" I said, gesturing between our chests.

"Yeah. I'm sorry. I think there's just too much pressure on the situation. I think I need to leave. I know I go cold with you, and I can't explain it, it's just . . . something doesn't feel right."

"You know what, Jon, I waited four years for you to fucking come around. If you're gonna bail on this the second the wind blows in a different direction, maybe I was wrong to begin with. Go. Do you. I won't be here waiting when you come back."

I stood up and went inside, stiff with anger, but a little relieved. I was prepared to fight for this love, but deep in my heart I knew he was right even if it tore at me.

A week later he was gone. He bought a used car, packed it with all his shit, and drove clear across the country.

I was gutted by the loss of the dream, but more than anything, I was shaken by the loss of my best friend. I was angry with him that he'd given up on us, but I missed my running buddy. We had done everything together for four years, and now he was just suddenly gone.

I went up to my pop's place in tears. He had been skeptical of the whole relationship to begin with, more astonished when I came out to him about being in love with a boy than with a girl. He didn't seem surprised that Jon had disappointed me in the end.

I sat on his couch and cried, telling him I felt like an alien, like I was too weird for everyone, a sexual hybrid that people are drawn to because I'm such a hustler, but no one can get close enough to actually understand me.

He went in to the other room and came back with a stack of books, told me that if I was gonna date men I was gonna have a rough go of finding one that was worthy. He handed me the stack and said, "Here. Forget Jon. These are your new boyfriends."

I've been floating in a gray zone between realities for the few months since. When I'm at the magazine, I'm the boss. We have recessed lighting and marble desks. When I go to my real jobs, I'm making twelve bucks an hour doing grunt work, shooting bullshit events and doing menial artist assistant crap, filing negs and fetching gear.

When my ma isn't home, Frankie and I have the run of the roost, blasting music, smoking weed and cleaning, going out dancing. The house smells nice, like Frankie's flowery candles, and we take herbal-smelling baths.

When Ma is in, she's screaming. The lights are off and the radio blasts. Frankie goes to her new man's and I do my best to stay out. Sometimes I'll drop in on Chico for long enough for Ma to pass out, but she still regularly burns the pots of rice.

I am eager to get out of town.

An opportunity comes up to go to Los Angeles. I've never been, and if I fly myself out, I could earn enough to cover my ticket shooting an event for a magazine, so I do it.

I have one friend in L.A., diminutive, hyperactive, handsome Jimmy, whose couch I sleep on. He's KGB's ex-boyfriend, and the one who initially introduced us all to 2C-I, the Prada of chemical psychedelics. He's a combination of mentor and bad influence, who I take some sick pleasure in making out with.

Tonight, he grabbed me when I got off work, put some mushrooms in my mouth, and said I needed to get my first lap dance. We slammed some drinks and came to this shitty strip club with a pink neon silhouette of a girl outside, just as the drugs hit their peak.

The cavernous room is dark, filled with the musty air of sex. Jimmy tells me to pick a girl. It's topless only, panties on. California, he explains, is one or the other; tits and booze, or pussy and sobriety. I can't imagine some girl's stank poon in my face being hot anyway, and I gratefully clutch my cold Corona.

I hesitantly take a seat a few rows back from the stage. A brunette in a thong appears on the platform in front of us. I don't have any money, so I try not to look at her. Jimmy pulls out a wad of singles and starts slapping them against his hand, licking his lips. This is becoming something out of *Fear and Loathing in Las Vegas*. One look at his pupils and it's clear he's off his balls. He probably can't even see her through the projections his mind is creating.

I can't help myself, I'm getting lost in thoughts way too deep for a strip club. I'm examining one girl's jazz shoes and perfect posture, and it makes me sad to realize she's a trained dancer, probably doing this because she can't get a legit gig. It leads me to thoughts of home, thoughts of class, thoughts of my ma.

Jesus, that's the last thing you want to think about when your friend is pounding on your shoulder, urging you to pay a girl twenty bucks to grind on your lap for one song. But I'm not in control, I'm just along for whatever ride my tired brain wants to take me on.

I start thinking about the apartment, how befouled it is, the ring of sludge around the inside of the toilet bowl that's been there since we moved in eleven years ago. I start to get angry, too high for empathy for my ma.

Green lasers shoot through the darkness, spinning and splitting into lines dividing the sparkling air. They lower down over my face and I'm lost in them, dreaming of what could be if my ma would just stop. Stop being wasted. Stop getting high. Deal with herself. Let me clean. Let me paint the place.

Jimmy won't let up, so I pick a girl with a blond bob. She looks soft, I tell him. He laughs at me and waves her over.

She leads me into a back room and pushes me down on a bench, straddling my lap. I am too high to be sexual and I'm finding this incredibly awkward.

"Let's wait for the next song, okay, hon?"

"Okay . . . what's your name?"

"We don't ask those things around here, baby."

"Oh. Got it. Sorry."

"Nadine. It's Nadine."

"Cool. Nice to meet you, Nadine."

She pushes her hips down onto me.

"Nice to meet you, too, honey."

I'm caught off guard by the feeling in my jeans. I realize I'm turned on by the soft, powdery smell of her skin, and when she grinds on me again, my breathing gets deeper without my permission. The song is taking forever.

"Where are you from?"

"The Valley. What about you?"

"New York."

"You visiting L.A.?"

"Yeah. How long have you been doing this?"

This is not how this is supposed to go. I know that. But I realize that I'm intoxicated by the closeness of her body. I find myself staring at her mouth. I want to kiss her.

"A couple years."

I realize I want to protect her. She reminds me of a blond Minnie Mouse.

In two seconds, stripper straddling my crotch, I understand what I've been avoiding all along: I prefer girls.

I put tentative hands on her lower back and look into her face, realizing she's older than I thought. She lets me do this. She's spacing out, looking away, chattering until the song starts.

"I started doing this to put my daughter through high school."

Oof. That's it. My hands come off her back, my body temperature drops. I want nothing more than for this nice-smelling lady to dismount me and to go take a shower. My skin feels creepy crawly. But an Usher jam kicks in and I grin and bear it as she rubs her now visibly wrinkled skin over my whole body.

When she finishes, I thank her politely and race back to Jimmy, who is having an incredible time showering a brunette with dollar bills. He has gone to the ATM to replenish his supply, half of which he presses into my hands.

As I'm standing over this girl, making it rain on her, I look down at her ass clapping, I look into her tired, checked-out eyes and realize I'm not destined for much better if I don't make some moves of my own. Something has to give, and it's not gonna be my ma. I can't wait for anyone to do it for me, it's gonna have to come from me.

## Chapter 49

— ⊹ ⊹ —

# Surgery

*New York City, summer into fall, 2007*

WHEN I COME HOME FROM L.A., SOMETHING HAS changed in my disposition. I'm not interested in fighting it out anymore. I've understood, deeply, that change will only come from myself. My ma has been this way nearly my entire life.

I avoid her completely. I can't erase my anger, but I do my best to keep it in. I spend my time working on the magazine, developing exit strategies: businesses I can start, careers I can embark on, ways out.

Then she breaks up with the reggae star. He convinced her to lend him her meager life savings and then it disappeared. She tells Frankie and me this one night, not even tipsy, and both of our hearts break. I get pulled right back in to caring for her, swearing to kill this guy, break his legs and drag him to a cash machine.

I look at her, hunched on her massage table, crying quietly. Such a proud back, slumped in pain from yet another disappointing man, and I feel so much for her. I would do anything to take her hurt, pull it out of her bones, and throw it away. I want her to know relief, at the very least from her physical pain.

We fetch her tissues and talk her through it tenderly, staying up for hours coaxing her out of her despondency.

My own hope fucks me. When her inevitable spiral back into psychosis happens, when her lip snarls back up and her eyes glaze back over, when the rice cloud seeps under the door, I'm crippled by the disappointment. I stop talking to her almost completely, but now she's in the living room every morning, and I can see how bad her hip has gotten.

When the singer douche bag finally returns the money, she pieces together every single dollar she has, borrows what she can from her family, finagles some kind of temporary insurance policy that will cover a hip replacement, and sets a surgery date.

The day of, I go up to the hospital with her. Standing at the window next to her bed, looking out over the East River, I am bouncing back and forth between immense guilt for not wanting to be there for her, and fury for everything she's done to damage my instinct to love and care for her. I ask her if she's stopped taking her pills and she sucks her teeth sarcastically.

"Psh. What pills. I don't know what you're talking about."

"Ma. This is not a joke. They're gonna put you under. You can't be on speed when they do that, it could kill you."

"I don't take any pills."

"Ma! The fucking pills I found under your bed! The Desoxyn! You think I'm a fucking idiot? I'm trying to help you right now."

Clearly, she intends to hold to her lie, so I push past her gurney and go out to the nurse's station in the hall.

I ask a petite middle-aged blond nurse who's in charge of my ma's care if amphetamines mixed with anesthesia can be lethal. I watch her hit the keyboard a few times.

"Am I right? Is she at risk?"

"Um, potentially. You never know. There could be respiratory failure if a stimulant and a sedative are mixed incorrectly."

"The bottle is in one of the plastic bags next to her bed. Maybe once she's sleeping you can check for the dosage or something . . ."

"How long did you say she's been on these pills?"

"Desoxyn. I don't know . . ."

She gives me a fleeting glance filled with so much sadness I pale. I want to disappear. I thank her quickly and retreat to the room, to the window, to the view.

Ma starts talking about dance classes and auditions and fantastical career bullshit that is never going to materialize. Anything to distract herself from the fact that she is in a hospital bed, about to go in for surgery, and her twenty-two-year-old child just had to warn the nurse about her amphetamine addiction. I can't do it anymore.

Turning around, I put both hands on the railing by her feet and look into her face. My tone is grave.

"Listen to me. I just told that nurse out there that you've been taking speed so that they know how to not kill you when they put you under. They're gonna probably detox you to be able to do the surgery. This is your one chance. If you start taking those pills again after this, once, even *one*, Ma, you will never see my face again. Do you hear me?"

She is silent, picking at her fingers. She shakes her head in the tiniest way, on autopilot. I won't let her feed me another line.

"Do you understand what I'm saying? You will *never* see your kid's face again."

She can't agree. If she agrees, she'll be confessing. She can't acknowledge that it's real, but I can see that something has reached her. She has been shamed enough by this proclamation that she falls quiet.

Guilt fills my throat, and I feel the desire to hug her. I want to hold her and erase her at the same time, and it's splitting me in half. I have to go. Before I can do something stupid, I bolt out the door, past the nurse, into the elevator, and onto the street. I throw my skateboard to the pavement and rip down York.

There's been an accident, so one lane of the FDR Drive is empty of cars all the way to Fifty-ninth Street. I jump the wall and skate down the center of the highway angrily. Part of me wishes they'd let the cars go, that I'd get swallowed up by them. The faster I ride, the less I have time to cry.

I'm racing home to pack my shit. I don't know where I'm gonna go, but I have to get the fuck out of there.

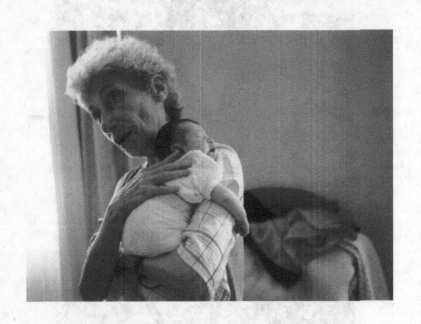

*Chapter 50*

# Around My Edges

*New York City, fall 2007 through February 2008*

THE FALL CREEPS BY SLOWLY. I TRY TO LEAVE, BUT MA gets escorted home from the hospital and put into bed, where she's supposed to stay for a while. My ma who I can hardly remember seeing sit down, even once. She's clean; I can tell because she's nice. Her eyes are clear, and she doesn't become dark at any point in the day. She can't get up to go buy any booze, so she's free from that, too. I'm quietly proud of her that she managed to pull off her insurance hustle and make her surgery happen. I feel like I have to care for her.

When she looks at me, it's with kindness and a twinge of embarrassment. We can speak to each other, have a conversation that makes sense and doesn't spiral into a fight. She doesn't want to ask me for anything, but she can't do anything for herself, so I bring her food and water, help her to the bathroom and into the bath.

To see my evil twin in pain flays me. Despite my roiling anger, I love her so much. No matter how she's hurt me, when the cloud of drink and drugs clear, she's my ma again, and I'm her cub. That's just the way it is. Unconditional.

Frankie has been keeping the apartment clean so my ma's hip heals right and doesn't get infected. We've been taking turns hanging out with her, and it's almost nice around there. But I know I've still got to go. The end is coming, though its shape is still amorphous.

Edie, meanwhile, has taken a turn for the worse. My beloved grandma has to be moved upstate to my uncle's house in preparation for her inevitable passing. My pop calls one day and tells me that she's stopped eating. She is ninety-two and proud, and she is stepping out of her own accord. No doctors, no illnesses—she has decided to go. He says it's only a matter of time.

Caught between the crushing trajectories of the two matriarchs in my life, I cry on the fire escape by myself, alternating cigarettes and joints. I listen to sad songs and try to figure out where to put all this shit while my ma quietly reads books on her massage table.

Pop says they're going to sell the house on Eightieth Street. That everything will be changing. I ask him why and he says something about letting things go, moving on from the past. It's a running theme right now. He says there will be a small inheritance for me. I don't know what to say to that.

"Nothing crazy, just a few thousand bucks."

A friend of mine is selling his low-slung, gray 1982 Mercedes diesel two-door for a grand. I ask Pop if he'll front it to me and he agrees. I don't have a license, but I drive it around on my permit constantly.

When I was seventeen I told my ma I wanted to get a driver's license and she laughed in my face. She said, "What the fuck for?" But when I pressed her, saying I needed a friend with a car I could practice in, she dug around her Rolodex and came up with Joey, our old downstairs neighbor, the paranoid schizophrenic with the .44.

He pulled up outside the building in a station wagon crammed with more crap than I've ever seen in one place (and I was raised by a hoarder). I got into the passenger seat holding the DMV driver's manual and he snatched it out of my hand.

"You see this?" he said. "Fuck this."

He threw it over his shoulder into the abyss that was the back of his car, then had me get in the driver's seat and zigzag up every block until we hit East Harlem, then back down Fifth Avenue in rush-hour traffic, even though I'd never sat behind the wheel of a car before.

So rules don't exactly keep me off the road.

One night I go to a party at some notorious loft in Brooklyn with Devin, my Canadian friend, and Jimmy, who's visiting from the West Coast and brought a fanny pack full of drugs. I end up taking mushrooms, doing coke, smoking weed, drinking a shitload of beers, and eating a small mystery pill that makes me feel like I need to stay close to the earth. Devin and I lie on the roof, watching white clouds of our breath billow up to the stars in a psychedelic haze, until she asks if I want to see her new apartment. I'm confused. She says she's moving into a loft two blocks away. It's in a building that's under construction and there aren't any locks on the doors.

We ring a bunch of bells and I yell gibberish at the intercom until somebody buzzes us in, and she takes me up a flight of stairs in what used to be a wool factory. The hallways are long and industrial, hung with raw bulbs. It feels like young lives are beginning here.

On the third floor, she takes me into a huge apartment with the best view I've ever seen of Manhattan and all its twinkling lights, the Empire State lit up in orange and blue stripes, the FDR with its necklace of headlights, the placid East River. It's a corner unit, with an entire wall of windows in the living room. Three bedrooms stretch out on the right, each with its own bank of factory windows.

The apartment is barren, save a few extension cords, aluminum scaffolding, and fragments of Sheetrock. We're both tripping our faces off, so Devin goes to feel the energy in the bedrooms while I post up on the windowsill in the living room and stare out at the city.

My heart is pulsing, because of the drugs, but also because I'm growing. I can feel the change coming, like my limbs are becoming elastic in front of my eyes, stretching out, reaching for something new.

There's a roll of paper towels on the floor and a pen in one of the kitchen drawers. I start to write. An avalanche of feelings, thoughts, fears, and longing pouring onto the soft paper.

I'm writing to Jonathan, telling him that he hurt me, but that he pushed me somewhere new. That I'm angry at him, that he didn't have to bail, he could have dealt with it differently, but that I still love him and I miss him in my life. I tell him it looks like I'm probably gay and maybe even a man anyway, so maybe I just wanted to *be* him more than I really wanted to be *with* him.

I write to my father, telling him what a disappointment he's been in so many ways. How badly I needed him to let me live with him when shit was so fucked up with my ma, that I needed to know he was my father, that he could be there for me, take responsibility, make a home for me. I tell the paper towels that his heroin addiction robbed me of the best friend I've ever had, the most charismatic, beautiful, intelligent person I've ever known, and wanted to know so much better. That it put a screen between us, like a two-way mirror. He could see in and out at the same time, but I was offered a lot of reflections of myself. I tell the paper towels how much it hurt that he wouldn't kick drugs for his kids, it took a girlfriend threatening to leave him to get him to put them down.

I write to my little brother, telling him I hope to know him one day, that I wish so badly that he would come and live in New York so I can take care of him and be there for him. I write about being angry at our dad for never showing up for him, and I apologize on his behalf. I write that I will buy us a Christmas tree one day and cover it in decorations. I'll load the bottom of it with enough presents with his name on them to make up for all the Christmases we never had together.

I thank my aunts Olivia and Alice for saving my life. I thank my sweet grandma Edie for her generosity and thoughtfulness, for showing me inspiration.

I can't even write to my ma. I write to Frankie. I thank her for being there, for helping me clean, for holding a lid on the pot when all

I could do was boil over. I tell her that I'm going to leave, because I have to. I know she'll stay on once I'm gone, and I tell her that's great, that's okay, it's wonderful really. I thank her for taking care of my ma. I explain that I need to have a home of my own. I need something clean. I need a life now. I've got to go.

When I'm done, I've covered twelve paper towels in scribble and I'm weeping in silence. I feel empty and so afraid of how it will all go once I bust out of the nest. I feel tremendous guilt about leaving my ma at such a fragile moment, but I can't stay on and take care of her insanity forever. I won't. The signs are telling me to jump ship now, and I have to while I can.

A few weeks later, Pop calls to tell me Edie has started to refuse liquids, so it's a matter of days. Olivia tells me I shouldn't come up, it would be too much of a burden, but I feel the urgent need to say good-bye. My pop calls me and says, "Listen to me. If ever something is burning in you that clearly, and you feel like you need to say good-bye to someone, you take that and you go. Don't let anyone stop you, because you'll regret that you didn't get to say it for the rest of your life."

So I get in my rusted, low-slung Benz and drive up there.

When I walk in, the shutters are drawn and the room smells like sterilized hospital gear. Edie wakes from her sleep and says softly, "Who's that?"

"It's me, Grandma, it's iO."

"Oh," she says, as I put my hand in hers, which is thin skinned and bird boned, "You look like a boy."

I laugh and ask her how she is, and she says she's fine. She agrees to take a sip of water from the strawberry-shaped cup next to the bed, but her way of doing it tells me it's a special favor to me. Poppa warned me that she is trying to die with dignity by sending herself over to the other side before her noble mind can disintegrate.

I ask if there's anything she'd like, and she says she wants to go for a walk among the turning leaves. Knowing full well she'll never stand up again, I turn to the window and say, "Oh, Grandma, you know, it's awful cold outside. I'm not sure you want to go out there. What about this—what if I just open the window and let some air in here? Will that do?"

Slowly, she turns her head, looks out into the crystal-clear fall day, and nods. I tuck the blanket in tightly around all her edges. Our ritual.

I say good-bye, trying not to cry. I rush to my car without a word to my uncle, unable to communicate any further, and peel out into the trees. Thirty minutes into the drive, I feel a pull in my chest, so I turn around and go back. I race up the stairs and into her room. I crawl into her bed and lay my head on her shoulder for a while, her delicate, papery fingers stroking my forehead, her eyes closed in reverie, and I tell her how much I love her and that I'll see her again soon. Tears roll over the cliffs of my cheekbones onto her soft pajamas and she holds my hand as tightly as she can. She nods and says she loves me, too.

"Good-bye, Grandma."

"Good-bye, iO."

Blasting music for the three-hour drive home, I am a mess. I know I will never see her again, that her final gift was to get me out of my hell, to give me the means to start my own life, but I can't handle that it comes with such a loss.

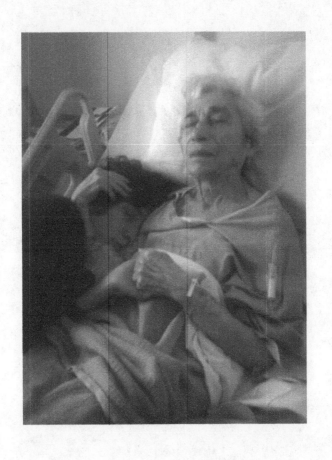

*Chapter 51*

# The Bridge

*New York City, February 2008*

As expected, Frankie says she will stay on. My ma takes the news of my leaving hard. She starts bawling, asking for an explanation of why I feel that's necessary, as though she truly can't imagine. I tell her I applied for the apartment above Devin's and I got it. I tell her I'm twenty-two, and it's time for me to live my own life.

I spend a week putting my shit into boxes scrounged from the deli and the wine store. Frankie helps me and Ma does what she can to pitch in. She is up and walking around again, using a cane, which means she's probably back to drinking because she can get to it. It doesn't seem like she's on her pills, because she isn't raging, and she is so down, so mournful.

When she pulls out drawings I made when I was a kid, old yearbooks, or my baby shoes, and starts crying, I take Frankie and leave. I can't go there; I can't walk her through all her regrets.

Frankie and I go up to St. Marks Place to get coffee from a big orange truck where a bunch of hippies blast rock music and sell drinks.

I discovered the Mud Truck and its mother ship, the Mud Spot, through the go-go dancer I chased onto the ferry so many years ago.

One day, when I'm sitting in the café, trying to get my thoughts onto a piece of paper, she walks in. The go-go dancer herself.

Awkwardly, we exchange hellos and she introduces me to her friend, a striking girl with short black bangs and giant, piercing brown eyes. She looks familiar somehow.

"I serve you coffee every day. I work on the truck. I'm Sadie."

"Oh. Shit. I'm sorry. Nice to really meet you. I'm iO."

They go to a table together and talk, but the truck girl suddenly appears back at my elbow.

"Hey. What are you working on?"

"Oh. Just writing some stuff."

"Yeah?"

"Yeah . . ."

She is standing too close to me, smiling too much. She's flirting with me. She's the type of girl no one realizes is five foot three because her personality is so big. She looks directly at you when she speaks, blinking long black lashes down over her huge, glistening eyes. She has a gruffness, a tomboyishness that plays well against her emphatic femininity. She is fucking me with her eyes and it throws me.

"What days do you work on the truck?

"Monday is my next shift. Come by."

That Monday, on my way to sign my lease, I stop at the truck. Despite my bumbling flirting, I order a coffee and I get a phone number.

We make a date to go to the Guggenheim and I pick her up on the corner of Ninth and First, where I find her leaning against a lamppost. As she piles into the passenger seat, I take stock of how stunning she is. She's an aching beauty, hiding behind baggy jeans and a wifebeater, her jet-black hair pulled into a single braid. She explains that she's just come from work and to please not judge her dirtiness. Actually, she says, she's into it, and if I'm not I can fuck off.

As we drive uptown, she tells me she's from San Francisco, that she is a trained dancer, a graduate of NYU Tisch, and that we probably shouldn't flirt with each other because my ex would be pissed. I tell her I agree, that us flirting is a terrible idea.

Sure.

We climb over a stone wall and sit in Central Park eating arepas. As I watch her type text messages into her flip phone with coffee-stained fingers, my emotions swirl together, indecipherable ingredients forming something significant.

Waiting in line at the museum, I tell her I'm going to do everything in my power not to be cute, and pretend to start picking my teeth with the pendant on my necklace. She says I am failing miserably. A droplet of affection swims down into the cocktail inside me.

The exhibition is an installation of wolf sculptures scattered up the entire winding spiral of the museum. Tourists mill around, taking photos and chattering in other languages. Sadie and I don't speak. We don't need to.

Seeking deliverance from the tension, I go to the bathroom to piss and be alone. When I open the door to leave, she pushes me back in and locks it behind her.

"Stay in here with me while I pee."

I stand in the corner, smiling at the floor. When she's finished, she pulls her pants up, sits down on the closed lid, and stares at me.

"I wish we weren't restricted."

"Oh yeah? Why?"

"I wish I could do whatever I wanted . . ."

"What would you do?"

"I'd tell you to come over here and straddle me."

I take the taunt, walking over and swinging my leg across her body. I sit down into her lap and press my hips against hers.

"Like this?"

"Yeah."

"And what else would you do, if you could do anything you wanted?"

"I'd tell you to kiss me."

When our lips touch, lava floods my veins. My eyelids close over detonations in every part of me. My being combusts. Her mouth is so soft, and when her tongue finds mine it is nothing short of perfect symbiosis.

We make out in every bathroom in the museum and she rides me so hard my back is black and blue.

I drive her downtown and we kiss at every red light, hungry for each other, insatiable. On Twenty-ninth Street, she takes my right hand and sticks it down her pants.

When I drop her off at the truck, we both know we're sunk. Something big has begun between us and it's unstoppable, regardless of the politics involved.

I go home and pull out my typewriter. A letter pours out of me, two pages long, that tells her I know what I've found. I have understood now that love is not something you design, it is something that finds you. I will wait as long as I have to, and once she is mine, I will give her this letter, and she'll know that I knew from day one. I put the letter into a box and tape it shut.

A text arrives from her as I'm loading up the backseat of the Mercedes with the last of my stuff. My ma is sitting in the passenger seat coughing. She has pneumonia and we've been bickering. She's being difficult because she doesn't want me to go. The text says, "Dinner tonight?"

My mother's voice recedes into background noise.

"Yes. I'll cook for you at my new apartment. Can you deal with Brooklyn?"

I sprint up the stairs with fire in my heels. The reply comes as I'm doing a final sweep of my cleared-out room.

"Ha. I live in Brooklyn. Send me an address and a time, and I'll be there."

Smiling, I turn out the light and pull the door shut. Frankie is out, so I steal a glance at her room. It's come so far since I used to sleep in here on that broken army cot, with her big candles everywhere and her shelf of creams and perfumes and makeup. They'll be okay, her and my ma. In a way, she knows how to handle my ma much better than I do. She can deal with it without exploding.

Taking in the kitchen, I know I won't miss it here. I'm going to a new place, with new floors, sinks that aren't clogged, and a shower I can keep clean myself. If anyone disrespects the house, it's my name on the lease so I can kick them out. I don't have a table, but I've got boxes, one of which I'll put a sheet over to serve Sadie dinner on tonight.

I can't believe my luck. I don't understand how this beautiful creature has surfaced at just this very moment, an oracle of the future that awaits me. She's like a spirit guide, an usher, showing me to my seat in the theater of my new life.

I help my ma to stand up, holding her cane. She tries feebly one last time to convince me to stay, but she knows it's done. She knows her cub is leaving the den. This story, this yarn, this torment between us is entering a new chapter.

I start the engine, smiling, my phone on the seat next to me, and pull out into traffic. My ma stands on the curb, in the very spot I imagine they loaded her into a cab to take me to my birth, watching me pull away. She is crying.

The trunk swings low to the ground, weighted with what little I own. The engine drags as I put on some music and light a cigarette. I feel one with this machine and with myself as I creep slowly down the Bowery, left on Delancey, and begin to climb the Williamsburg Bridge. I watch Manhattan receding in my rearview, a mausoleum now, a mausoleum of malady that I disburden with each block I pass.

I can't wait to get to my new home, unpack my things, lay them out as I want to, to grocery shop and cook, to welcome this new woman into my world. I can't wait to close the door tonight, to lock it behind me, to turn the radio off, and to sleep in peace.

*There but for the grace go I,*
*that I was not down there looking up.*

*Me*

## Acknowledgments

My ma, my great muse and my protector.

My father, my best friend, my guide, and my collaborator.

Katie, for keeping me alive so many times.

Nea and Leslie, who went into battle for me when it mattered the most.

DD, the originator. The rock.

Bill, for pointing out that I've been a writer all along.

Dan, for trusting me and giving me the chance.

Every person in this book who played a role in my life and let me attempt to describe them.

The beautiful faces around my chosen family dinner table, who have given me a foundation.

Claudia, for living a life that has resulted in such wisdom, that is now generously shared with me.

Kashi, my general, in life, love, work, food, and Drag Race.

Everyone at Ecco.

Sara, Nan, and Diego, for being godparents when I needed them.

Ale Zuek, for inspiring me and never resenting my bites.

Eve Ensler, Alix Browne, and Kathy Ryan, for giving a scrappy kid a moon shot.

For my two goddaughters, Nina and Lucia, and my godson. I cherish you.

Every person who had the opportunity to force me into a box in my formative years and didn't.

Thank you.